MW00574408

PRAISE FOR
ISRAEL: A CHRISTIAN GRAMMAR

This is a visionary proposal from Paul Griffiths, with all the wisdom, precision, and erudition we have come to expect from him. It sets out a map for how Christians might see themselves as part of Israel along with the Jewish people—and the many implications this has. It is exacting, profound, and very provocative.

—Gavin D'Costa, emeritus professor of Catholic Theology, University of Bristol; visiting professor of interreligious dialogue, Pontifical University of St. Thomas Aquinas, Rome

In this theological tour de force, Paul Griffiths argues that the synagogue (the Jewish people) and the church (Christians) are both essential parts of God's divinely favored people, Israel. While writing from a Christian vantage point to a Christian audience, Griffiths highlights that the church after its lengthy history of mistreating Jews and maligning Judaism should be listening to, not instructing, the synagogue. I highly recommend it!

—Joel Kaminsky, Morningstar Family Professor of Jewish Studies, Smith College

There are at the end of the day perhaps only a handful of ways Christians can understand the place of Israel in God's economy. Of these, some have proven to be deeply flawed, while others have yet to be fully explored and tested. In this book, Paul Griffiths puts us in his debt by displaying the logic of an account in which "Israel" names God's elect beloved, jointly constituted by the synagogue and the church.

Everyone who cares about a rightly ordered Christian doctrine of Israel will want to read and weigh this original and provocative book.

—R. Kendall Soulen, professor of systematic theology, Candler School of Theology, Emory University

This is quintessential Griffiths—polished and lively prose, abundant gems of insight, deeply original and thought-provoking. Griffiths writes to awaken mind and heart; he stirs up on every page a strong response from his readers—sometimes "Yes!" and sometimes "No!" but always grateful, always enriched. No future Christian theology of Israel will be able to proceed without this touchstone book.

—Matthew Levering, James N. Jr. and Mary D. Perry Chair of Theology, Mundelein Seminary

ISRAEL

ISRAEL

A Christian Grammar

Paul J. Griffiths

Fortress Press
Minneapolis

ISRAEL
A Christian Grammar

Library of Congress Control Number: 2023932815 (print)

Cover image: Abstract Painting Art ©Giorez | Getty Images
Cover design: Kristin Miller

Print ISBN: 978-1-5064-9105-9
eBook ISBN: 978-1-5064-9106-6

This book is for Lauren, without whom I would not have written it

Israël est présent. Israël est sa présence, on ne peut pas inventer Israël. La réalité, révolutionnaire, abolit les fantômes.

—Paul Celan

Israel is a mystery. Of the same order as the mystery of the world or the mystery of the Church. Like them, it lies at the heart of redemption.

—Jacques Maritain

CONTENTS

CONVENTIONS

Most of the conventions adopted in these pages are clear on their face. But it is worth noting the following.

I write *god* always lowercased and never replace the word with a pronoun. I treat the word, that is, as a kind-term, not as a proper noun. *The god* is always the god of Israel, the one among the gods who has adopted and been adopted by Israel. LORD is the representation in English of the proper name of that god.

When I write of *the Church* (always with majuscule initial; pronominalized feminine), I intend primarily Christians taken collectively, whether or not observant or believing; and secondarily the Catholic Church as the paradigmatic and fullest expression of that body. I offer many descriptive generalizations about Church doctrine, ecclesial grammar, and the like (*the Church's position is . . .* ; *Christian doctrine claims . . .* ; and so on), as well as some recommendations as to how the Church ought speak, write, or act about this or that (*the Church should now . . .* ; *it is no longer proper for the Church to . . .* ; and so on). None of these generalizations and recommendations will find anything close to universal acceptance by Christians, Catholic or otherwise. I canvass and respond to objections when they seem to me pressing or to have other kinds of interest; but I neither intend nor provide a depiction of or response to all objections, possible or actual, and many are therefore absent from these pages. This is neither an encyclopedia nor a survey of a field; it is, rather, a sketchbook whose task is to display a particular ecclesial grammar from a number of perspectives, to show what the landscape—the landscape of Israel, that is—looks like if spoken and written about in a particular way; and to indicate, without fully developing, patterns for future writing and speech about Israel that become visible when the landscape is depicted in this way.

When I write of *the Synagogue* (always with majuscule initial; pronominalized feminine), I intend primarily Jews taken collectively, whether or not observant or believing, as they show themselves to my ecclesially formed imagination and thought. I do not presume to describe the Synagogue from any perspective or position other than that of a Christian theologian trying to think Israel through. I have no special expertise in the Synagogue's history or archive; I read Hebrew badly; my invited presence at Jewish liturgies has been occasional and untutored; I am largely ignorant of what I would need to know in order to describe the Synagogue as historians might variously see her; and it is both improper and impossible for me to try to describe her as Jews might variously see her. I sketch her, rather, as a conundral figure in the Christian theological landscape, and I do that with the principal goal of clarifying the conundrum for the Church. Still less do I presume to make recommendations to the Synagogue of the kind I am happy to make to the Church; I am not a Jew and I am a Christian, which means that I have no standing whatever to recommend anything at all to the Synagogue.

All quotations from the (Christian) canon of Scripture are my translations from the Latin of the *Nova Vulgata*, and all discussions of scriptural passages are responsive primarily to that version.

I quote and discuss few written works, and mention few names of writers. That is because I seek clarity of line, and diversion into representation and exegesis of what others have written would smudge the line. There are, of course, antecedents to what I write here, and, no doubt, others who have made some, or many, or all the points I here make, better than I have or can; I have, too, been stimulated by reading the work of others to write things I would not otherwise have been able to write; the list of works consulted at the end of this volume, together with its prefatory comments, is intended to discharge debts of gratitude, so far as I am aware of them, for this stimulus. There is, however, a place, the place I should like this book to occupy, for written work that shares with pencil sketches a concern for form that requires neither explicit identification of antecedents nor commentary on what they might have meant or what their context made it possible for them to say. Walter Benjamin writes somewhere in *The Arcades Project* that his work has not yet perfected the art of citing without quotation marks. That is an important and difficult art, and I too am very far from perfection in it, though I do seek it. Why? Because pencil sketches don't quote. The intense blue of Giotto's skies is precedented; Giotto's paintings, however, make no explicit acknowledgment of those precedents, and would be worse paintings if they did.

PREFACE

Theology as I practice it here is a *Glasperlenspiel.* The glass beads are lexical; the game is to arrange them syntactically; and the purpose is to show the kind of theological writing that a particular arrangement of the beads encourages. I have no interest in convincing readers of anything. I want only to show how Christian theological writing looks and where it might go if informed by this grammar rather than that. I should like this writing, and the grammar that informs it, to be provocative of thought and talk and writing on the part of those who read it. That is a good deal to hope for, more, I expect, than is realistic; I certainly don't hope that readers might be dazzled or persuaded by what is written here, and as a result find themselves adopting this grammar in their own theological writing. Deflation is better than inflation, and on a properly deflationary account what is written here is certainly no more than and perhaps no less than an instance of theological writing that might stimulate more of the same.

The grammar unfolded in this book is a Christian one. It is a lexicon and syntax of Christian discourse about Israel, which is the constitutive conundrum for the entirety of Christian theology, and it proposes some fundamental adjustments to the several Christian grammars of that matter which have been lively since the effective separation of Synagogue and Church. If the glass beads are arranged in the manner suggested here, some other areas of Christian theological writing coalesce around the pattern produced in distinctive and, as it seems to me, interesting ways. I indicate some of those changes, though without unfolding them fully, in the second part of this book. This, as all good theology should be, is a book of sketches rather than an attempt at a system.

Catholic doctrine about Israel has developed since the beginning of the Second Vatican Council in 1962. Two points are central to this development: first, that since the effective separation of Church and Synagogue each continues to receive the god's blessing and favor and to remain in possession of the god's irrevocable gift of election; second, that the Church's god and the Synagogue's god are the same. These two points are by now largely uncontroversial among Catholics. Subtending them are two more, long accepted and taught by the Church in various ways. The first of these is that Church and Synagogue have a common lineage; and the second is that they have a common purpose, even if the meaning of that purpose and the methods proper to its prosecution are only in part agreed between them.

These four points taken together, two recent and two ancient, bring Synagogue and Church close in substance as well as in form. They appear in the territory of Christian theology as forms of life with a common lineage, a common purpose, a common god, and a common promise. Or, to say the same thing with different emphasis, they show themselves as modes or variants of a single form of life, in something like the same way that the language spoken by the majority of those who live in North America and that spoken by the majority of those who live in Australia appear as modes or variants of a single language. This book is a sketch, from a Christian point of view, of elements central to the form of life to which the Church and the Synagogue both belong, and which they conjointly constitute. I call that form of life "Israel," and the book is therefore an ecclesial grammar of Israel: a sketch of the lexicon and syntax of well-ordered Christian speech and writing about Israel, so understood.

An element central to that grammar is that although Synagogue and Church are each intimate with the god, loved by the god, chosen by the god, and irrevocably guaranteed continuance in that condition by the god, they are differently so. One element in that difference is explicit knowledge of and relation to Jesus, the second person of the Trinity the god is, which is central to the Church's life with the god in

Israel and not to the Synagogue's. That difference has long been obvious to the Church, even if typically misconstrued and misrepresented. A second element in that difference is that the Church is in most significant ways less intimate with the god than is the Synagogue. The Church's grammar of Israel ought present her place in it as peripheral to the Synagogue's center, a paraphrase of the Synagogue's poem, and a gloss on the Synagogue's sentence. There is a theological grammar at play in saying such things, and it, taken with an understanding of the long and violent history of the Church with, and largely against, the Synagogue, suggests that the Church ought now adopt penitence, subordination, and service as her fundamental attitudes toward the Synagogue. It is a central task of this book to sketch this grammar (chapters 1–7) and to indicate some of the actions this grammar suggests for the Church (chapters 8–11).

The theological grammar offered here is speculative: it is not taught by the Church, and it stands in tension with some things that are taught, particularly with some aspects of ecclesial doctrine about Jesus and about the Church. The grammar is there, however, as lexical and syntactical seeds in the subtextual soil of what is magisterially written, seeds that that might germinate. Those seeds are fertilized and watered when the Church's teachers and speculative theologians ask what follows from the affirmation that the Synagogue has been liturgically and halakhically and theologically intimate with her god, who is also the Church's god, for many centuries independently of the Church; what follows from the affirmation that the principal damage to the Church's body has since its beginning been done by a violently inadequate theological grammar of Israel; what follows from the affirmation that the Church, since Israel's complication into Synagogue and Church, has laid the foundation for attempts to remove the Synagogue from Israel, and has often participated directly in such attempts; and what follows from the fact that the Church has sometimes been complicit in, and has laid most of the conceptual groundwork for, attempts to make the world itself *judenrein*.

The theological grammar depicted and advocated here is both revolutionary and conservative. It is the one because it is the other. It is also an ecclesial grammar: a churchly artifact. It proposes nothing directly to the Synagogue; her interest in it, should she have any, is hers alone to determine. Israel is not now, and has not been for a long time, such that the Church has standing to propose anything to the Synagogue.

1

ISRAEL AND THE GENTILES

ISRAEL IS AN English word borrowed from a Hebrew one (*yisrael*). In current English it has at least three significant ranges of meaning.

The first has to do with a person, initially called Jacob, who has a nightlong wrestling match at a river ford with an unnamed opponent. Jacob is wounded on the thigh, or perhaps the hip, but nonetheless keeps his grip on the opponent; the opponent demands release, but Jacob refuses to let him go unless he provides a blessing. Perhaps Jacob's opponent is also Jacob's god, or some emissary of that god, for from whom else would he ask a blessing? The blessing is eventually given, but is preceded by a dialogue:

> *He said to him: "What's your name?" He replied, "Jacob." Then he said, "Jacob won't any longer be your name, but Israel: for you have struggled with God and with humans, and have prevailed." (Genesis 32:27–28)*

The passage is not entirely lucid in its details—there is the characteristic scriptural reluctance to specify the antecedent of pronouns; but it does show with clarity that Jacob's new name, Israel, is given because of what the story is about, and that the new name encapsulates the meaning of that story. The Semitic roots that make *yisrael* are *ysr* (to fight, to struggle), and *el* (one of the many words for a god, or the god, or one of the many gods), and so *yisrael* and its calques suggest fighting with god, or struggling against god, or something of that kind.

Three other things of importance about the passage: first, even though the opponent says that Jacob-Israel wins the match, he is nevertheless wounded by it; second, wrestling is a matter of close fleshly intimacy, closer than almost any other physical connection; third, Jacob does not choose the fight, but is chosen for it, for no discernible reason. Other scriptural stories about Jacob, which set the scene for this one, show him as a trickster and a deceiver. He is not a man of high virtue, or unusual powers, or any other out of the ordinary goods, and that he is chosen as the one to fight and be marked and be renamed by the god is perhaps (the text does not say) to be seen as a love choice—largely inscrutable, that is, as to reasons, for the lover and the beloved as much as for anyone else.

If Jacob is any guide, to be called *Israel* is to be named as chosen for close fleshly intimacy with a god without seeking or deserving it; to experience that choice as a painfully wounding struggle; and to be transformed by it sufficiently that a new name is needed and given.

The second sense of *Israel* in contemporary English extends from the first. It is the name of a group of people derived from the individual so named. The people in question are those appropriately related to Jacob-Israel, or, extending backward, to his grandfather Abraham. Exactly how you need to be related to Abraham in order to belong to Israel is a complexity about which more below. For now it is enough to say that the relation in question includes both descent and recruitment. That is, you get to belong to Israel if you are conceived and born with the proper degree of consanguinity (typically by matrilineal descent) or are recruited by the proper means (typically liturgical). Every group of human creatures maintains itself by descent or recruitment or both; lacking both, a group ceases to be in a short time. Israel, as a whole and on the whole, uses both, though she argues with herself and with the world about the particulars and relative weight of each.

The people of Israel is, like Jacob, severally and collectively called (chosen, elected, set aside, and so on) by a god, their god, one of the many gods, for peculiar intimacy with a fleshly aspect; that people is, again severally and collectively, marked by that setting aside; and its election is a struggle with and against the god who chooses it. The whole business is a matter of unmixed pleasure neither for the people nor for the god, being in that like most love affairs; but it is unlike most in that some, at least, in Israel are born into it and therefore have no say in their implication.

The third sense of *Israel* is related to the first and the second. It is the name of a tract of land given by the god to the people in which they are to live their lives as that god's people. The tract's borders are inexact and fluid, but it has generally included some part, occasionally all, of the territory between the Jordan and the Mediterranean, and between the Sinai and the Golan, with Jerusalem as its most significant city. The post-1948 sovereign state of Israel, with its changing and conflicted borders, can be seen as an instance of Israel in this third sense, as can some other polities during the last three millennia. The people of Israel has at different times lived in the land as a loose tribal federation, a monarchy, a satrapy under various colonizing powers, and, now, a late-modern neoliberal democracy with some totalitarian tendencies; there has also, for more than two millennia, been a substantial portion of the people outside the land, often, as now, amounting to a large majority of them. Whatever polities are found in the land, and whatever the portion of the people that lives there, the land as promised and given has the same relation to the god as Jacob-Israel and the people derived from him: a relation, that is, of choice and gift. The people and the land are chosen by the god, and they are chosen for one another: the land of Israel is the arena of the people of Israel's life with her god. So, at least Israel's archive often says, and such sayings belong at least to the penumbra of this third sense of *Israel* in English.

A convenient name for a member of the people of Israel is *Israelite*. It is not the only possibility. *Jew* might seem more natural, but I reserve that word for a more specific use, discussed below; and since *Israelite* has good credentials and deep roots in Israel's own archive, I adopt it here and throughout what follows. Every member of Israel is an Israelite, and there are no Israelites outside Israel—Israel the people, that is, not Israel the land.

By definition, not everyone is at the moment an Israelite. Israelites are a subset of human creatures, constituted as such by the god's choice. Everyone else, everyone not an Israelite, is a gentile. That is a word derived from the Latin *gens*, which indicates what we might call a people, or an ethnic group, or a nation (*gens* often renders the Greek *ethnos*). To have *gentilitas*, which in Yiddish might be *Goyischkeit*, is to belong to a *gens*, to have, that is, non-Israelite peoplehood. To be a gentile, then, is to be one of the gentiles; and that word came, as this semantic complex passed into Israel's archive, to indicate all peoples other than Israel. A gentile is a non-Israelite; an Israelite is a nongentile; and there is no tertium quid.

• • •

So far I have not gone much beyond ordinary English usage in considering the uses of *Israel*, *Israelite*, and *gentile*. But now, drawing upon some elements in Israel's archive, I'll give the words a little taxonomic polish. What follows is not the only Christian way to specify the use of these words; there are many ways of doing that in the archive, not all compatible one with another. What follows is, as it seems to me, at least a possible synthesis of the writing about Israel with which the ecclesial part of Israel's archive is replete, and a more suggestive synthesis than its principal rivals.

First, on the nature of the distinction between Israelites and gentiles, or, what is the same, between the people of Israel and the gentile peoples. That distinction is established by the god as brightlined and binary. That is, at every moment subsequent to Israel's establishment, every human creature belongs to just one of the two categories. No one is neither Israelite nor gentile, and no one is both Israelite and gentile. Once the god has called Abraham and renamed Jacob, thereby establishing and naming Israel, everyone, at all particular times, is either an Israelite or a gentile, without any mixed cases or third possibilities.

The distinction need not have been like this. It could have been nonbrightlined or nonbinary. Had it been, then even after Abraham there might have been people neither Israelite nor gentile, or people both at once. In establishing the distinction as both brightlined and binary, the god acts in a way familiar to us. Parents do something similar when they distinguish between their children and those who are not; so do sovereign states when they distinguish between their citizens and those who are not. In both these cases, there are duties and rights in play: parents and sovereigns need to know from whom they can expect what is owed them by children and citizens, and to whom they should give what they owe. Allowing mixed cases, multiple allegiances, and fuzzy lines makes this difficult. Our practice of parenthood would be very different if we allowed that there are some children who have no biological parents, or some who have more than two. Similarly with citizens and sovereigns. These analogies are not perfect (there is always some fuzziness in the parental and sovereign-state cases), but they help, perhaps, by showing that the more intimacy and reciprocity present in a relationship the stronger the tendency toward binary brightlining. Reading the god's establishment of the Israel/gentile distinction as brightlined and binary suggests that the relation between the god and Israel is marked by close intimacy and much reciprocity. These, the god effectively says, and no others are my people. And the god knows which human creatures at any particular time fall on which side of the line.

It might be objected that a brightlined distinction of this kind is of little use if it's unclear who belongs on which side of it, and that it often is unclear. It certainly is sometimes unclear both to third parties and first persons whether someone is Israelite or not, gentile or not. And if it were always unclear to all human knowers in every case, then the distinction between Israelites and gentiles would have no purchase upon human life. Nothing about that life could be ordered in terms of it; it would be as though we could define what a prime number is but could not tell in the case of any particular number whether it meets the definition. But this is not so. There are accessible criteria for telling whether someone is Israelite or gentile, and we deploy them with sufficient confidence and consensus that various forms of human life can be and are ordered in terms of our use of them. Sometimes, no one can tell whether a particular person is Israelite or gentile; and sometimes differences in criteria for telling lead to differences in conclusion about particular persons—not even those who agree that there is a distinction between Israelites and gentiles, and that it is binary and brightlined, always agree among themselves about either the criteria or their application. These are limitations, certainly, but not disabling ones, and in spite of them we do well enough in distinguishing gentiles from Israelites that we can order, fairly smoothly, some forms of human life in terms of the division. It is a familiar state of affairs that a binary brightlined distinction in the order of being is not always transparently applicable to particular cases in the order of knowing. And in this instance there is a skyhook: the god who called Abraham and renamed Jacob knows, we may say perfectly, in every case who among human creatures is a gentile and who an Israelite, and this entails that there is, at every moment, a fact of the matter about who is which, even if it is sometimes and in some respects occluded so far as we are concerned.

More can be said about the god's establishment of Israel. It is doubly irrevocable, and is so by promise. A talismanic text from the archive says (Paul is writing to the Romans about the difficulty of Israel): *Sine paenitentia enim sunt dona et vocatio Dei* (The god's gifts and call are not taken back). That is: the god who called Abraham and fought with Jacob established a people called Israel by those acts, and did so as sheer, promise-accompanied gift. The promise is that the gift is not to be taken back. Nothing Israel has done, is doing, or will do can remove her peculiar intimacy with the god that is the principal content of the gift; nothing the god will ever, future-perfectively, have done removes it either. The promise is irrevocable. Israel remains Israel. For ever? At least until the end, until the heavens and the earth are rolled up like a scroll and all things become as they should be. Until then, Israel endures.

That is the first irrevocability. The second applies not to Israel as a collective, but rather to individual Israelites. It is equally striking: once an Israelite, always an Israelite; once in, never out, so long, at least, as this life lasts. The promise to Israel collectively is that she will not come to an end; the promise to Israelites individually is the same: so long as they live, they are Israelites. Nothing they or anyone else can do is capable of removing that condition, and nothing the god will have done removes it either.

There are other conditions like this. Arguably, membership in a particular biological family (having these parents and those siblings) is a condition that, while you live, cannot be called back by anything you or anyone else might do. You are marked by it in something like the same way that you are marked by being of Israel. But most group belongings are not like this. Citizenship and marital status are often revoked or otherwise altered, as are attributions of gender and race. These have only the status that imagination, which includes the imaginings that make law, gives them, and so they alter when imagination does. The irrevocability of being an Israelite for the course of a life does not, however, entail anything about knowledge or conduct. Particular Israelites may forget or never have known that they are Israelite; they may apostatize; they may have no interest in the question. They nonetheless remain Israelite. They are tattooed indelibly and sealed irremovably by the god's inscrutable choice.

So understanding being an Israelite makes familial tropes attractive for its elucidation, and they are widespread in the archive. Such tropes are appropriate to the thought that Israel comes from the god, issues from the womb, as it were, of the god's choices and desires, and is in that way marked as the god's own, the god's offspring, the god's family extended through the generations. But there are other tropes for the god–Israel relation in the archive as well: Israel is the god's servant, slave, emissary, spouse, lover, vineyard, garden, harvest, clothing, adornment, and so on. Many of these sit better with the thought that being Israelite, collectively or individually, is revocable, even contractual. On such a view, Israel and the Israelites remain what they are, the god's chosen, so long as they do what the god wants. Should they cease to do that, they thereby cease to be what the god for a time made them. It is possible to construe Israel in this way, though the weight of the archive's testimony is against it. It is also possible, though less elegant and consistent, as well as less responsive to the archive, to make the gift-promise to Israel collectively irrevocable (there will always be an Israel), while affirming revocability for individuals (if you don't continue to do what the god wants, you can be removed from Israel at any time). Israel looks very different if her condition, whether at the individual or the collective level, is so understood.

The Israel sketched and burnished here, however, is chosen with a doubly irrevocable promise: collectively, she always bears the relation she has to the god who chose her; and individually, all Israelites remain so at least until death. The god repents of the gifts and the call at neither level, and that is because of the god's love for and delight in Israel, and because of the importance of the purposes for which Israel is called.

One implication of this view of Israel is that removal from the condition of being an Israelite is not possible, even by apostasy. If it were, that would make being an Israelite revocable. Another is that *gentilitas* must be understood differently with respect to revocability than being an Israelite. If you can become an Israelite by recruitment from without, as the archive is consistent in affirming, and if there are only Israelites and gentiles in the world, then *gentilitas* must be revocable. Removal from that condition is possible, and such removal can only mean recruitment to Israel because that is the only other possibility. Gentiles, then, are not, as individuals, irrevocably such. Neither should they so be thought of collectively: there is no promise to them that there will always be gentiles. Further, the claim that the set of gentiles may become null is required by the hope, scattered broadside in the archive, that before the end, or at the end, all gentiles will come in to Israel—will come in to Zion, as is also said. Israel hopes for that, and since god-given hope entails possibility, there is no necessity that there will always be gentiles. The condition of the gentiles is the condition of those not chosen by the god, those to whom no promises of irrevocable intimacy have been made by the god, and those who may, individually, at any time join the god's chosen people that is Israel. To be a gentile is always to be inchoately an Israelite. The reverse is not true.

• • •

It might be objected that this picture of a people distinguished from all others by the inscrutable and doubly irrevocable choice of a god, a people in large part maintained through time by matrilineal descent, tends toward hard-identitarian racism. It is, on its face, an understanding of Israel and Israelites like that held by the classical antisemites of the nineteenth and twentieth centuries, and it may seem to biologize and reify being an Israelite as if the Israelites were a race in the way that, for instance, Nazi theorists took Jews to be, or in the way that one-drop racists in the Americas understood negroes to be. Even if this kind of understanding of Israel and Israelites is suggested by the archive, and even if many Christians have held something like it, don't those affinities and that lineage provide sufficient reason to picture Israel differently, perhaps by diluting or abandoning both the brightlining and the double irrevocability? Why not think of Israel as a community of taste and affinity and practice with a long history, fluid in membership and boundaries, rather than in this unpleasantly hard-identitarianly biologized fashion?

It is true that the understanding of Israel and Israelites sketched here is identitarian; it is also in a limited way biologized, transmitted by matrilineal descent, that is, even if not exclusively so (there is also recruitment from without); and it is in essentials very like classical antisemitic understandings of Israel, many of which are still lively. That this is so explains the power of those classical antisemitisms: they trade on, and distort, what Israel says about herself. But there are, nonetheless, some important distinctions to be made.

First: to say that the condition of being an Israelite may be transmitted matrilineally is not to say that being an Israelite *is* a biological condition, whether of physical form or genome or anything else. What it is to be an Israelite is to be beloved of the god, chosen for particular purposes by the god. It is to be understood by and related to the god in a particular way, independent of any biological variables. It is to be a not-gentile, related to the god in ways that no other human creatures are. The means of its transmission are neutral with respect to this fundamental point. An approximate analogy here is with citizenship: that too, for most sovereign states, can be transmitted by birth. But that need not, and typically does not, lead to the thought that what it is to be American or English or Togolese by citizenship is any collocation of morphological or genetic conditions. Rather, to be a citizen is to bear a particular, legally definable, relation to a sovereign state; to think otherwise is to make a mistake destructive of the very idea of citizenship. Just so for being an Israelite: however transmitted, it is to bear a particular, theologically definable, relation to a god; to think otherwise is to make a mistake destructive of the very idea of Israel. This point is buttressed by considering that liturgical recruitment makes Israelites of gentiles as naturalization makes citizens of aliens. No biology is in play in these cases, and Israelites recruited liturgically are as much Israelites as those born so, as much beloved of the god, as closely intimate with the god.

Second: that bad use has been and easily can be made of a position is never by itself reason enough to abandon it. It is true that understandings of Israel like the one sketched here will continue to be distorted and used by antisemites. Nevertheless, the sketch given here makes better sense of the archive's abundant materials about Israel than does the fluid one canvassed in the objection, and it makes possible some patterns of speaking and writing about Israel, the Synagogue, and the Church, otherwise barred. Becoming an Israelite, whether by birth or liturgical recruitment, is not at all like joining a golf club. Israel is not a free association of people for the purpose of worshipping a god. Israel is a people chosen, set aside, and especially beloved by the god: once so, never not; placed on one side of a brightlined binary by becoming so; and so independently of race or sex or gender or age or any other broadly biological variables.

• • •

There is another serious objection to the picture of Israel and the gentiles here sketched. It is that it seems to leave the gentiles without blessing, without positive relation to the god, as nothing but fodder for recruitment to Israel, or, if not that, as detritus left aside by the inscrutable choice of an incomprehensible god. Can such a god also be the god of the Church? The god of Jesus Christ? The god of universal love and compassion? The god of all creatures? Isn't such a god rather a local deity, a god of some but not all, a god who gives support and succor only to some among human creatures, leaving the rest to founder? Should the god not distribute grace equally, indiscriminately? Perhaps, instead of this, the god continuously pours out the fullness of grace upon all creatures, without distinction.

A full response to this objection will have to wait for the treatment of the god of Israel to come. A brief response here has two parts.

The first acknowledges that there is something right in the objection. The sketch of Israel here given does show her god as one who works locally, through particulars, here rather than there, not everywhere in the same way. This is not a god whose presence and action are evenly distributed, whether among human creatures or across timespace. This god is one of local intensities and rough ground. Action in time and space requires this; it is only the dislocated and timeless spaces of number and other abstractions that suggest the possibility that grace might be evenly distributed. Places of intense and particular presence include the ark of the covenant, the temple(s) in Jerusalem, the flesh of Jesus; places of diluted presence tending toward absence include abattoirs, gas chambers, killing fields, and places of torture. But that is compatible with the god having and showing concern for everything and everyone. A means of health or healing or repair may be directed at the whole person to whom it is given, but nonetheless be given first and fully only to a part: food comes through the mouth and is savored only on the tongue, but its nourishment is for the whole body. The choice of Israel may be of that kind: a particular means of addressing a universal problem. The gentiles, recall, may come to Zion. Perhaps that is the long-term and final purpose of Israel.

And second: nothing written here so far implies or suggests that the gentiles are without blessing; only that whatever blessings they have are not like Israel's, and that they do not include Israel's intimacy with and wounding by the god. It is axiomatic for the Church that no creature can come into being or remain in being without the god's action, which is, first and last, one of love. That applies to gentiles. They are not the god's particular and peculiar intimates as Israel is; but they are nevertheless the god's creatures, and they may have gifts for Israel that Israel cannot give to herself and are not given directly by the god, as well as knowledge and skill, even knowledge of the god and skill in relating to the god, which Israel lacks. The question of the gentiles' blessings lies almost entirely outside the scope of this book (standard tropes within the archive for attending to it include the god's covenant with Noah, and fugitive Israel's need for the gold of the Egyptians), but it is a good question, deserving a good and full answer. That the question presses, however, does not at all suggest that the sketch of Israel, Israelites, and gentiles here given needs fundamental revision.

• • •

To recapitulate: Israel is chosen by a god from among human creatures with a doubly irrevocable and largely inscrutable choice. It is a peculiar, promise-heavy election. As soon as she is chosen, human creatures are divided by binary brightline into Israelites and gentiles. Israel then perpetuates herself by matrilineal descent from the first Israelites, and by liturgical recruitment from the gentiles. That is, to a first approximation, how Israel should appear in Christian discourse. It is a sketch of what philosophers would call the ecclesial intension of "Israel": the meaning of the word; the sum of the attributes indicated by it.

But the sketch does not much clarify the extension of the word—that is, which human creatures should be taken to belong to it. The proper answer to that question so far as the Church is concerned is that Israel includes both Synagogue and Church, which is also to say both Jews and Christians. Everything written in the preceding paragraphs about Israel's intension therefore applies to Christians as much as to Jews. Understanding the extension of Israel in this way runs counter to strong currents in both secular and ecclesial usage of the word. Those currents tend to restrict the word's present extension to the Synagogue with her Jews. This is certainly so in secular usage, and to a considerable extent also in ecclesial. Those patterns of usage make it odd, grating, perhaps, to English-using readers, to write that Israel includes the Church and the Synagogue. It is likely, as well, that the Synagogue will have her own objections to such usage, and if that is so, the Church should attend closely to them. But although there are these strong countercurrents, the usage here recommended is not a novelty. The Church has often called herself Israel, and she has been right to do so, sharing as she does a lineage and a purpose and a god with the Synagogue. Her inclusion of herself in Israel has too often been accompanied by the claim, or the implication, that the Synagogue no longer belongs to Israel—as when the Church calls herself the new or true Israel. There is no such implication in the usage suggested here: to write that Israel includes Synagogue and Church need imply no superiority of Church over Synagogue in Israel, nor any displacement of the Synagogue from Israel by the Church. The claim here is different: that the Church and the Synagogue complementarily constitute Israel; that the Synagogue is more intimate with the god in Israel than is the Church (a claim to be taken up at length later); and that it is essential to a rightly ordered ecclesial grammar of Israel for the Church to see and to say both things.

This depiction of the intension and extension of Israel in ecclesial discourse needs one more element: a comment on Israel's purpose.

What is she for? Why has the god chosen her and given her the promises?

The scenes of Abraham's call, and, a short time later, of Jacob-Israel's fight at the ford, are ones of devastation. The world has been severely damaged by a double fall, one of angels and one of humans, and that double falling away has brought defect and loss to everything. Death is the clearest evidence of the damage done: everything living now dies, and everything not living is subject to other kinds of destruction, whether by violence or entropic decay. The world, everything that is the case, is not as it should be: it is a theater of violence and death and blood and decay, and the god's principal concern is to find a way of repairing it. It is not that the world is only those horrors; it also contains threads and vestiges and traces of the beauty with which it was endowed by the god who made it. Even human creatures, bloodthirsty power-drunk marauders though they are, at once terrified of their mortality and pain and isolation and eager to inflict suffering on others, can still occasionally see beauty, act lovingly, and work order in the world. The world's devastation does not mean the complete draining of good from the world. A world with no good in it would not be. Rather, the world after the fall is a tattered garment, becoming more tattered by the day; and the god is there to reweave it, to make it whole, and therefore holy, again. Israel is the god's principal instrument for that. That is what she is for. She, as the god's beloved, responsive to the god's choice, is supposed to be drunk on love for the god so that she has no desire to do anything other than what the god wants. The god chooses Israel so that she will show to a devastated world what it is like to be capable of nothing other than the god, and by so showing call the gentile world to herself, to live as she does and to know the god as she does. That will be the world's repair. That is Israel's purpose.

• • •

This is a strange view of things. In its words appears a fevered dream, a fantasy of such first-blush implausibility that the only thing a gentile reader not already tutored in the archive, not already accustomed to talking in this extraordinary way, can do with it is look at it with some admixture of puzzlement, surprise, and ridicule. You mean, such a reader will say, this is what Christians think about Israel? It piles implausibility upon peculiarity: it makes the doings of an obscure clan in western Asia three or so millennia ago the axis upon which turns the repair of the entire world, with its billions of years of time and billions of light-years of space and billions of galaxies; it makes contemporary Israelites, whoever exactly they are, the ones to be met on the streets of New York or Jakarta or Delhi or Jerusalem, the love-drunk heralds of a god who will heal us and save us if only we, too, enter Israel. Is there any reason to take any of this at all seriously? There is not. No reason at all. It can be displayed. That is all. Its display might please, dazzle, offend, puzzle, repel—but there are no arguments for it. Those who offer arguments for this way of talking, or against it, misconstrue the nature of such talk and writing. What is given here is a picture: this is how the Church, when she speaks as she should, speaks about Israel. It is characteristic of ecclesial ways of talking and writing that they appear exceedingly strange to those unfamiliar with them. It is sometimes difficult for Christians to remember this, good though it is to keep in mind. Christian talk and writing is to the world of gentile talk and writing as Israel is to the gentiles: implausible, strange, wounded, alien, often provocative of violence, and sometimes itself violent. Gentiles would be rational (but mistaken) were they to wish both Israel and Christian talk about her further.

2

ISRAEL'S FUGUE

ISRAEL HAS SO far shown herself as undivided, and largely by contrast with the gentiles, who have also appeared monolithically, as not-Israel. But Israel is not, as the Church sees her, undivided: she comprises both Synagogue and Church. How has this distinction emerged, and how may it productively be characterized? To answer these questions, two terms of art are useful: *complication* and *fugue*.

As to complication: the word is used here first to indicate the folding together (*com* + *plicare* in Latin) or mutual entwining of two or more things in such a way as to make an internally complex, as opposed to simplex, whole; and second to suggest, as modern use of the English verb does, that the result is perplexing, less easy to understand and account for after the complication's complexity than before. After the complication there are Christian Israelites and Jewish Israelites, as well as some Israelites who are both Jewish and Christian; but no Israelites who are neither. The Church and the Synagogue together exhaust Israel. The irrevocable promise of Israel's endurance means, minimally, that there will always, until the end, be some Israelites of one kind or another: the world, while time and space last, will never be empty of both Jews and Christians. That conclusion is not altered by the complication. It remains a central element of Israel's grammar. But the texture of Israel's postcomplication life is different from what it was before the complication, and that difference is given principally, as the Church sees things, by the knot of the Synagogue's and Church's co-constitution.

As to fugue: in everyday English the word has two ranges of meaning.

A fugue state, in the psychological sense, is forgetfulness brought about by flight. Behind the English word lies the Latin *fuga/fugere,* "flight/to flee." Some afflictions cause fugal flight: violence, trauma, disappointment, betrayal; anything too painful to remember or otherwise acknowledge, whether done to or by the one who flees. Acknowledgment of and attention to a past affliction is incompatible with the forgetfulness of it that fugue seeks. You might have been tortured or been yourself a torturer; raped or been raped; betrayed others or been betrayed; stolen or been stolen from; inflicted or undergone something sufficiently horrible, sufficiently difficult to attend to, that you run from it to the waters of Lethe. There, bathed and washed clean, freed from the burden of recalling the parts of the past you want to forget, you become someone who did not suffer or inflict that affliction, whatever it was.

You carefully clean the bloodcaked machete with which you hacked your neighbors into pieces, wrap it in silk, place it in a closed box on a high shelf, and live out your life, becoming, fugally, a person who did not do those things, had no such neighbors, never wielded the machete.

Or: you carefully and thoroughly expunge from your life all traces of connection with someone you had thought your friend but turned out to be your betrayer, someone who wrote your name into the files of security services that disgraced and imprisoned you; you carefully scrub your memory of that person, and live out your life friendless, understanding yourself always to have been so.

Or: a nameless and unknown assailant beats and tortures you, leaving you naked, bleeding, and in pain; when at last a Samaritan cares for you and heals your wounds, you have forgotten the person who was wounded; you know nothing of your name or your past, and they never return to you because your deep-down desire is not to have been the person whose life led to that suffering.

These are fugues understood as flights. They all involve, more or less, a passion not to be the person who was afflicted in that way, or who afflicted others in that way. And they all involve, again more or less, flight from the past into forgetfulness. Forgetfulness is rarely complete, however, and never final. It takes unremitting and exhausting imaginative effort to keep buried those aspects of the past from which fugitives flee. Sometimes it is easier, less exhausting, to rewrite rather than to forget, and so it is commonplace for fugitives to edit the manuscript rather than put a match to it; there is no memory without such fugal edits, and so we are all, to some degree, fugitives. Murderers may recall what they did but retell it as a necessary defensive act; those betrayed by people they'd taken for friends may retell the friendship to show that they were always aware that something was not quite right about it; those beaten and tortured and left in the ditch might recall what happened, and yet retell it by emphasizing the degree to which they resisted, recovering thereby a sense of agency and making the memory more endurable. These too are fugal flights. They involve flight from the unendurable and an aversion from the texture of what happened. They are flights into forgetfulness, even if scripted rather than amnesiac.

The sense of fugue so far explored, the psychological sense, has to do with damage: trauma, flight, and forgetfulness. There is a second, musical sense: a fugue in this sense is a polyphonic composition in which one theme, the subject, is played or sung by a single voice and then answered, or repeated (depending upon the degree of similarity), by a countersubject belonging to another voice or voices, each of which is discernible separately by the ear, yet at the same time heard in relation to the others and altered by that relation; the relations and interweavings, echoes and modulations and differences, typically contrapuntal, of the various voices, make the whole more complex and beautiful than would be possible were there only a single voice present to be heard. Musical fugues gather momentum and move toward resolution: their composers work at weaving the fugue's voices together so that the whole, in the end, works as a whole, and the hearer, having heard the whole, retrospectively hears what at first might have seemed other to the initial theme, alien to it, even contradictory of it, as an integral part of a whole that takes up into itself all the voices that conjointly constitute it.

• • •

The history of the Synagogue and the Church together within Israel can productively be understood by the Church as a fugal complication, which is to say as at once a flight threaded with fear and violence and forgetfulness, and a concordant harmony. A schematic history may begin to show how. That given below is responsive to materials from Israel's archive, and to the conventional historiographic wisdom of the present; but it is also written out of a peculiar Christian-theological grammar, and it will have served its purpose if it provokes further writing that extends and ornaments that same grammar. It depicts the past, and is historical in that sense; but it pretends to no neutrality or objectivity or comprehensiveness (no historiographic act should pretend to any of those chimeras), and is best taken as a lightly sketched framework within which instances of the Synagogue's and the Church's exchanges may be placed.

The schematic history to come requires use of two pairs of words not yet attended to: Synagogue and Jew; Church and Christian. Some clarification of the usage of these words here is in order.

These two pairs of words indicate on their surface the depth and strength of the parallels between them. "Church" is derived distantly from a Greek word, *kuriakon*, meaning "lord's thing"—something owned by or having to do with a lord; and since *kurios* is the Greek rendering of the name of Israel's god, the word indicates at root something that has to do with, or is for, or belongs to, that particular god. It can then easily be taken to mean, as it does in current English, both a place or building where Israel's god is to be found, and the assembly of those who gather in such places for the god's liturgical service. "Synagogue," similarly, is Greek-derived (from *sun* + *agein*, to bring or lead together; to assemble), and while it lacks immediate resonance with Israel's god's name, the word does suggest on its face an assembly brought together, or led, by one who might be Israel's god; and, like "Church," "Synagogue" has come in current English to indicate both the places where Israel's god's liturgies are performed, and the assembly of those brought together in such places for the performance of those liturgies. Church and Synagogue are fundamentally alike on this understanding of them. They differ in liturgy and theology and habit, but they are alike in the formalities of what they do, and in the god they do it for. That is the sense in which the words appear here. I make the initial letter of both nouns majuscule, and pronominalize them as feminine, mostly because of the grammatical gender of the words in Greek and Latin, but also to allow space for the long Christian tradition of thinking of the Church in terms of Mary, and to provide parity of orthography and gender for the two. These, now, are the two liturgical assemblies that together constitute Israel. There is no third. (Islam provides a particular difficulty here, but one that falls outside the purview of this work.)

Who gathers in these assemblies is different, however. In the case of the Church it is Christians, which word bears its meaning on its sleeve: Christians are followers of the Christ, the anointed one who is Jesus. They are, in short, the baptized. In the case of the Synagogue, it is Jews, which is a rather more complex word. The English word is derived, via Greek and Latin borrowings, from Hebrew *yehudi*, which in turn means at root those who descend from Judah, one of Jacob-Israel's sons from Leah, Jacob's less-favored wife. The word also comes to mean those who inhabited that part of the promised land called Judah (later Judaea), after the patriarch. But eventually, already in the canon of Scripture and clearly later, it comes to be used as a label for any descendant of Jacob-Israel—for all those, that is, I have so far been calling Israelites. As Israel complicates, coming to include Church and Synagogue, the word *Jew* can be used for the Church's purposes to indicate all those descended matrilineally from Jacob-Israel or recruited into Israel otherwise than by baptism. Collectively they constitute the Synagogue, as the baptized collectively constitute the Church. Together, Synagogue and Church constitute Israel.

It is possible, and tempting (many yield), to add a third to each of these two pairs of words: "Judaism" for the form of life that Jews inhabit (the Jewish thing), and "Christianity" for the form of life that Christians inhabit (the Christian thing). I resist the temptation for two pressing reasons.

First, writing and speaking in that way leads those who do it almost ineluctably toward writing and speaking of Israel as a form of life that contains two religions, namely the Jewish one (Judaism) and the Christian one (Christianity); and that in turn entangles discussions of Israel with the word *religion* as it has come to be construed in late modernity, in ways that yield nothing but confusion for the Christian-theological enterprise under way here; all that makes it more difficult than it need be to maintain the sense of intimacy between Church and Synagogue that must be theirs if each belongs to Israel. That is the first reason for renouncing such language.

The second reason for not adopting "Christianity" and "Judaism" is if anything more pressing. Neither Synagogue nor Church is here restricted in extension to those who have a halakhic and liturgical life. You can perfectly well be a Christian or a Jew without such a life, and without knowing that you are a Christian or a Jew, just as you can be an Israelite without having any idea that you are. That is because Jews and Christians, being Israelites, are what they are by the god's choice: by election, that is. They are what they are in the order of being whether or not they or anyone else knows it. Linking the Synagogue with her Jews to Judaism or the Church with her Christians to Christianity obscures this by removing the space in which it might be said. I consign such locutions, for the purposes of this book, to the flames. (There may be other purposes for which such locutions are useful or necessary; none among them, so far as I can see, are Christian-theological ones.)

The gradual coming to be of the Church and the Synagogue as halakhically, liturgically, and theologically distinctive forms of life within Israel, therefore, did not bring into being gentile communities of any kind, but instead complicated, by way of both damage and gift, the internal ordering of Israel, the god's elect beloved.

The Synagogue, with her Jews, is bound to the god by her halakhic and liturgical observances, and by her theology, all of which are offered to and received by the god with delight. The Synagogue belongs to Israel, as do her Jews. She and they are, therefore, in receipt of the irrevocable promise and blessing, and their liturgical and halakhic and theological response to that promise is the principal means by which they participate in the god's holiness and bring that holiness to the world.

So also for the Church and her Christians, the other kind of Israelite: they too are of Israel, which means that all Christians are also Israelites, and are so because they are Christians; baptism in the triune name, which effects incorporation into Jesus, is one way in which a gentile may enter Israel (the other is by whatever liturgical means the Synagogue uses to recruit gentiles). The Church is like the Synagogue, therefore, in her receipt of the irrevocable promise and blessing, and like her, too, in that the liturgical, halakhic, and theological response of Christians to that promise and blessing is the principal means by which they participate in the god's holiness.

Christians and Jews together, which is the same as to say Church and Synagogue together, now complementarily constitute Israel, which is to say that they exhaustively constitute it: there are no Israelites who are neither Christian nor Jewish. That is the correlate within Israel of the complementarity between Israel and the gentiles that exhaustively accounts for human persons. Further: since the mark of being an Israelite is indelible, rooted in the god's irrevocable promise, it is also the case that being a Jew and being a Christian are each similarly indelible: once a Christian, always so; once a Jew, always so; once in, never out.

• • •

Israel's history is Janus faced. In one direction, Israel looks to her god, and in the other, to the gentiles who surround her. As a people among the gentiles she has waxed and waned. Her beginning was minuscule, including only Abraham and his family. With time she increased in the land given her; there was war and conflict and famine, and the people, in the persons of Jacob-Israel's offspring, went down into Egypt and were eventually enslaved there: a first exile. Under Moses's leadership the god liberated them, and they returned to the land, bringing bloodshed and slaughter; they established themselves there, eventually under the leadership of kings beginning with Saul, with Jerusalem as their central city. But there were marauders and invaders (Assyrians, Babylonians, others), and the people, or some part of it, was taken in servitude to Babylon: a second exile. Israel returned from Babylon and reestablished herself in the land, but there was again an ebb and flow of invaders and occupiers of the land (Persians, Greeks, others), culminating with the Romans, who eventually, after the failure of a final, large-scale revolt in the land against their rule, instituted what they intended to be a final and forced removal of the people from the land. Coins issued by the Emperor Hadrian in commemoration of that event bear the legend *Israel capta*, and thereafter Israel is largely scattered: a third exile. Then, in 1948, with premonitory rumblings, the State of Israel was established, in large part in response to European attempts to slaughter all Jews within her territories. Though in theory a secular state (there are definitional difficulties), Israel provided and still provides a right of return from exile for those among the people who wish it, though none for Palestinians displaced by her founding—there are definitional difficulties here, too: Israel as sovereign state continues to find it difficult to define the criteria that suffice to provide such a right in particular cases. By 1948, the people had spread to all parts of the world, and had often been subjected to violent persecution, including, in twentieth-century Europe, a systematic attempt, partly gentile and partly Christian in inspiration, to exterminate the Jewish part of Israel altogether: the Shoah.

As a people with her god, Israel moved and changed too. At first, her god was present with her as she moved, guiding her out of Egypt, accompanying her in the ark of the covenant. Then, a temple was built for the god in Jerusalem, and the god's liturgies were centralized there, though never exclusively: Israel's liturgies continued, as did holy places in the land other than Jerusalem. The god took up apparently permanent residence in the Jerusalem temple, with the ark installed there. But that first temple was destroyed by the armies of Nebuchadnezzar, as precursor to the second exile, and then rebuilt at approximately the same site after the exiled portion of the people's return from Babylon, though now without the ark, which may have been destroyed during Nebuchadnezzar's razing of the first temple. Israel's liturgical life centered upon that Second Temple until it was, in its turn, destroyed, this time by Roman forces. That Second Temple has not been rebuilt, though its ruins remain.

Two generations or so before the destruction of the Second Temple, Israel's life was complicated by Jesus of Nazareth. He, whom the Church came to recognize as the anointed one promised to Israel, and to worship as the god enfleshed, the second person of the Trinity the god is, was born into Israel as an Israelite. The turn of the calendrical eras dates from that birth, and it was also a pivotal event in Israel's life. Jesus was, perhaps in the twenties or thirties of the new era, tortured and judicially executed by crucifixion by the Roman authorities, and then rose from the dead and ascended into heaven, where he remains until his anticipated return at the end of things. Jesus was and is, in the Church's view, a person both fully human and fully god—the god of Israel, that is. His followers, those who confessed and worshipped him in these ways, came at first mostly from Israel, but before long they included gentiles in large numbers, and a more or less standardized liturgical form developed, by means of which aspirants, Israelite and gentile, could be incorporated into the body of Jesus's followers, which was also understood to be Jesus's own body. That liturgical form was baptism in the triune name of the god of Israel: Father, Son, Spirit. These Jesus followers shared with those in Israel who did not acknowledge Jesus as Christ and god (a large majority) the third exile: removal from the land into the world prompted by the destruction of the Second Temple and the final Roman victory over Israelite rebels in the second century of the new era.

This account is much too neat. All such complex processes are more gradual, more nuanced, more conflicted, and effected by more causes than such heuristic periodizations recognize. Israel's Diaspora had certainly been under way long before the second century, and the events of the first and second centuries did not issue in the complete removal of Israel from the land. Nevertheless. The Second Temple was destroyed in AD 70, the revolts of the second century against Rome did end in bloody failure, and Israel's scattering, ecclesial and synagogal, did accelerate thereafter. The schema has heuristic value for the purposes of this book, and I assume it in what follows.

The event of Jesus can be understood as an occurrence within Israel, and that is how I take it here. If it is understood in that way, then the body of Jesus's followers incorporated into him by baptism are Israelites, and baptism is one of the means by which Israel brings into herself those not born into Israel—gentiles, that is.

The separation, within Israel, of those who acknowledged Jesus as Messiah and as Israel's god enfleshed from those who did not caused a fugue of sorts. The separation of Church from Synagogue is sometimes described, by Jews and Christians both, with anodyne phrases such as the parting of the ways, as though it were a painless and bloodless happening, two paths diverging in a wood, something almost casual, a topic for disinterested memorial contemplation. But the traces of the divergence are mostly bloody and agonized, and such calm and dispassionate descriptions of it occlude that feature of them. Suppose, instead, Israel's internal division into Church and Synagogue to have been, and to some extent to continue to be, a fugue, something painful to attend to otherwise than by rewriting, and something painful enough often to require flight from it and selective forgetting of it. Then those traces can be attended to and accommodated, not fully, but better than is possible under anodyne descriptions.

Among the roots of the Church's flight from the Synagogue, as the Church sees it, is the refusal of a majority within Israel to acknowledge Jesus. This lack of acknowledgment ranged from the overt and active collaboration of a few Israelites with the Roman occupying power in the judicial torture and execution of Jesus, to a simple lack of interest in Jesus, whether during his time enfleshed in Israel or proclaimed by the nascent Church after his ascension. It extended to an occasional use or advocacy of violence against those who did acknowledge Jesus by those who did not: the fear of Jews among the first Christians is a frequent presence in some strata of the New Testament. And then the followers of Jesus began to baptize gentiles in his name, and were themselves divided about whether doing so made gentiles into Israelites, and, if it did, what that might mean for their halakhic and liturgical lives. Those in Israel who did not acknowledge Jesus, and who gave the matter any thought, were mostly clear that baptism in Jesus's name could not make an Israelite out of a gentile; and the Church, soon enough, for her own reasons, moved toward the same conclusion, at least to the extent that she took those among the baptized who had not been Israelite prior to their baptisms not to be required to (and, soon enough, to be required not to) participate in the nascent Synagogue's liturgical and halakhic life. A similar and equally tense set of disputes occurred within the Church about its baptized members who had been Israelite before their baptisms: Should they, or might they, participate in the liturgical and halakhic life of the Synagogue? The answer arrived at by the Church was negative, though then as now with less unanimity about the baptized who were already Jews (a term now with purchase) than about the baptized who had been gentiles; about the former some Christians thought that they might, and fewer that they should, live as Jews.

• • •

Thus the fugue's beginning. The Church turned her back on the Synagogue and developed her own liturgical and halakhic life independently of the Synagogue's, and to some degree in opposition to it. She attempted to become not-Synagogue, to present herself to herself as proud and happy possessor of Jesus, whom the Synagogue had spurned, and of a liturgical and halakhic life superior to that of the Synagogue because hers was centered upon Jesus and theirs was not. The Church began to inveigh against both Jews and Judaizers (those who advocated Jewish practices as possible, or appropriate, or required, for Christians, whether Jews or not); to flee with increasing speed from the Synagogue; to forget her place in Israel; to occlude even the fact that Jesus, her god enfleshed, is an Israelite, or, now, a Jew; to develop and deploy a repertoire of negatively stereotyped images for the Synagogue and for individual Jews; and to call into question, or outright to deny, the Synagogue's place in Israel as, still, recipient of the irrevocable promises to Abraham.

There is in all this both fugal amnesia and fugal rewriting: the Church in large part (never without remainder) is fugitive from Israel and from the Synagogue, and is damaged by that flight. She also damages the Synagogue by it: her stereotypes of the Synagogue fund theological error by the Church's speculative theologians and sow confusion among her faithful, as well as too often stimulate them to bloody violence against Jews. Her self-blinding by this fugue is projected, in an archetypal fugal move, onto the face of the Synagogue: when the Church's cathedrals are decorated with images of the Synagogue blind to Jesus and incapable of understanding the promises her god once gave her, the Church shows herself blind to the nature of her own place in Israel, which is in the arms of the god of Israel, incorporated into the circumcised flesh of Jesus; she shows herself, too, incapable of reading with understanding the promises her god has given her. The fugue of the Church's separation from the Synagogue has damaged both of them, though the Church more deeply. (It is for the Synagogue to speak to what she understands to have been the damage done to her and by her in her separation from the Church, and for the Church to attend to what she has to say, even if what is said appears to her wrong or incomplete.) That the fugal flight occurred at all is damage, an artifact of sin; and the damage begun then has proliferated since, winding

a shroud of suspicion and a mantle of violence around the Church's approaches to the Synagogue.

If Israel includes both Synagogue and Church, then each is in her distinctive way a friend of the same god, each increases in holiness by way of her liturgies and her halakhah, and each responds by way of them to the god's addresses and overtures to each. If that is so, then root-and-branch contempt for or violence toward the Synagogue and her Jews on the Church's part is clear evidence of sin on the part of the Church and her Christians. Sin requires contrition, confession, repair of damage when possible, and amendment of life. That is how the Church's sacraments treat the sins of individual Christians; it is also how the Church ought treat her own sins, performed corporately. Seeing Israel as including both herself and the Synagogue permits clearer recognition on the Church's part of the damage she has suffered and inflicted by her flight from the Synagogue, and permits clarity, too, about her need of repentance.

However, seeing both the Synagogue and herself as the god's beloveds does not require the Church to abandon her central doctrines, or to pretend that she and the Synagogue are in agreement about the god they both worship, or about what life as that god's elect entails. If Jesus was Israel's Messiah, and is the second person of the Trinity the god is, and if the Synagogue denies those truths, or shows no interest in them by living its life as if they were not so, then the Church must conclude that the Synagogue is mistaken about these matters. (The Synagogue may have similar judgments about the Church's doctrine and life, but it is for her to make them explicit.) These are not small matters. Consideration of them, and of what they require the Church to do and say, proceeds differently when Israel is imagined to include herself along with the Synagogue than it would were it imagined otherwise. A Church that imagines Israel in this way knows that what she says about her disagreements with the Synagogue, and how she acts upon those disagreements, cannot call into question the Synagogue's irrevocable election, and that if it begins to do so something has gone wrong. That is, imagining Israel in this way provides the Church with a rule of recognition for doctrinal and practical error. It may also, though with less clarity, provide her with an imagination attuned to seeing how to go on with the Synagogue in a situation in which each has been damaged by mutual amnesia and fear—by, that is, the fugal flight that has for so long been the texture of their mutual suspicion and fear.

Application of the first sense of fugue, as flight, to the Synagogue/Church question is straightforward enough. Before Jesus, Israel's liturgies and life were her holiness; they also, though this could only be seen retrospectively and then not clearly, prepared for Jesus by figuring him, and prepared for the priestly work of the Church, which is the work of Jesus, or, more fully, of the Trinity, by figuring that work; when, fugally, fugitively, what might have been one, an Israel undivided in its acknowledgment of Jesus as Messiah, separated into two, each developing apart from the other so that neither could recognize or acknowledge the other for what it is (the god's beloved, the god's elect), the god's work was, and could only have been, to reweave them as voices no longer in flight from one another, no longer discordant, but distinct, each made more distinctive by separation, each capable of hearing patterns in the liturgy and halakhah and theology of the other that recapitulate, develop, and deepen its own, and each moving, with the other, toward the same consummation. The harmoniously resolved fugue flows from the fugue of flight, which was its necessary condition; and it will be, perhaps (it is convenient to say so), eventually more beautiful in its harmony of differences than would have been the liturgy and life of an uncomplicated and unperplexed Israel.

This second sense of fugue suggests that the flight of the Church from the Synagogue and her construction of the Synagogue and the Jews as figures of failure and defect and vice in whose light the Church can sleekly and contentedly admire her own success and virtue, though itself a matter of sin and damage, may nonetheless yield good that would not have obtained had the initial flight not occurred. It suggests, too, that the now largely independent liturgical and halakhic lives of Church and Synagogue may have come, just because of the extent of their independence and ignorance of one another, to enshrine developed modes of intimacy with Israel's god, each of which may instruct and reform and deepen the other. Receiving instruction in this way, were it to occur, would require attention to particulars. The Church would, if the harmonious beauty of her own liturgy and halakhah were to be contrapuntally intensified by that of the Synagogue, need to know something of the particulars of the Synagogue's liturgy and halakhah and theology—not just that they are offerings by the Synagogue to Israel's god received with delight, but how those offerings are made, with what habits and attitudes, and in response to which particular blessings. Imagining the mutual flight of Church and Synagogue as a *culpa*, a fault, should lead, given standard Christian axioms about the way in which Israel's god responds to faults, to an eagerness on the Church's part to discover the felicities the god brings from that fault (the Synagogue may wish to do the same; but that is for her to decide, and to speak to, should she wish)—for all *culpae* bring *felices* with them: honey comes from bees hiving in a lion's corpse as blessings do from sins, which is neither apology nor excuse nor justification for death or sin, but an observation about what the god typically brings from them.

Israel's complication, then, may productively be seen by the Church as a fugue: lamentable, but resolvable. Two implications of depicting the complication in this way need to be underscored: first, the limits it places upon the Church's current standing to intervene in the Synagogue's life; and second, the capacity it provides Christians, should they wish to use it, to look at the Synagogue, and at her own habits of depicting the Synagogue, in ways that might gradually transfigure their depictions of and responses to her, moving them away from contempt and contrastive self-aggrandizement, and toward a perplexed admiration.

• • •

The taxonomy provided so far can be restated formally: Since the complication, there are within Israel Israelites who are Christian only (they are born to a gentile mother and then baptized into Jesus), Israelites who are Jewish only (they are born to a Jewish mother or are gentiles received liturgically into the Synagogue), and Israelites who are both (they are Jews first, and then baptized; or Christians first and then received into the Synagogue). Outside Israel there are only gentiles, who are by definition neither Jewish nor Christian. Since Israel's complication, the Israel/gentile distinction remains as it was before, and as it will be until (should it happen) all gentiles enter Israel; and the indelibility of the mark of being in Israel is present in two ways, Jewish and Christian, each mark also indelible, Israel thus being no longer simplex but complex—or at least more complex; she never was simplex, marked since Abraham by internal divisions and differences of various kinds; but the complication marked by Jesus and what stemmed from him is, from the Church's standpoint, deeper and more thoroughgoing than others. It is this last feature, the indelibility and irrevocability of Jewishness and Christianness, which explains the strange, perhaps monstrous, perhaps utopian, perhaps overweening, almost certainly excessive, existence of Jews who are also Christians, who are the same people as Christians who are also Jews. They can be differentiated only by the order in which they became each: Jew first, and then also Christian; Christian first, and then also Jew—the upshot is the same. Christians who become Jews do not thereby cease to be Christian, and Jews who become Christians do not thereby cease to be Jewish. This also means that such people belong, postcomplication, to both Church and Synagogue, and this leads to perplexities of a liturgical, halakhic, and sometimes, too, of a properly theological kind, for them as individuals, for their local communities, and for Church and Synagogue in a broader sense.

• • •

This way of taxonomizing Israel raises some questions about the god's irrevocable promise of endurance to Israel. Does that promise apply only to Israel as a whole, in which case the world might be emptied of Jews or of Christians, though not of both? Or should it rather be said that Israel is now, since her complication, defined by the complementary presence in her of Church and Synagogue, in which case there will, until the end, be some, at least, of both Jews and Christians in the world? Each of these three possibilities—Israel with only Jews; Israel with only Christians; Israel with both Jews and Christians—is grammatically possible within the constraints of Christian speech and writing; but consideration of the archive, together with analysis of the advantages and drawbacks of each possibility, ought dispose the Church to affirm the third possibility and to reject the first two: since her complication, her new and perplexing complexity, Israel is complementarily constituted by Church and Synagogue, and therefore there will, until the end, always be some Jews and some Christians in the world.

The first possibility, that there might cease to be any Christians in the world before the end, is ruled out for the Church by the seriousness with which she takes the promise that Jesus will find followers in the world when he returns to it; if that is so, the world will not then be empty of the baptized. The second possibility, a world empty of Jews before the end, is one envisaged by Christians from time to time (altogether too often); but there are strong reasons not to affirm it, and for most of Christian history the thought that such a state of affairs is either possible or desirable has been a minority view, even if the reasons for rejecting it—principally that the Church needs the Synagogue to witness to her own fulfilment and understanding of the promises made to Israel by the god (almost the standard view in the Western Church for the last sixteen centuries), and to the fact that she is more intimate with the god than the Synagogue is or can be (also a standard view, sufficiently axiomatic for most Catholic Christians that it seems puzzling how any Christian might think differently)—have been bad ones. That leaves the third possibility: that Israel's irrevocable election means that since the complication it is certain that she will continue to harbor, and be exhaustively and complementarily constituted by, both Church and Synagogue, until the end.

That is about the endurance of Israel as a collective. There is, postcomplication, an individual version of the same point. The Church has long claimed that the liturgy for making Christians, baptism, does something to those who undergo it that cannot be undone. It tattoos them with a mark invisible to the eye that cannot be removed, in something like the way that soldiers in the Roman legions were tattooed. The Church does not rebaptize, therefore: it is not possible for a Christian, or for the Church, or for the god, to do anything that would make rebaptism necessary. Once a Christian, always so. For the Synagogue it is the same: evidently so in the case of becoming a Jew by being born so; less evidently, but reasonably, in the case of recruitment by whatever liturgies the Synagogue uses for that purpose. The gift of Jewishness or Christianness given by the god to individuals is in form irrevocable in just the same way as the gift that brought Israel into being. Said differently: following Israel's complication, there will always have been at least one Jew and one Christian; and no Jew and no Christian can cease to be what they are, can be separated from their Jewishness or Christianness by any state of affairs: *Certus sum*, Paul of Tarsus writes in his letter to the Romans immediately before embarking upon his most extensive and nuanced treatment of the question about Israel, *enim quia neque mors neque vita neque angeli neque principatus neque instantia neque futura neque virtutes neque altitudo neque profundum neque alia quaelibet creatura poterit nos separare a caritate Dei, quae est in Christo Iesu Domino nostro* (For I am certain that neither death, nor life, nor angels, nor principalities, nor things present, nor things future, nor powers, nor height, nor depth, nor any other created thing, can separate us from the love of God which is in Christ Jesus, our LORD). This certitude, from a Christian point of view, embraces Jews as well as Christians. The Synagogue has her versions of it, even though, postcomplication, they do not include the name of Jesus.

Both Church and Synagogue can in theory exist without any of the liturgical, halakhic, and theological distinctives that mark them as a form of life. That could happen if all their members, all Jews and all Christians, that is, were ignorant, apostate, forgetful, or otherwise secularized—conformed, that is, to the halakhic norms, liturgical exercises, and theological speculations of this or that gentile community without any specifically Jewish or Christian remnant or aspect. Jews and Christians like this, conformed without evident remainder to the world, would be no less Jews and Christians for being so. That is because their identity, the god's irrevocable gift to them, is not constituted by what they do, or think, or intend. Deserters from the army are still soldiers even if they no longer live under military discipline; pear trees remain what they are even when placed in an environment that makes it impossible for them to blossom or fruit; amnesiacs remain the offspring of their parents even if they cannot recognize or acknowledge them. But none of that suggests that the halakhic, liturgical, and theological norms and practices of Israel, whether in ecclesial or synagogal form, are unimportant to her, or to her god. If the god's purpose in electing Israel is her holiness, and through that holiness the repair of the devastated world (there is also, it must always be said, the purpose of inscrutably offering Israel love without respect to what she might do for and in the world: election has a universal and a particular dimension, and to forget either is to offer an inadequate view of it), then a Church or a Synagogue composed exclusively of the nonobservant would be severely damaged. They would not be nothing (there would still be Jews and Christians), but they would be incapable of intentionally and overtly and explicitly returning the god's love; they would be beloveds who had forgotten their lover's name and face, and would be correspondingly incapable of offering the gift of holiness to the world.

Is it possible that Church or Synagogue or both could ever be in this condition? Even that at the end Jesus might find in Israel only apostates and amnesiacs? This, I suppose, is a theoretical possibility; perhaps it is even the case that Church and Synagogue have at times approached it. But it is not something that appears likely. There will be, as there seems since Abraham so far always to have been, a remnant of the observant in Israel, both ecclesially and synagogally, and the Church should be confident, even if not apodictically or irrefragably so, that this will continue to be the case—that there will always be an observant remnant. More can be said from the Church's side: should the Church become such that the last observant Christian has a choice between maintaining her observance and abandoning it in support of the observance of the last observant Jew, she should choose the second alternative. That the Synagogue should continue to have observant Jews is, for the time being and the foreseeable future, more important for the Church than that she should herself continue to have observant Christians.

• • •

This taxonomy yields some clear formal similarities and differences between Church and Synagogue—clear, at least, as they appear to the Church (the Synagogue may characterize them differently should she wish to characterize them at all).

As to the similarities: each has the other as its complement in the constitution of Israel; each is in receipt of the god's irrevocable promise that she will endure as the god's intimate beloved until the end; each has a liturgical, halakhic, and theological life given her by the god, by the living of which she becomes holy and calls the gentiles to herself; each can be instructed by the particulars of the other's life; and each has the other as the form of human life with which it is most intimate, and places, or should place, the interests and needs of the other, therefore, above the interests and needs of any other form of human life—each, that is, is, or should be, the other's most particular and intimate love within the human sphere.

As to the differences. The first is about the acknowledgment of Jesus as Messiah, and as the god enfleshed. The Church makes such an acknowledgment, while the Synagogue does not. The second is that the Synagogue recognizes biological descent as the ordinary (not the only) way of entry into herself: birth to a Jewish mother makes you a Jew (perhaps other, more distant, forms of descent also do; whether or not that is so—it is for the Synagogue, not the Church, to decide—direct matrilineal descent suffices). The Church does not recognize this means of entry into herself. You can become a Christian only by recruitment, which is to say ordinarily by the liturgy of recruitment, which is baptism. The Synagogue also recruits liturgically, but as a subsidiary, or extraordinary, means—an accommodation, perhaps, to circumstance, rather than a fundamental commitment. Since the complexification of Israel's division into Church and Synagogue, it is likely that a large majority of Jews has come into being by way of procreation rather than liturgical recruitment.

This last is a significant difference. What is common to, or at least characteristic of, human communities that perpetuate themselves only or principally by procreation? The first, and obvious, point is that such communities will likely be interested in the regulated encouragement of procreation among members. Such encouragement looks different depending on whether only matrilineal descent is recognized, only patrilineal, or both. Matrilineal descent is, naturally, easier to observe and regulate than patrilineal, and it is probably for this reason that most procreation-perpetuated communities tend toward establishment of matrilineal rather than patrilineal descent. Such communities are likely to encourage procreation by providing scripts for male/female relations in which it is a positive norm, and, correspondingly, in which celibacy, understood as abstention from potentially procreative sexual relations, is treated with suspicion or sanction, or at least made a minority and idiosyncratic interest. These are tendencies only. It is not difficult to imagine a procreatively maintained community within which positive place is provided for some celibates, male or female; but it is harder to imagine such a community within which celibacy is scripted as the norm for its members. Such a norm would, if effective, ensure the community's rapid end.

In addition to this positive norming of procreation, procreatively maintained communities are likely to show an interest in the marking and forming of their babies from birth onward, for they are already, then, members of the community, whereas that is not so for recruitment-only communities. Further, there is likely to be a strong correlation between the degree to which a community is maintained procreatively and the degree to which it discourages out-marriage—marriage, that is, between someone who is a member of the community and someone who is not, with the possibility of procreation in such a situation. The reasons for this are obvious for communities in which membership is assured only if both parents are themselves members; in the case of those for which either matrilineal or patrilineal descent suffices for membership, the reasons are less clear and pressing, but are still likely to be present in some form and to some degree. And lastly, procreatively maintained communities are likely to maintain stronger and more clearly marked boundaries between themselves and others than are those that maintain themselves at least in part by recruitment. That is because those outside can never enter communities exclusively maintained by procreation, and are thus without interest as potential recruits. And even for those among the procreatively maintained that do, extraordinarily, allow recruitment, barriers are likely to be higher and identity markings clearer than in the case of those communities that perpetuate themselves only or mostly by recruitment. Most generally and fundamentally: the degree to which a community is maintained procreatively is also the degree to which it positively validates the biological family—for it is, as a whole, itself a large family.

As to recruitment-only communities, of which the Church is one. These are in no sense biological families. Interests they have in regulating procreation will therefore be distinct from interests they have in self-perpetuation, and this is likely to mean that norms for the regulation of procreation and the ordering of the biological family will be drawn from sources external to the community, as is evident in the length of time it took for the Church to develop an interest in regulating and performing the weddings of Christians, and in her dependence, by and large, upon legal and practical norms for marriage and procreation external to herself. By contrast, Israel before the complication, and the Synagogue since, have shown an interest in regulating such matters from the beginning, and given them greater importance than has the Church. Recruitment-only communities have more space for celibacy than procreation-only or procreation-dominant ones, for obvious enough reasons, principal among which is that the celibacy of even a large portion of members is no threat to the community's perpetuation if all new members are recruited. Here too the Church and the Synagogue perform approximately as expected: the former has developed scripts for celibacy, and has often, perhaps even typically, elevated it above the sexually and procreatively active life. The latter's scripts for celibacy, by contrast, are scarcely evident, and Jews who live a celibate life do so against the Synagogue's norms. One manifestation of this difference is that there has been less concern about out-marriage on the part of the Church than on the part of the Synagogue. Another is that the Synagogue has been, and remains, more concerned than the Church to distinguish the appearance of her members from the appearance of those who are not.

All these differences have to do in various ways with the means of self-perpetuation adopted and validated by the Synagogue and the Church, respectively. They are tendencies only, and I have overemphasized them for clarity, and for suggestiveness about the significance these differences have for a theological understanding of Israel post-complication. In order to correct this overemphasis, it is important to note that the Western Church, at least, has in recent centuries, since the Reformation on the Protestant side and the Council of Trent on the Catholic, diluted its sense of itself as a recruitment-only community, and regressed to the norms of procreation-dominant communities. This dilution and regression is most evident in the elevation and positive validation of the biological family as of great significance for the Church's life; and in a concomitant downgrading and marginalization of the scripts for celibacy. It is not that the Church has rejected or otherwise seriously called into question the thought that entry is ordinarily by recruitment, which is to say by baptism—which entails that no one is born a Christian; neither is it that the Church has abandoned the idea that celibates have a significant part in the Church's life. But it is the case that the elevation of the celibate life above the procreative has been deemphasized and sometimes called into question; and that there has been and continues to be an explicit magisterial emphasis on the biological family as the core and norm of the Church's life here below. In these ways the Church has over time become more like the Synagogue, and the significance of baptism as a rite of recruitment, a rite that brings gentiles into Israel in its specifically ecclesial form, has been attenuated. It is difficult now to imagine a homily or a magisterial teaching document that would advocate celibacy as the highest norm for Christian life, or that would instruct Christians to stop having potentially procreative sex. Such teaching and advocacy were commonplace during the first millennium of the Church's life.

• • •

The texture of the Synagogue's and the Church's life now with respect to these differences is complex—a good deal more complex than I have made it seem (this is no empirical study). The Church is not a pure type of the recruitment-only community, and the Synagogue is likewise not a pure type of the procreation-only community. Nevertheless. There remain real differences: Israel, since the complication, contains Jews who tend toward procreation only, and Christians who tend toward recruitment only. The Church ought not and need not depict this difference as if it were to her advantage and to the detriment of the Synagogue. She can, and she ought, try to discern what there is of benefit to the mission of Israel as a whole in this difference, which is also to say what the god, hers and the Synagogue's, might do with it. Here are suggestions along that line, here given only as an illustration of the kind of thinking about Israel proper for the Church now.

First. The recruitment of the gentiles is among Israel's central purposes. The effecting of that goal is one of the reasons the god called Abraham and renamed Jacob. The world is devastated; it needs to be made whole; its repair requires, inter alia, that all human creatures become the god's beloveds and the god's lovers; and that means that all human creatures should enter Israel. If, as seems the case, the Church is ideal-typically, and sometimes actually, a recruitment-only community, she may be the form Israel takes, postcomplication, when recruitment is the principal purpose at hand. She is equipped to offer Jesus—an Israelite, and since the complication also a Jew—to the gentiles; she has shown herself effective in doing so; and when she does what she does in this connection she incorporates gentiles into Israel by baptism, and in that way makes them into the god's intimate beloveds, which until then they were not. The Synagogue, in the forms she has come to take since the complication, is less good at this: her self-offering to the gentiles does not appear to be among her central purposes, not among those enterprises proper to Israel for which she is best equipped.

Second. Israel is to be holy, drunk on love with the god's intoxicating presence, radiant with a way of life that shows her to be the god's beloved, capable of nothing but the god. That, too, is among the god's reasons for calling Abraham and renaming Jacob: the world is devastated, it needs to be made whole, and holiness is its repair—or at least the beginning of a necessary condition for its repair. If, as seems the case, the Synagogue is ideal-typically, and sometimes actually, a procreation-only community, she may be the form Israel takes, postcomplication, when holiness is the principal purpose at hand. She is equipped, with her liturgical and halakhic concern for a life marked and identified as holy, focused upon a familial community perpetuated mostly procreatively, to be holy and to show holiness to the world. Her life, when ordered as it should be, shows in the details of its texture what holiness is like. The Church, in the forms she has come to take since the complication, is less good at this: holiness of life, sharp and clear, does not appear to be among her central purposes; her intimacy with the gentile world perhaps precludes it for her, and so she moves through that world camouflaged, hard to see, hard, therefore, to learn holiness from.

I am extravagant here. Recruitment of gentiles is of course not absent from the Synagogue; the transfiguration of life's particulars toward holiness is of course not absent from the Church. But extravagance can be clarifying, and the instance of it provided here begins, sketchily, a task essential for the Church—that of determining now, in the state of perplexity about Israel in which she finds herself, what the differences between herself and the Synagogue may be taken to mean for her.

Third. As the Church should see it (she too often forgets or ignores it), the only human flesh that is also the god's flesh is Israelite flesh, and not Israelite by recruitment but, rather, flesh in direct descent from Abraham. That is, the flesh of Jesus Christ. The Church's god, Israel's god, took human flesh, certainly; but also, and necessarily, Israelite flesh. Once Israel had been called into existence by the god, the god's enfleshment had to occur there, within Israel. The canon of Scripture as the Church reads it (not, of course, as the Synagogue does) is clear about that: the flesh of Jesus, which is also the god's flesh, is Israelite flesh, and a Christian is anyone who has been incorporated by baptism into that flesh, and in that way incorporated into Israel. Another way to put this: what gentiles become when they are baptized is a version of what Jews already are: participant in the flesh that makes Israel Israel, the flesh that descends by procreation from Abraham, and which is taken up by the god as Jesus. Jews and Christians are now, since the complication, participant together in one flesh, a flesh in which gentiles do not participate. When the Church prosecutes its work of making Christians, which is the god's work first, it makes gentiles into what Jews already are in respect of the flesh. This makes the Church dependent, both logically and temporally, upon the Synagogue for its very existence, and for the most basic particular of that existence. And this is not a point to be made only about what baptism is and does; it applies also, though in different mode, to the Eucharist: the body and blood of Jesus given and taken in the Eucharist is Israelite flesh and Israelite blood. The holiness and health the Church has is sustained in her mostly by that flesh, and in this respect also the Church depends on the Synagogue—Christians on Jews for their existence and sustenance as such. If there is a judgment of value to be made about this difference between the Synagogue and the Church, it is certainly not to the detriment of the Synagogue. This is an ecclesial imagining of the Synagogue, and as such may or may not (very likely not, I should think) be acceptable to the Synagogue. But it does not represent the Synagogue as lacking something the Church has. Rather the reverse. The Church, in order to become what she should be, must work to see clearly that she stands in need of what the Synagogue always and abundantly has—the flesh the god loves.

• • •

There are, however, a number of significant objections to this use of the tropes of complication and fugue to schematize both the history of Israel and the nature of the connections between Synagogue and Church within that history.

One is that this use of the fugal metaphor runs counter to a widely held ecclesial view of the Synagogue by suggesting that the flight of Synagogue from Church and of Church from Synagogue was and is symmetrical—that misunderstanding and error, at least, are equally distributed. The more widely held view, which might even be called the standard view, is that the Church knew then, at the fugue's beginning, and knows now, more than two millennia later, something of fundamental significance about Israel's god, which is that Jesus is both Israel's Messiah and Israel's god enfleshed, and that the world's salvation, including, therefore, the salvation of the Jews, comes from the god's work in and as Jesus. The Synagogue, this standard view continues, refused then and refuses now to acknowledge these truths. There is nothing of such fundamental importance about Israel's god that the Synagogue knew then and knows now, and therefore nothing of such importance that the Church denies. Where then the symmetry with respect to error and ignorance? Is not the fugal flight better understood as occurring principally in one direction: the Synagogue's flight from truth, while the Church moves into ever-fuller understanding of truth? It is here that the almost standard ecclesial trope of fulfillment for her relation to the Synagogue finds its application.

This objection has something right: the Church does teach these truths about Jesus, and takes them to be fundamental and essential. Her entire liturgical and halakhic life is ordered around them to one degree or another. It is true, too, that the Church has often, perhaps typically, imagined the Synagogue as constituted at heart and in essence by their denial. But that act of the imagination does not follow from the fact that the Church acknowledges Jesus while the Synagogue does not. The Church might, and perhaps can, imagine the Synagogue's life not as resting upon a denial, but rather as constituted by an affirmation: of her god's continuing gifts and promises to herself, and of her attempt to live responsively to them. Those gifts and promises include liturgy and theology and halakhah; the Synagogue's response includes waiting for a messiah yet to come, and growing in holiness by attention to her god's address and demand and caress. That there is error and incompleteness in all this is inevitable, and the Church has no need to deny it or minimize it. If what she teaches about Jesus is true, then the Synagogue's denial of it, insofar as the Synagogue is interested enough in Jesus to deny him, is false, and the Synagogue's life with Israel's god without an acknowledgment of Jesus (not, of course, without Jesus: if Israel's god is triune then the Synagogue's life with that god is a life with Jesus, whether the Synagogue sees it or not) is incomplete.

The Church might, however, and can, imagine herself also to be as yet partial and incomplete and subject to error not yet discerned in her understanding of and response to the gifts given her, including the gift of seeing and acknowledging Jesus. One clear sign of that error, increasingly discerned and discernible, is the Church's expressed contempt for and frequent misprision of the Synagogue. She and the Synagogue ought be imagined alike in their subjection to incompleteness and error, and necessarily so: the god's beloveds do not, because they cannot, comprehend what the god has given them; and the god's beloveds always, in their attempts to understand and respond to what the god has given them, make errors. That there is sin and error in Israel's complication is a claim integral to the Church's imagination of Israel; the fugue is, in this respect, like Israel's flight from Egypt with Egyptian gold, which was both blessing (it was used to ornament the ark of the covenant) and curse (it was used to make the golden calf). The distribution of error between Church and Synagogue, however, is not fully known to the Church, and a view of it neither need nor ought contribute to her imagination of the Synagogue. The fugal flight was bidirectional, and lamentable (not only lamentable, but at least so) in both directions.

Those should be the essential elements in the Church's imagination of the fugal flight. Imagining herself as more holy than the Synagogue, more intimate with the god, more virtuous, more lovely—none of that is needed for an ecclesial imagining of fugal flight and gradual fugal reconciliation. The Church knows Jesus, and should say so, with passion. She knows the Synagogue as beloved of the god, and should say so, with passion. She knows that the extent and particulars of what the Synagogue has come to know of the god are in considerable part hidden from her, and should say so, with passion. She has no need, self-aggrandizingly, to depict the Synagogue principally as a creature of lack and loss, and she should cease doing so, with passion.

There is another objection to the fugal metaphor, from the opposite direction. It is that study of the historical record shows that while the Church has often defined herself over against the Synagogue, and has often, in doing so, been rhetorically and actually violent toward the Synagogue and her Jews, the Synagogue has, for the most part, been without interest in the Church's construals of Israel's god, without interest in the pretensions of the Church's Jesus, and without interest in the Church, except as something dangerous to herself. The question of the Synagogue, and more broadly of Israel, is of continuing and obsessive concern to the Church; but the question of the Church has no parallel place in the Synagogue's life, which, for the most part, shows no interest at all in the Church and her Christians. Should not, then, the fugal metaphor be construed as a one-way flight? It is the Church, after all, that did the running, and the Church that shows concern about what to make of it. The Synagogue had little interest then, and has little interest now.

This objection involves an empirical question addressable by study of sources and events across the long history of interactions between Synagogue and Church. It is likely correct that the energy devoted by the Church to imagining the Synagogue these last sixteen hundred years or so is greater than that devoted by the Synagogue to imagining the Church. But the Church's imagination of Israel is not an activity to the prosecution of which empirical, historical studies are central (they are not irrelevant, either). Whatever is the case about the objection raised here, it remains important to the Church's Israel (an entity distinct in the orders of thought and imagination from the historian's Israel, and from the Synagogue's Israel) that she is constituted by both Church and Synagogue; that their separation is a matter of damage and flight to which each has contributed; and that the transfigurative repair of that damage can only be an act of the god both acknowledge. The Synagogue may imagine differently, and may in part do so because of a lack of interest in the Church, and because of the fugue here sketched, as this objection suggests. It is her privilege to do so. The task here is only to sketch lightly one version of Israel as a guide to the Church's future life with Israel's god. For that purpose, the fugue as bidirectional flight is important. This in no way undercuts the truth in the objection, which is that the Synagogue is of interest to the Church in ways that the Church is not of interest to the Synagogue. That is a claim the Church can endorse.

It is also possible reasonably, though wrongly, to object theologically to the musical sense of fugue in play here, which suggests that felicities always come from faults, that the felicities prompted by a particular fault would not have occurred had the fault not occurred, and that the healing in which particular felicities consist exceeds (sometimes? typically? always?) the fault-produced damage that catalyzed them. It might be said that this is an absurd and inadequate theology that suggests that no fault is lamentable and each is to be celebrated because from each comes grace that would otherwise not have been.

A theology such as that would be pollyannaish. It is, Christianly speaking, flat-footedly ungrammatical: a solecism. It should, therefore, have no place in the Church's imagination of Israel or the Synagogue. That felicities have come already, and that more will, from the fugal flight of Church from Synagogue does not remotely suggest that the flight should be celebrated. The felicities flowing from it should be celebrated; the proliferating damage in which it consists, including the bare fact of it, should be lamented. Christians do not celebrate the judicial torture and execution of Jesus simpliciter. Good Friday is not a celebration, but a lament. And yet, from that pain-filled event came something to be celebrated. So also here: there is no contradiction. Difficulties arise when the coexistence of fault and felicity, together with the complex connections between them, is systematized into a doctrine of providence, or some other supposed answer to the so-called problem of evil and its many deformed cousins. But that need not be done. All that need be done here, in the case of the Church's imagination of Israel, is to acknowledge the coexistence and interweaving of fault and felicity in the double fugue that relates Church to Synagogue; and to acknowledge the Church's incapacity (the Synagogue's too, no doubt; but that is for her to speak to) to distinguish, in particular events, with anything approaching apodictic certainty, fault from felicity. The Church can be sure that both are present here; her speculative theologians can suggest (as I am doing here) trajectories and methods for distinguishing them; and her magisterium, at times, may specify with authority instances of each as such. The objection rightly rejects an unacceptable position; but it is not one required or suggested by the second, musical sense of fugue in play here.

A fourth objection to the sketch of the history between Church and Synagogue given here is that it overemphasizes the Church's responsibility for the violence done to the Synagogue in the West these past sixteen centuries or so, while at the same time minimizing gentile violence done to Jews on strictly gentile—that is, non-Christian—grounds. Christian violence toward the Synagogue, the objection might continue, has more often been done by Christians as an outflow of ambient gentile hatred of Jews than because of specifically ecclesial understandings of the Synagogue and her Jews, and so it is misleading to depict such violence as an act of the Church.

Some disagreement on this question is reasonably possible. It's clear that not all violence directed toward Jews because they are Jews need be intimate with specifically ecclesial patterns of speech and writing. Much about the pseudoscientific racism that informed and prompted violence toward Jews in, for example, Germany in the 1930s and 1940s, had no direct precedent in the Church. It is abundantly possible to act violently toward Jews, and to seek to empty the world of them, without being Christian or using Christian tropes and doctrines. But it is much less clear that widespread gentile violence directed at Jews could have come into existence without the traditional ecclesial grammars of Israel against which this book is in significant part written. Those ways of talking about the Synagogue and the Jews at least provided the soil in which the gentile versions grew, and often fertilized them as well. It has been, for much of the Church's history, normal for her to depict the Synagogue as blind, weeping, and dispossessed. The Church was in error when she did this, and it is possible to provide (as here) a Christian grammar of Israel which neither requires nor suggests it. But it is hard to deny that the patterns of speech and writing about the Synagogue's place in Israel commonplace in the Church for many centuries are ingredient to the fugal flight depicted here; and almost as hard to deny that those patterns have often informed, and continue to inform, nonecclesial (gentile, and particularly Islamic) patterns of violence directed at the Synagogue and hatred directed at Jews. The exact balance between ecclesial and gentile hatred of Jews of the kind canvassed in this chapter may remain a question; but not the fact that the Church has been the principal offender in this matter.

A final objection. The lexical stipulation made here, that *Israel* extends to both Synagogue and Church, runs counter to most English usage of this word now, at the end of the first quarter of the twenty-first century. It will seem strange to most users of English, for whom, when the word doesn't indicate the sovereign state of that name, it tends to indicate the Jews, for whom it can stand as an umbrella term. That is true, too, for the majority, perhaps a very large majority, of English-using Jews now. The usage suggested here will therefore appear to most who read it somewhere on the gamut that runs from idiosyncratic to insulting. It isn't, quite, on a level with Humpty Dumpty's stipulation that *glory* means "a nice knock-down argument"—or, at least, his stipulation that this is what he, Humpty Dumpty, means by it. But it isn't far from that. And so perhaps it would be better to find a different word for the form of life which the Synagogue and the Church conjointly constitute.

Everything in this objection seems correct, save for its recommendation. The usage of *Israel* here is at least idiosyncratic; most readers of English are likely to stumble over it; and many, perhaps most Jews, will find it offensive or something similar. But I can see little choice. If Israel is the name for the god's chosen, the god's beloved community, then it must, as the Church sees things (or ought), extend as suggested here. And so far as I can see, there is no other good candidate for the name. If the Synagogue, or some part of her, does find this usage objectionable, then it is the Church's task to attend to her objections and to take them seriously. But at the moment the stickiness and counterintuitiveness of this usage is a desirable feature of the enterprise under way here, not a difficulty to be removed.

3

THE CHURCH'S STANDING

THE FUGUE WITH its consequent complication, which includes the particular patterns of violence and hatred directed by the Church toward the Synagogue, has effects upon the Church's standing in Israel.

Standing is something you might have, or lack, with respect to some action. To have it is to be competent with respect to that action: to have all the capacities required for its effective performance. To lack it is to be incompetent: to lack at least one of the capacities required for its effective performance. Examples: teaching a class at your local college while not on the faculty; marrying someone when already married to someone else; calling a strike at a baseball game while not being the umpire; voting in a precinct while not registered there; receiving the consecrated body and blood at Mass while not baptized; bringing suit for damages against a municipality while never having visited or lived or paid taxes there. In these instances the lack indicated removes standing for the action attempted, and thereby removes competence for the action. Should you attempt an action for which you lack standing, what you do will not be that action but, rather, some other. That is the typical case.

Suppose, for instance, that you successfully impersonate a legatee and receive a sum of money left to the person you are impersonating. You bank the money and happily spend it; the impersonation is never discovered. You have not received a legacy, however, because, not being a legatee, you cannot. Only legatees have standing to receive legacies; you are incompetent to do so. What you have done might be described as theft or fraud or both; you do have competence for those. Or, suppose you tutoyer me in French even though we have never met before and you haven't asked my permission to do so, which means that you lack standing to address me in that way. The form of address remains the same as if you did have standing to use it; but because you lack it, what you effect in using that form is a solecism or even an insult rather than the address of one intimate to another. A similar analysis, mutatis mutandis, can be applied to the other examples canvassed.

On this analysis, lack of standing for some action guarantees at once failure in doing it and success in doing something else, something typically distant from the action for which standing is lacking. The examples also suggest that it is most natural and appropriate to say of someone that they lack standing for some action only when they meet almost all the conditions necessary for the performance of it, lacking, typically, only one. It would be odd to say that Jane lacks standing to compete in the 2021 Olympic Games because she died in the seventeenth century; it would be less odd to say that she lacks it because she does not meet the International Olympic Committee's current standards for competition in women's events. The difference is given by the fact that in the former case Jane lacks so many of the necessities for Olympic competition that the possibility that she might compete does not arise; such competition is simply impossible for her, for many reasons. In the latter case, by contrast, she might have all the necessities save one: she can, let's suppose, run the race, and do so faster than anyone else, and she is barred from entering women's competition only because of her testosterone levels, or something similar.

Discussion of standing ordinarily occurs in contexts in which it seems at first blush that there is standing—that this person is competent to undertake the action in question. For this reason, analysis of what happens when a mouse nibbles the consecrated host is less likely to use the concept of standing than is analysis of what happens when an unbaptized person receives the sacrament. The ordinary scene for discussions of standing, therefore, is one in which people do something for which, and at which, they are at first blush entirely competent: there they are, apparently doing it. Should they in fact lack standing it will be for reasons not immediately apparent, not written on the surface of the event. That is why the idea of standing has its principal locus and its most baroque development within the sphere of positive law. It is typically used there as a device to distinguish those who appear competent for some action and in fact are so, from those who appear competent and in fact are not. It is not ordinarily used to distinguish those who evidently cannot do something from those who at first blush can: the incarcerated are not discriminated from those who have standing to drive on a public highway by saying that they lack standing for that activity. It is the licenseless unincarcerated who are distinguished in that way.

Standing is not a permanent possession; neither is its lack. It may be that once you had standing to marry, but now you lack it because you're already married. You may come to have it again, following divorce. So also for the other examples canvassed. Standing varies, then, according to the history and circumstance of the persons, individual or corporate, to whom it might apply.

• • •

Suppose, with this idea of standing in hand, we ask about the Church's standing now, whether corporately or in the individual persons of Christians, for interventions into the life of the Synagogue. What is the Church competent to do in this respect, and what is she not competent to do? For which kinds of intervention has she standing, and for which does she lack it? What does the depiction of Israel's fugal complication do to ecclesial standing with respect to the Synagogue? This is not a question about what the Church may do by way of intervention; it is more pointed than that. It is a question about what the Church might effect if she attempts it, and what she cannot now effect because she is incompetent. Instances of the latter kind, if attempted, yield, inevitably, something other than and usually distant from what they putatively aim at.

The question about what the Church has standing to do to, for, and perhaps with the Synagogue is, given the taxonomy in play here, a question about affairs within Israel. It is a question, that is, about what one body of Israelites (Christians) has standing to do to, for, and with another (Jews). It is also a question whose answer is dependent, among other things, upon a construal of the long history between Church and Synagogue since their fugal flight from one another. This is normal: the standing of one spouse for intervention in the life of the other is in part dependent upon what they have done to, for, and with one another over time; likewise for sovereign states with one another, pastors and their congregations, children and their parents, banks and their debtors, and so on.

The history of Church with Synagogue is fugal and violent and agonized. It was, at first, a matter of error and blindness, whose damage then proliferated. No complete account of that damage is now possible, but it is clear that, from the side of the Church, violence has been a frequent, almost ordinary, feature of her interventions into the Synagogue's life. Christians have coerced Jews into baptism; have falsely accused Jews of host desecration and acts of violence against Christian bodies; have directly slaughtered Jews, sometimes in large numbers; have ghettoized and otherwise limited the lives and freedoms of Jews by the soft coercion of law and custom as well as by the hard coercion of physical force; have been complicit in, as well as sometimes initiating or being actively participant in, the large-scale slaughters of Jews of which the Shoah is the paradigmatic but not the only instance; and have sometimes done all these things, and more, for what they have wrongly taken to be Christian reasons, reasons given by misconstruals of their baptisms and of the status and nature of the Synagogue.

Also, until very recently Christians have depicted the Synagogue in such a way as to deepen and make violent divisions between Church and Synagogue. The Church has painted the Synagogue as principally responsible for the death of Jesus, and as bereft of intimacy with her god. These depictions (they are as often pictorial or sculptural as verbal), together with their various assumptions and entailments, lead easily enough to the conclusion that the Synagogue has had no reason to continue in existence since Pentecost; or, in more moderate form, that the only reason she now has to continue in being is to point to the Church as her inheritor and successor.

The Church's life with the Synagogue has not been exclusively one of contempt, suspicion, fear, and violence, even though those are the dominant notes. There have been occasional works of corporal mercy, some of them self-sacrificial, offered by Christians to Jews, and, less often, by the Church corporately to the Synagogue corporately. The Church has begun, slowly, to see and acknowledge and apologize for the extent of her violence toward the Synagogue and the Jews, and to develop her doctrine in ways that make some of the patterns of thought and practice that subtend and justify that violence less plausible, or even to rule them out altogether. Sometimes, and more often since the end of the Second Vatican Council in 1965, the Church has recognized the Synagogue for what she is and Jews for what they are, and has advocated and sometimes performed love for both. (She has less often recognized herself for what she is within Israel's economy.) But these are recent and as yet inadequate attempts at contrition, repentance, and penance. The long history is predominantly one of hatred, fear, violence, coercion, and lies.

The Synagogue may accept everything, something, or nothing about this condensed version of the Church's history with herself. She may have her own version or she may find the question insufficiently interesting to attend to. The Church's task with respect to the Synagogue's accounts of their life with one another, should any be offered, is to attend to them; nothing more. Nothing written here impinges in any way upon that. It is, rather, an attempt to show the Church how the Synagogue has appeared and appears within the space of her own imagination, as prelude to further consideration of the Church's standing with respect to the Synagogue.

This history of the Church with the Synagogue limits her standing with respect to interventions in the Synagogue's life. She is, with respect to the Synagogue, like a verbally, physically, and psychologically abusive spouse, whose abuse has extended over much of the couple's life together; the abusive spouse may also have occasionally been loving, and may now profess understanding of what he has done and repentance for it; but his standing for such things as cohabitation, sexual exchange, commensality, and the offering of advice about or recommendation of norms for the life of the spouse he has injured, is radically compromised by the history of violence between them. Or, the Church is like a priest who has, for decades, raped and otherwise abused children supposedly in his pastoral care; he may also have shown them occasional warmth and support, and may now profess understanding of what he has done and repentance for it; but his standing for such things as in-person pastoral interactions with children, and perhaps with anyone, is radically compromised by his history of violence. Or, the Church is like a sovereign state that has, over generations, colonized, occupied, and exploited, economically and otherwise, another such; it may also have provided the colonized state and its inhabitants some material benefits; it may now renounce control over or intervention in the internal affairs of the once-colonized state; and perhaps it now professes repentance for its performance of such actions in the past; but its standing even for normative intervention of any kind, and certainly for such things as presence of troops or advisors, is radically compromised by its history of violent colonization.

These are imperfect analogies, but they provide something of the flavor of the situation. In the version of Israel provided here, the Church has, for most of her history, been a consistent and unambiguous abuser of the Synagogue, as Christians have of Jews. It would not be in the least surprising if, for most Jews, the Church generically, and particular church buildings, should appear, still, not as places of refuge and support, but as places of danger; and if Christians, individually or en masse, should seem to be occasions for avoidance, so that when

Christians or churches are in sight, the appropriate thing is to do whatever is necessary to avoid them. The violent spouse may have ceased to use his fists; the pedophile priest may no longer be raping children; the colonizing state may have replaced troops with aid. But when these changes are recent and not yet to be trusted if ever they can be, they alter the standing of those who have done these things with respect to those to whom they have done them.

Particular ecclesial interventions in the Synagogue's life (proselytism, the giving and receiving of instruction, participation in shared liturgies, works of corporal mercy, cooperation in case of external threat or shared enemy, and so on) each require their own discussion, and some of that discussion is provided below. Here it suffices to write that the Church now, and for a long time to come, has full standing to intervene in the Synagogue's life only penitentially. Penitence for her history of violence wrought upon the Synagogue, publicly expressed and often repeated, is something she has standing for, can do, and to some degree is doing. That penitence should have penance as its correlate, which means, in turn, that the frequency and range of the Church's nonpenitential interventions in the Synagogue's life should be reduced and guarded; that they should move as far as possible from the coercive toward the exemplary; and that those who teach the Church and administer its disciplines should take particular care to foster this sense of how churchly interventions into the Synagogue's life should now go. This is penance for the Church, correlative to its public penitence; it amounts, often, to a deliberate moratorium (perhaps for centuries, and perhaps longer; it is convenient to say that it should last at least as long as the abuse did) upon other interventions into the Synagogue's life that the Church has often taken to belong to her nature and mission. Should she attempt those now, and for the foreseeable future, her lack of standing for them will mean that she effects something else, in something of the same way that the abusive spouse's caress may unavoidably seem a blow to the one who receives it, the pedophile priest's instruction of a child may unavoidably seem like grooming for rape to the one who receives it, and the colonizer state's distribution of vaccines to the once colonized may unavoidably seem an offer of infection to those who receive them. These things (caresses, instruction, care of the flesh), are good, and good to do; but history may remove or compromise the standing of some persons or corprorate bodies to do them at a time and for a time. The extent to which this is the case for the Church's particular interventions into the Synagogue's life remains to be investigated.

• • •

There are reasonable objections to this view of the Church's standing with respect to the Synagogue.

One has to do with the Church's self-understanding as placed under her god's nonnegotiable mandate to offer Jesus to the world, and to baptize everyone who is either willing or whose willingness can be represented by appropriate proxies. It might be thought that "everyone" includes the Jews, and if it is so understood the claim that the Church lacks standing for this kind of intervention into the Synagogue's life stands in tension with this mandate. Does the god's mandate not still stand?

Even if the Church is under mandate to offer Jesus to the world, and even if the world is taken to include the Jews (an antecedent not affirmed here), the position on standing taken here amounts to a moratorium rather than a cancellation. It may at the same time be that the Church is under some evangelical mandate, and yet that for the time being she is, because of her own sins and lacks, unable to do what would be necessary to fulfill it in the case of the Jews. The Church now, and for the long future, has abrogated her standing to proselytize Jews, and has done so because of her sin. She is to this obligation, if she has it, as an abusive spouse is to the abused: should she attempt to fulfill it, she will effect something else, something worse.

A further objection to this view of the Church's standing with respect to the Synagogue is that it suggests a denial that the Church has standing even for efforts to succor the Synagogue, or individual Jews, by corporal works of mercy. If that is the conclusion, what then is to be said about, for example, the occasional support offered by the non-Jewish baptized to Jews under threat by the totalitarian movements of the twentieth century, or by the ambient antisemitism of the twenty-first, which is now producing increasing numbers of acts of violence against Jews? Does the Church lack standing for such acts? Is she incapable of them? And, further, might not this view of the Church's standing call into question the particular love she should have for the Synagogue as her co-constitutor of Israel? Is she incapable, now, of showing that particular love?

Corporal works of mercy are, for the Church, good to have provided and to provide; performing them, when possible, is a constitutive element of the Church's halakhic life; and the only thing that should influence the Church's decision to undertake them is that their recipients seem to her in need of them. This entails at first blush that when it seems to the Christians that a Jew, or some Jews, or Jews in general, stand in need of food or shelter or protection from violence or other corporal help, she is bound to help them as she would help gentiles. And further: Christians are, in the order of being, as the objection suggests, closer to Jews, more intimate with them, than with gentiles. That is so even if they have often not recognized it; it is so because Christians and Jews are both Israelites. That closeness carries with it, or should, a greater concern for the well-being of Jews than for that of gentiles, in something like the same way that I have, or should have, a greater concern for the well-being of my children than I have, or should have, for that of yours. That is what it means to have a particular love, and to act in accord with it.

The objection is right in its suggestion, therefore, that the Church's current standing with respect to intervention in the Synagogue's life does not place under the ban corporal works of mercy offered by the Church to the Synagogue. It does mean, however, that when such works are not framed and accompanied by penitence, and even sometimes when they are, they will fail by appearing to the Synagogue as so compromised that they are themselves dangerous, and perhaps unacceptable. Everything depends on the texture of the occasion. Among the serious damages effected by the fugal flight of the Church from the Synagogue is that the Church's particular love for the Synagogue, which sometimes, now, she is able to see, as through a glass, darkly, may not be expressible in action. All the Church can do, and it is something, is self-effacingly to do what she can for the Synagogue while bearing the burden of knowing that it is less than it should be, less than it could have been, and yet still necessary.

4

ISRAEL'S GOD

THE WORLD IS full of gods. That is so if a god is a nonhuman agent served (appeased, complimented, beseeched, celebrated, interrogated, manipulated, praised, cursed) liturgically by us. There is the market with its invisible hand; there are sovereign states; there are transnational corporations; there are sports teams; there are humans who become something more when served liturgically—monarchs, presidents, charismatics, immortals, prophets, heroes, martyrs; there are naiads, dryads, piskies, fairies, elves; there is truth, beauty, love, power, violence, rationality, revolution. And that is very far from an exhaustive list, whether of types or tokens. All these have their liturgies, and many of them demand something approaching worship.

We humans like liturgies, and are energetic and imaginative in finding occasions for liturgical service and in making and using representations of our gods. We designate places and times as holy, we are possessed by our gods, we invoke and hymn them, abase and exalt ourselves before them, show them the violent madness of acolytes massed. We are, almost without exception, enthusiasts, and there are many gods ready and waiting to fill the hearts of the faithful, to deepen and shape and direct their enthusiasm. Being full of gods, the world hums with their liturgies, is saturated by the blood of their sacrifices, and resounds with invocations of their names, which rise like the fumes of incense from our world to that of the gods.

Israel too has her god, and because Israel includes Church and Synagogue, each of these is a liturgical servant, a worshipper, of that god. The god the Synagogue invokes and worships and the god the Church invokes and worships is the same. Israel's god is for all Israel, and all Israel is for Israel's god. That is definitional: the liturgies of both Synagogue and Church are gifts from Israel's god to each of them, returned to and received with delight by that god as a kiss from a beloved, even though neither Church nor Synagogue understands more than a small portion of what it does liturgically, even though the liturgies of each are damaged and half-hearted and weaponized, and even though the liturgies of the two are in many respects different, contradictory, noncompossible. There is, for the Church, no question about whether the god Jews worship in their synagogues and the god Christians worship in their churches is the same: that is given by the taxonomy that informs the ecclesial grammar of Israel, and especially by the irrevocability of the god's promises to all Israel.

There is no question, then, about which god Church and Synagogue serve. The question, rather, is about how to account for the fact that they serve the same god, given the deep and significant differences between the Church's and the Synagogue's understandings and imaginings of that god, the god of Israel. An approach to this question may be had by considering the central features of the Church's imagination and understanding of Israel's god.

• • •

The god of Israel is in many respects like other gods, including those of the gentiles. Those gods, like Israel's god, are typically local: they belong to and in a particular time and space, and they have an intimate relation with a particular people. Their liturgies, like those of Israel's god (at least until the scattering following Israel's complication), are also typically local, intimate with the particulars of place: the gods of Shinto belong to and in Japan, and their liturgies can only fully be practiced there; so also for those of Hinduism and India, and the god of Israel and Jerusalem, again until the Diaspora. These are gross generalizations, and they preclude neither relocation (Aeneas brings the *lares* and *penates* from Troy to Rome), nor reconstrual in such a way that the significance of place is changed (Israel's god is related differently to place and places after diaspora than before); they remain true as generalizations, however: Where is Zeus without Olympus, the White Sox without Chicago, the emperor of Japan without Mount Fuji?

This location in time and space sits well with and is almost always accompanied by narrated identifications of the gods. This god, the story goes, is the one who once called Abraham; or once arrived at the truth of things in Bodhgaya; or once seduced the gopis on the banks of the Ganges; or once crossed the Delaware toward victory; or runs as a bull in the exchanges of London and New York; or won the World Cup at Wembley in 1966 and then declined into senescence. The gods, Israel's and the gentiles', do this and then that, are here and then there. They move in the world and find place there in most ways as we humans also do.

So far, the gods appear within the spatial and temporal horizons of the world that we also occupy. They may be more powerful and less comprehensible than we (who grasps the powers and movements of the market?), but like us they are always somewhere and somewhen, doing something and not everything. Their being, like ours, is in and of the world, which is to say that they are always, in principle, findable. They are within the world's horizons. But some among the world's gods are not exhaustively accountable in this way. Who and what they are is not to be found only, and in some cases not at all, within the world's horizons, and therefore cannot be comprehended by story, which works within the confines of time and space. For these few (Israel's god is among them), what they have tensedly done, are doing, and, future-perfectively, will have done, is not all they do. They also are and also act, these two not easily distinguishable for this kind of god, entirely outside the confines of the world, which is also to say entirely outside the confines of space and time. Gods like this are related to the world contrastively, as its other, while gods of the former kind are related to the world by membership in it, inhabitation of it. Some, like Israel's god, are both; and the ordinary way, not confined to those who theorize Israel's god, of saying something further about how a god such as that can be related to the world—"world" here understood to indicate *alles, was der Fall ist,* following Wittgenstein in the *Tractatus,* which implies that Israel's god is not among the states of affairs that are the case, or, as also may be said, that there is no univocal predication of being that joins the world to the god—is, first, to claim the god as the world's creator, and the world as the god's creature.

Many gods have this said of them. Fewer, many fewer (how few is an empirical question to which those imagining the god of Israel need no answer), are said to be not merely the world's creator, but also to create (here a tenseless form of the verb) the world out of nothing. This additional move is a guard against attributing to some god of whom this is said creation as an act of making out of already-extant materials. That is what we humans do when we create: we take what is already there (words, wood, stone, paints, chemical elements, and so on) and form it, shape it, order it. Those are our makings: we bring nothing into being out of nothing (whence the maxim *ex nihilo nihil fit*), and to differentiate some god's makings from ours, to make them more godlike and less human, we may say that the god creates the world *ex nihilo*. Such gods do not shape the cosmos from prime matter or any other kind of ur-stuff; that would suggest the existence of something such gods did not create, or make, but existed already, independently of anything they have done. And then (there are some gods like this, so it is said), such gods are once again, or remain, inhabitants of the world they have made, much as the builders of houses live in the houses they have built. Such gods are not other to the world they make; they are demiurges, shapers of clay they found but did not make.

The god of Israel is not like this. That god is creator *ex nihilo*, and it is convenient to reserve the verb "to create" for bringing into being *ex nihilo*, and the verb "to make" for all other kinds of bringing into being. (The Church's archive does not consistently make such a verbal distinction, and it seems likely that the Synagogue's archive also does not; it is nevertheless appropriate when speaking and writing of Israel's god.) Writing in this way of what the god does has some immediate implications.

A first is that the god is not finally and fully locatable, not completely findable within the manifold of timespace that is the world, not an object or a being in the world. The world, all that is spatiotemporally the case, is not created at a time by the god, which would incoherently make the world already the container for the god's act of creating it; it is, rather, brought into being by the god with and as timespace: timespace begins with the world and is coextensive with it, which is also approximately what contemporary astrophysics says when it considers the beginning of things. The god is, then, definitively and necessarily neither spatial nor temporal, and therefore not exhaustively specifiable in terms of space and time.

A second implication has to do with the lexicon proper to specification of the relations the god who creates *ex nihilo* bears to what is not that god. If the verb "to create" is reserved as suggested, the world as an ensemble, together with all the particulars that conjointly constitute that ensemble, can appropriately be called a creature. Everything that is not the god is, then, a creature; were there anything other than the god that is not the god's creature, the god would not, properly speaking, be creator.

A third implication of such an understanding of Israel's god has to do with the relations between that god and other gods. There are two possibilities here. One has to do with putative other gods who are not creators *ex nihilo*, who are, that is to say, creatures. Israel affirms these, or at least can easily do so: the world is indeed full of gods in this sense, some largely beneficent and many less so; they provide a problem for the Church or the Synagogue only when their liturgies conflict with or infringe upon her own, as sometimes they do. But the other possibility is different. It concerns putatively other gods whose liturgies and acolytes identify them as creators *ex nihilo* (perhaps they are called Vishnu, or Allah, or Buddhadharmakaya). It is not logically possible for there to be more than one such: if the god of Israel does not create Vishnu out of nothing, then there is something the god of Israel does not create, so that, ipso facto, Israel's god is not creator out of nothing; if the god of Israel does create Vishnu out of nothing, then Vishnu is ipso facto a creature, and not the god who creates out of nothing. So, mutatis mutandis, for the others: there is and can be only one such god, whatever that god's name is, and however many names are used to address that god.

Israel's god is, therefore, in one sense a local god with a particular history, one among many, one nonhuman agent served liturgically by humans among many such; and in another sense creator of all that is out of nothing, the only god there is and can be. This is the position of Israel's ecclesial archive (perhaps also of her synagogal archive), scriptural and otherwise: gods other than Israel's are there both affirmed and denied, for the reasons given. Israel's god is a great god, a *rex magnus super omnes deos*, as the ninety-fifth Psalm has it. This is to say both yes and no to the question of whether Israel's god is the only god.

A further tightening of the conceptual screw is necessary at this point. There is, for Israel, nothing but the god and creatures. But this ought not be taken to mean that the sense in which the god is and the sense in which creatures are is just the same. An account of creatures would ideally enumerate them exhaustively, classify them into kinds, again exhaustively, and provide a definition of the properties essential to each kind. A property essential to every creature is exactly creaturehood, being the god's gift. That is one way to say what a creature is: creatures have from the god the gift of being what they are, as well as the gift of being anything at all. That relation is not commutative: the god is not dependent for who the god is upon anything about creatures. Creatures exist participatorily and by gift; the god is in virtue of nothing other than the god. There are no categories predicable univocally of the god and the god's creatures, and this is true of existence as well as the rest (love, beauty, truth, creation, and so on). It is then not the case that a world without the god would have one fewer thing in it than one with the god (the god is not a thing in the world); neither is it the case that existence is a simple toggle concept, possibly on and possibly off for all (if the god is said to exist this does not entail the possibility of the god's nonexistence). Better to say, in light of Israel's god, that a world without the god is a circle without a circumference; that if something can fail to exist, it is a creature; and that the god without the world is simply the god. That is the god, the only one of that kind (the many gods are all, by definition, creatures). That god, the god (the definite article does some work here), is the one who chooses, in the atemporal present, Israel, and whose promises to Synagogue and Church, Israel's constituents since the fugal complication, are irrevocable.

Such an understanding of Israel's god, like much about the Church's Israel, can be made to hang together and, when appropriately burnished, to look beautiful, even to dazzle and compel. It is certainly productive of thought about many interesting things: the nature of existence; the modalities of necessity and possibility; the nature of damage, evil, suffering, and lack; and much more. But this understanding, like so much about the Church's doctrine, has no first-blush plausibility, and cannot but seem, especially to those who encounter it for the first time in the context of talk of Israel as chosen and irrevocably promised, excessively strange, outré to a degree that makes it hard to take seriously. It comes to this: the world as the scientific orthodoxy of the twenty-first century depicts it is very large: every observer in it sits at the center of an expanding sphere whose diameter at the moment—it gets larger as the world expands—approaches ten-to-the-eleventh-power light years; it has many particulars in it: more than two billion galaxies, each with something on the order of one billion stars, among which, ours, Sol, is one; and it is very old: approaching fourteen billion years, of which our planet has existed for between four and five, harboring animate creatures for most of that time, including hominids and hominins for the last few hundreds of thousands of years only. It is this, all of it, that Israel's god has brought into being out of nothing, and this, all of it, whose being is necessarily and definitionally participatory in that god. And within these spatiotemporal vastnesses the god chooses and promises irrevocable intimacy with Abraham, one hominid on a tiny planet in a single solar system at a moment when the clocks had already been ticking for fourteen billion years or so. To find it reasonable to say this you must already be saying it. It is what the Church teaches. Perhaps it is also a version of what the Synagogue teaches.

• • •

Gods ordinarily have names, even one who creates all that is out of nothing, and Israel's god is no exception. The word *god* is not a name. It is a simple, one-syllable Old English expectoration or grunt, a kind-term like *dog* or *mountain*. It is true that God, with uppercase initial, has come to be used as a name by English-using Christians and, more complicatedly and with more reservations, by English-using Jews, who appear sometimes to prefer G-d, perhaps as a hedge against blasphemously using the god's name—though of course *god* (the English word) is under no reasonable construal the god of Israel's name, or a name at all—but treating it instead as a kind-term, a sortal or taxon, permits clarity about Israel's god otherwise not attainable. One way to distinguish a particular god from others appropriately labeled by the sortal *god* is by name. The god of Israel, as understood by the Church, has many names, but among them two are of central, revelatory importance.

The first is given by the god to Moses. Moses has just been commissioned to liberate the Israelites from slavery in Egypt, and wants to know the name of the god who has given him this commission. Moses acknowledges that he is being addressed by a god, and not just any god, but the god of his ancestors—he is an Israelite, a descendant of Abraham. But that is not enough. Moses wants a name. And the god provides one:

> *God said to Moses: "I am who I am." He said: "You will say this to the sons of Israel: I am sent me to you." God also said to Moses: "You will say this to the sons of Israel: the* LORD*, the God of your fathers, the God of Abraham, the God of Isaac*

> *and the God of Jacob, has sent me to you; this is my eternal name, and this my memorial from generation to generation."* *(Exod 3:14–15)*

The passage is not pellucid, but a possible reading is that the god self-identifies in two ways: by name and by narrative.

The name is given in three forms: first, I Am Who I Am (*ego sum qui sum* in Latin; *ehyeh asher ehyeh* in Hebrew); second, Who I Am, which is, verbatim, the latter part of the first name (*qui sum* in Latin; *asher ehyeh* in Hebrew); third, (the) LORD (*dominus* in Latin; YHWH in Hebrew; no definite article in either language, which Latin in any case lacks). This third is the name, *stricto sensu*. It is four consonants in Hebrew when seen on the page or the scroll; and when voiced in that language by and in the Synagogue it sounds as *Adonai* (the voicing deliberately occludes the consonants of the written form because the name is too sacred, to weighty, to say; *Adonai* is a vocalized avoidance, a pronoun-like placeholder). The four consonants, YHWH, are rendered into Latin with a word, *dominus*, that belongs to the Latin of the gentiles as well as that of Israel, and there indicates a person of authority—a paterfamilias, an emperor, a potentate. One among the ordinary English renderings of that Latin word (and of its Greek equivalent, *kyrios*) is lord, and I use it above, in small capitals, to suggest that this is not just any lord, but the one who is called LORD, who has LORD as proper name. That word chain—YHWH, *kyrios*, *dominus*, LORD—is, in the Church's canon of Scripture, the short form of the name. Israel's god, the god, is the one who is called LORD, and the very frequent scriptural phrase LORD god (YHWH *elohim*; *kyrios theos*; *dominus deus*) can then be read, rightly, as applying a generic term (god) to a proper name (LORD). The LORD, Israel says, is our god, our instance of what everyone else has one or many of. LORD is what our god is called.

The core name, YHWH, has semantic content as well as capacity to indicate the god whose name it is. It is hard to say, though, just what that semantic content is. It clearly has to do with being, or existence; in both the Latin and Hebrew forms of the longer version of the name, that connection is explicit. The Lord self-names as the one who is. Many interpretations are possible; it suffices to write here that if, as argued, the god of Israel's creation of the world—everything that is the case—out of nothing implies that the mode of existence proper to that god is distinct from that proper to everything else, that no univocal predication of being or existence (themselves capable of reasonable differentiation, though that will not be undertaken here) of the god and creatures is possible, then the name itself can easily be read to cohere with this, for it indicates explicitly at least that invoking Israel's god involves invoking a god whose mode of existence is distinctive. This act of naming is, or can easily be read to be, centrally concerned with the distinction between god—the Lord—and creatures, and then, by implication, between this god and other gods, who cannot say *ego sum qui sum* of themselves, and do not claim that state of affairs as a proper name. The first naming in the passage quoted above from the book of Exodus takes the god out of the world and away from creatures; it designates the god (there can only be one) who has created everything out of nothing.

But the god does not, in the passage under discussion, self-name only in that way. Intimate with that first name is a second, which belongs to the sphere of time and narrative. To repeat: it is the Lord, the god of Abraham, Isaac, and Jacob, who sends Moses to the Israelites. That god, the god, says that such a description is also the god's name, and is so forever, never to be abandoned. Again, the passage is suggestive rather than definitive, but it is at least clear that Israel's god includes in the act of naming reference to that god's history with Israel. This god is the one who called Abraham and guaranteed that call for ever. These are events in time and place, and they mean that as well as being the god who is what that god is, creator of all things *ex nihilo*, the god is the one who always, atemporally, will have been what that god has been, caller and lover of Israel. Tense and tenselessness are here interlocked inseparably. To think about Israel's god is to think at once about that god in the world, doing this and that and then something else, and about that god as outside the world, its presupposition and possibility and goal. To forget either is to forget Israel's god. The giving of names—specifying that Israel's god is this one, and not one of the innumerable others—shows that the two must be held together because they are given together. To forget or ignore or fail at one or the other is to forget half of Israel's god's name, and, almost inevitably, then to begin to talk about some other god.

Israel's god self-names, then, both as LORD and as the god of Abraham who has done all the things claimed as that god's work in the canon of Scripture. The Church has another name by which she calls this god: Jesus. Jesus is LORD is a fundamental confession of the Church, and it indicates not only, and not primarily, a relationship of dominance and power between Jesus and those who call him LORD, but rather that Jesus is the god of those who so confess him, and not just any god, but precisely Israel's god. Thomas, the one who doubts, identifies, in John's Gospel, the resurrected Jesus as *Dominus meus et Deus meus!*, which captures one key element of the relation between calling Jesus *dominus* and calling him *deus*. Jesus is not only that. He is also a man of Israel, born to an Israelite woman in the line of David the king; and he is the Messiah, the anointed Savior-redeemer promised to Israel. As the Church considers these matters and develops her doctrine of god, and as her theologians speculate, a preferred formulation emerges: Jesus the anointed one, Mary's son, is fully the god and fully human, the god enfleshed, a single person (Jesus) with two natures (god-human), the second person—the Son—of the Trinity the LORD is, himself therefore fully LORD. The Synagogue, the Church imagines, does not share these namings of her god. For her, Jesus was not the anointed one, is not the LORD; and the LORD, the one who created all that is out of nothing, does not and cannot take flesh. These differences are central to the Church's imagination of the Synagogue; they are provided here as instances of that imagining, not as statements based upon study of what Jews have said and say, have written and write, about these matters. (Whether what the Church imagines the Synagogue to claim, and to deny, about her god is at odds with what she in fact claims is for her to say.) A further caveat is important: attributing to the Synagogue a denial of the god's enfleshment, as fact and possibility, is distinct from attributing to her a denial of the god's triune nature. That is because some versions (not Christian ones) of trinitarian theology do not require incarnational theology: the Church's attribution of a denial of trinitarianism to the Synagogue is therefore still weaker, still more tentative, than her attribution of a denial of the god's incarnation to the Synagogue. But both are tentative: offerings to the Synagogue rather than weapons with which to attack her.

The Church's double identification of her god as the Lord who is what the Lord is (*sum qui sum*), and as the Lord who is Jesus, brings together the two registers in which Israel's god self-names in response to Moses's question: the one that distinguishes god from creatures (creator of all that is out of nothing), and the one that distinguishes this god from others (god of Abraham, who is Jesus). Both registers are essential to the Church's worship of her god, and they are both present, often startlingly juxtaposed, in her liturgies, as when, in one of her standard liturgically deployed confessions, the Niceno-Constantinopolitan Creed, she uses elevated language about Jesus Christ as the god's only-begotten son, and so forth, and then shifts suddenly enough to produce conceptual whiplash to talk of crucifixion under Pontius Pilate, a Roman procurator in a particular place at a particular time. This is a good example of the combination of the two registers, and the frequency with which this confession is said shows how important each is in the Church's liturgy.

The Church's teaching that the Lord is triune also brings the two registers together in a different way. To treat a complex matter too simply we may say that the specification of the relations that define the differences among Father, Son, and Spirit, the Church's preferred terms of art for the Trinity's three persons, is a way of talking about

Israel's god as that god is independently of creation; while the idea that the LORD takes flesh as the Son, the Trinity's second person, is a way of talking about the LORD's presence in the spatiotemporal manifold—though always with concern to emphasize that since it is the LORD, the *trinitas quae dominus est*, who takes flesh and acts in the world, it is and must be all three persons who do so, not just the second. There are technicalities involved here, both trinitarian and christological, which need not detain us. The importance of even this much detail is to show the skeleton—the bones, the pattern, the shape—of the Church's depiction of her god. According to the pattern of the musical fugue, the Church anticipates that the Synagogue's identification and depiction of her god, also the god of Israel and hence her own god, will share the pattern of her own, even if it differs in many particulars: if the two voices together make a double fugue, that must be so, for the subject and countersubject in a double fugue share a structure, a fundamental form, and a consummation.

• • •

It is now axiomatic for the Church that her god, the one who is the LORD, is also the Synagogue's god. That has been true since Church and Synagogue fled from one another, it is true now, and it will, at the end, always have been true, even though the Church has rarely seen it clearly. The Church has not, however, shown much interest in or taken much trouble to become acquainted with what the Synagogue says or writes about her god, whether in the person of her rabbis or of her speculative thinkers. Some Christians have taken such trouble throughout the Church's history, but they have been few and marginal, and their studies have not much informed the development of ecclesial doctrine about the Synagogue or the Synagogue's god. I am like most Christian theologians in this respect; I have some Hebrew and no Arabic; I have read little in Mishnah and Talmud, and only somewhat more in what I would call Jewish speculative theology. I therefore have nothing of depth or interest to say about the range and course and sweep of Jewish thinking about the god of Israel. The version of the Synagogue's god imagined here is not inflected by knowledge of that sort. That frees me to depict the Synagogue's god imaginatively, from the Church's viewpoint, as consisting essentially in three aspects, each as it appears in relation to the Church's understanding of her god. (The Synagogue, now as ever, is unlikely to have much interest in this; should she have, it is for her to speak and for the Church to listen.) The first aspect is harmony of form; the second is difference about Jesus, and, by extension, about the possibility of the god's enfleshment and perhaps of the god as triune; and the third is the development of the Synagogue's doctrine of god toward truths about the Lord not explicitly known to the Church and now learnable by her only through instruction from the Synagogue—or, at the end of things, by seeing their truth.

The first of these three can be treated briefly and formally. The Church expects that the double fugue of her own and the Synagogue's response to the god of Israel will at the end be resolved into a single note of perfection that summarizes, recapitulates, and resolves the differences and reversals and contrapuntal echoes that have informed the body of the fugue. This view of things requires a fundamental similarity of structure between what her voice says about Israel's god, and what the Synagogue's voice says. Such structural or formal similarity is not identity: all the particular notes of one voice's contribution may be different from all the particular notes of the other's. But it does require similarity of shape, of the spacing and relation of elements, of, to transpose the figure, lexicon and syntax. And the similarity must be sufficient to permit resolution. It is not necessary, and perhaps not possible, to specify formally what the required degree of grammatical or harmonic similarity is; but it is possible to give an instance of it.

I have written above that the Church's doctrine of god requires two registers, one in which her god is differentiated from creatures, performed by abstraction; and the other in which her god is differentiated from other gods, performed by narrative; and that it requires both because her god is at once the god who has brought everything that is the case into being out of nothing, and the one who initiated and remains involved in a narratable sequence of events that began with the call of Abraham and the establishment thereby of Israel. Both registers must be present in what the Church says and writes about her god. The extent to which one of them is forgotten or left aside is the extent to which the god of Israel is forgotten and some other god talked about instead. The Church anticipates that the Synagogue's talk and writing about her god will exhibit the same two registers, and find the same difficulties in resolving them at the theoretical level. Should that not be the case, should, per impossibile, the Synagogue have forgotten or come to forget the god who identifies as *sum qui sum* or the one who identifies as *deus patrum vestrorum*, then the resolution of the Church's song of god with the Synagogue's will not be possible. But all that is at a very high pitch of abstraction. The Church also anticipates that the ways in which the narrative register is developed by the Synagogue will be different from, and in some ways incompatible with, the ways in which she has herself developed that register; and she expects, too, that the Synagogue will not differentiate the creator from creatures in just the way that she does. But she does expect that the Synagogue will undertake both enterprises, since those enterprises, taken together, are what it means to speak of the god of Israel; their presence in both the Synagogue's and the Church's voice is necessary, too, for the fugal resolution of subject and countersubject.

This first aspect of this act of imagining the Synagogue's god involves structural similarities pointing toward, or at least capable of, harmonic resolution. The second aspect has to do with difference. The Church names the Lord not only as such, but also as Jesus, and specifies the implications of that act of naming by way of doctrines about enfleshment and Trinity. The Synagogue, as the Church sees her, also names her god as Lord, but does none of the rest. Even knowing that the Church speaks and writes in these ways, the Synagogue does not. The Church invokes her god as Jesus while the Synagogue does not herself so speak; and the Synagogue may sometimes deny that her god can be invoked as Jesus.

Does this provide a problem for the Church's axiomatic commitment to the claim that her god and the Synagogue's god are the same? No. Difference in naming does not entail, and need not suggest, difference in reference. If, on a crowded train, you and I both see across the carriage a person we know, and when we mention the fact to one another we discover that I think she is called such-and-such and you know her as so-and-so, this doesn't mean that when we've invoked her in past conversations by different names we were talking about different people. Perhaps it turns out that she publishes under both names, and you've read her poetry, published under the name so-and-so, while I've read her phenomenology, published under the name such-and-such, neither of us knowing (and there being no indication in her publications) that she also publishes the other kind of thing under the other name. Our conversation in that train carriage might convince one of us, both of us, or neither of us, that the person we know does indeed publish under two names, and that the poet and the phenomenologist are the same person. But no matter who comes to agree about what with respect to naming, the fact remains that there is just one person we're talking about, just one person sitting across from us in the train; and that, in the thought experiment at least, she does publish in both genres under different names. There is no principled difficulty here: Church and Synagogue can agree that their differences about invocation do not entail, and need not suggest, that they are addressing a different god; and if either of them takes herself to have decisive reasons for saying that the two of them are invoking the same god, as is the case for the Church (the Synagogue can speak for herself), then differences about naming stimulate further thought about what that difference comes to and how it is to be accounted for; such differences do not provide any doubt as to whether the god invoked is the same one. It of course remains the case that if the Church is right about who Jesus was and is, it follows that the Synagogue is mistaken if she denies it, which it seems she sometimes does; and that she is missing an opportunity to learn something more about her god if she fails to attend to it, which she more often seems to do. If you're interested in the author, why not read the phenomenology as well as the poetry?

Fugal harmony of form tending toward resolution; difference about the place of Jesus in the economy of the god's life with Israel. Those are the first two aspects of the Church's imagination of the relation between her own and the Synagogue's understanding of the Lord they both acknowledge. There is a third aspect: the understanding of the Lord developed by the Synagogue since her flight from the Church by way of her halakhic, liturgical, and theological response to the gifts her god continues to give her is in some ways richer and fuller than that of the Church, and is instructive for her. If, as the Church takes to be the case, the Synagogue has lived with the Lord, the god of Israel, for sixteen hundred years or so effectively apart from the Church, and if that life has consisted most intensely in close liturgical and halakhic intimacy with that god, then it is at least likely, and perhaps inevitable, that the Synagogue as a result knows things about the Lord the Church does not know, or at least does not explicitly know.

Suppose you've been studying a corpus of poetry closely for forty years. It's elegant, aphoristic, compressed, saturated, and violently suggestive—as though, perhaps, Cavafy, Mallarmé, and Celan had collaborated. There's a substantial literature interpreting this corpus, and you're familiar with it and have contributed significantly to it. You've devoted much of your life to the study of this corpus. Not only that. The author of the poems still lives, and you're in occasional correspondence with her. The letters you get from her are, for you, sacred objects, and while they raise as many questions about the poems as they solve, reference to them is an essential part of the interpretive enterprise. Then, as you begin the fifth decade of your study of these poems, you learn something dramatically new. Their author, you discover, has also written a series of philosophical works of a phenomenological sort; she has published those works under a different name, and has taken care to conceal the fact that the philosopher is also the poet; and there is, as with the poetry, a large and energetic community of interpreters, some of whom are also in correspondence with the author, though without knowing that she is a poet as well as a phenomenologist.

What now? Your mouth waters. You want to read the phenomenological work as well as its interpretations. You want to study closely the phenomenologist's letters to that community of interpreters as you've studied the poet's to yours. You hope and expect that new light will be shed upon the poetic corpus that interests you, and that you will come to know your author more fully and closely by reading her philosophy. Writing in a different genre and in a distinct idiom requires differences in focus and trajectory and method even when the fundamental concerns that drive the writing are the same, and attention to those particulars promises to be instructive. Now that you've learned, and are sure, that the poet and the phenomenologist are the same, you can see with equal certainty that those who've devoted their energy to the phenomenological corpus will know things about the author you share an interest in that you do not—even though you cannot yet see what the particulars of that knowledge might be. (It is also true that you expect your own interpretive work to be instructive for the phenomenologists; but that is for them to speak to.)

The analogy limps, but is not useless. It shows something of why the Church ought expect the Synagogue to know things about Israel's god that she does not know herself, even though she knows the name of Jesus while the Synagogue does not. It also suggests that the Church ought yet be modest both about the particulars of her own understanding of the god, and about those she might hope to learn from the Synagogue; while some Christians who are not also Jews have learned about the god from the Synagogue in the relevant ways, and while some Christians who are also Jews have brought with them into the Church knowledge of the relevant kinds, the Church's enterprise of seeing that it needs instruction from the Synagogue about the god is still relatively undeveloped. It is far, as yet, from becoming what it needs to be, which is close to the heart of the Church's theological enterprise.

This third aspect of the Synagogue's understanding of Israel's god shows the Synagogue over time coming to relate to and understand that god in ways the Church does not, and thereby to know things about that god which the Church does not. An informing assumption here is that comprehensive understanding of anything is not possible for finite knowers. That is almost self-evident. I can understand a good deal about the positive integer two: that it is an integer, that it is even (not odd), that it is one less than three and two less than four, that every even number is divisible by it, and so on. But I cannot know all truths about even something so simple because there is an infinite number of them: the set of positive integers, for example, to which two belongs, has an infinite number of members, and two has relations to each of them. I can say, formally and abstractly, what those relations are; but I cannot exhaust them in their particularity. There is neither world nor time enough for that. The same is true, though not for precisely the same reasons, for my understanding of my children: I know who they are, that they are my children, a good deal about their histories, and much else. I understand them more fully, probably, than do almost all other human creatures. But my ignorance about them nonetheless exceeds my knowledge. It includes such things as how they appear to someone not their father. And for a god such as the Lord, the one who created all there is out of nothing and who inscrutably chose Abraham and enfleshed as Jesus, the limitations of my understanding are still clearer. When the Church says of herself, as sometimes she does, that the *depositum fidei* is complete and without need of supplement, the claim should be interpreted to imply that she has not yet made explicit, to herself or to the world, most of what she has been entrusted with about the Lord; and that she does not herself understand fully what she has made explicit, whether to herself or to the world.

But the limitation under discussion here goes beyond these universal and relatively uninteresting formalities. If the Lord self-reveals distinctly and distinctively to different communities, as is the case for the god's continuing self-revelation to Church and Synagogue respectively, then those who respond to what the god gives to only one of these communities do not and cannot see an aspect of the Lord that is knowable to human creatures, which is what it is like to respond to what the god gives to the other. And if, as is the case for the Church's Israel, the Lord's postfugal self-communication to both Church and Synagogue is part of a design to repair not only the damage done by the fugue, but also that done by the double fall, then it seems that the present condition of Church and Synagogue as partly hidden from one another in their responses to Israel's god is in part a felicity produced by the fault of the fugue, and in part damage produced by that fault which will, finally, be overcome. That, in any case, is the assumption under which the Church should now work in considering her understanding of the Lord as it relates to the Synagogue's. Each is necessary as things are; each complements the other; each is damaged in some ways and lacking in some ways; and they will be brought together and resolved in the end. The god of Israel is god of both Synagogue and Church, and the liturgical, halakhic, and, yes, even theological intimacies each shares with that god are the principal means by which each increases in holiness. The first and last notes in the Church's response to the Synagogue's theological life—her life of reflection about her god—should be one of gratitude that there is such a life, coupled with eagerness to study it and to learn from it.

• • •

The world is full of gods. The god of Israel, which is to say of Synagogue and Church, is named Lord. And that god is the only one who has, or could have, created the world out of nothing, called Abraham, enfleshed as Jesus, and burnished the holiness of Synagogue and Church. Gods other than this one are, necessarily, godlings, creatures, local deities. They are not nothing, but they are not, and cannot be, the Lord. The Church and the Synagogue can join in seeing and relativizing these other gods, as they also can in seeing and offering loving liturgical service to the god who has irrevocably chosen and loved each of them, and as they also can in learning from one another how better to understand the god. A caveat is necessary, however, because of the weight of the violence instigated by the Church against the Synagogue in Israel's fugal complication. It is by now familiar: the Church lacks standing to instruct the Synagogue about anything, and therefore also about the god. The attitude of penitence before the Synagogue now required of her provides her the penance of listening to the Synagogue rather than speaking to her, and learning from her rather than teaching her. She should open her theology to the world (as I am doing here), of course, for there can be no tincture of the esoteric in her speech and writing; but the only circumstance in which it is now proper to offer her understanding of god to the Synagogue is when she is asked by the Synagogue to do so—and then with fear and trembling. The Church before the Synagogue should now and for the foreseeable future be a form of life with ears only, eager to listen, not one with voice, eager to instruct.

5

ISRAEL'S HOLINESS

THE HOLY IS whole: complete, undamaged, perfect, just what it should be, no more and no less. The unholy is wounded, lacking, less than it should be, imperfect because damaged. These words identify a spectrum rather than a toggle: holiness is a matter of more and less, not of either/or: (almost) no creature is, since the fall, holy without remainder, just as none is unholy without remainder; each is located somewhere on the spectrum of holiness; only the god is entirely holy, and all creaturely holiness is a gift of that god, effective by participation in the god's holiness. What substantively counts as holiness for one kind of creature is not the same as for another; angelic holiness (angels, like us, are more and less holy; the least holy among them are demons) has not much of substance in common with human holiness, just as human holiness is very different from that proper to a carpenter ant. Christian life (and, as it seems to the Church, Jewish life too) is fundamentally about holiness: to be a saint (a word derived from the Latin *sanctus*, which is often rendered into English as "holy") is a universal Christian vocation, and among the more striking exhortations of the New Testament is the one from the Sermon on the Mount that enjoins Christians to be perfect as the god also is (*estote ergo vos perfecti, sicut Pater vester caelestis perfectus est*); that is not an injunction to be the god, or to be a god; much less to be a carpenter ant or a swift; but rather to be as one should be, to be whole, which is to say holy.

That is a condensed churchly grammar of holiness. It captures the fundamentals of the etymology and semantic range of the English adjective *holy* and noun *holiness*. In an undamaged world where everything is just as it should be, where there is no distinction between fact and value, every particular is holy, as is the world, which is the ensemble of particulars. Holiness would, in such a world, not be a term of contrast, for there would be no unholiness (lack, damage, unwholesomeness, unwholeness, rot, loss, death, suffering, sin, violence, slavery) to contrast it with. In a world without sickness there would be little need of talk about health (other, perhaps, than for those with speculative tendencies), and none at all for doctors. But in a devastated world like this one, to call something holy is to separate it from most things, because most things are not whole, not undamaged, but rather riven in various ways with lack. In a world such as ours, to be or become holy, or to seek holiness, is to be unusual, to go against the stream. Holy people, holy places, and holy things are, therefore, things set apart. The degree of their holiness is the degree of their difference from the world, and, ordinarily, the degree of difficulty and danger involved in interactions with them, particularly on the part of the deeply damaged (unholy) things of the world. A dark-adapted eye may be blinded by exposure to light, as cancerous flesh may shrink in pain from the surgeon's knife. Approaching and otherwise having to do with what is holy is, therefore, for the unholy a dangerous matter, and we are all unholy, more or less; such approaches and encounters require a mixture of circumspection and fear.

A good illustration of this reading of holiness is the prophet Isaiah's vision of the god in the temple in Jerusalem. The Lord—the god is so named in the account—is high up on a throne and surrounded with seraphs, angels of fire, who say, *Sanctus, Sanctus, Sanctus Dominus exercituum; plena est omnis terra gloria eius*—"Holy, holy, holy, is the Lord, the god of armies; all the earth is full of his glory." Isaiah, seeing the Lord, laments *vir pollutus labiis ego sum in medio populi polluta labia habentis ego habito*. He is a prophet, charged with speaking the Lord's words, but his vision of the Lord's holiness convinces him that he cannot speak such words because of his uncleanness. One of the seraphs then flies to him from the Lord's throne and scalds his mouth with a red-hot coal. Now he can say what the Lord wants him to say: his lips have been burned clean, and so he can speak cleanly.

Holiness is here linked with Israel's god as its paradigmatic possessor. That holiness shows itself to others—to the seraphs and to Isaiah—as glory, which is a kind of radiance, represented in the passage as fire: the angels are angels of fire; the temple is full of smoke; and a glowing coal is used to purify Isaiah's lips. Holiness, showing itself as glory, is evident as a dangerous power that the world and its damaged creatures and artifacts can scarcely endure and can certainly not contain. The temple shakes because the LORD is in it. The passage uses the language of impurity (the unclean lips) and shows the danger to what is unholy and inglorious that comes from what is holy and glorious. Faced with the holy's glory, what is unholy is in danger of being consumed by it as a rotting corpse may be rendered into ash's purest white by a crematorium's fire. But the holy and the unholy need not be likened only to the clean and the unclean; they may also be to one another as health to sickness, light to darkness, harmony to discord, life to death, truth to lie, grasping to letting go, eating to looking. Common to all these tropes is the sense that what is unholy cannot tolerate the close presence of the holy without being radically transformed by it; and that it may seem to the unholy that being made holy involves its end: before Isaiah can say to his god *Ecce ego, mitte me*, he has to endure his lips being burned, and he is convinced that he will die because he has seen the LORD. That is the ideal type of a well-ordered reaction by an unholy creature (every creature is more or less unholy) to the presence of holiness unadulterated—which is to say, the god of Israel.

Unholiness for creatures is also interpretable as distance: distance from the god. Holiness, then, contrastively, is a matter of intimacy: intimacy with the god. Christian talk and writing typically has it that some kinds of creature are generically more capable of intimacy with the god than other kinds. They are more like the god than others—in the god's *imago* and *similitudo*, image and likeness, in their distinctive ways. Christians have tended to say that the two creaturely kinds most like the god are angels and humans. These are different from one another, and therefore different in the likeness they bear to the god, but each is significantly like. In the case of humans, likeness is evident most clearly in the enfleshment of the god as Jesus, a human male and a Jewish human male. If human flesh is the flesh the god chooses to take (not avian, not cetacean, not fishy), then there is comfort and convenience in the thought that human creatures are closer to the god than others, and thus in principle already more holy than others and capable of more holiness yet.

A doubt should be registered here. It is easy for Christian talk of this kind to be assimilated to Linnaean talk about species, and then to say that it is *Homo sapiens* that, generically and in its particular members, is more like the god than the other species in their members. But talk of species is problematic in its own right. We lack apodictic clarity about what a species is, and it is becoming increasingly clear that the concept has dubious purchase and use even in biology, and much less in theology. Biologists are happy to say, for instance, that members of the species *Homo neanderthalensis* have procreated with members of *Homo sapiens*; and Israel's archive says that the *filii dei* have done the same with human women. These claims, each of which the Church should take seriously, though not for the same reasons, make the idea of what a species is, and that of how to allot individuals to one, fuzzy. Christians have no need to construe the claim that some kinds of creature are closer to the god than others as exchangeable with the claim that some species are closer to the god than others. It is better to take the route of the exemplary case, and say that the flesh of Jesus of Nazareth provides the clearest case Christians have of flesh intimate with, and like, the god, and to extrapolate from it as occasion and knowledge demand. There is no reason why, for example, creatures inhabiting planets in other solar systems might not be as close to, as much like, the god as members of *Homo sapiens*—and there is good statistical reason to think that there are such creatures.

With this significant caveat in mind, however, the fundamental point that holiness is unevenly distributed among creatures, according to their kinds and in their individuality, remains. There is rough ground here too, and it is part of the god's intention that this should be so: among creatures, humans (with Jesus as the exemplary case) are closer to the god than all others; and among humans, Israelites—which means Christians and Jews, together and complementarily. Within Israel also there is a hierarchy of holiness. Some Jews are holier than others, and holier than some Christians; some Christians are holier than others, and holier than some Jews; and it is a distinctive mark of Christian talk about holiness to say that claiming it for oneself is an instance of its lack; and that, except where the Church has provided decisive magisterial guidance in particular cases (by canonization, for example), claiming to be able to identify others as particularly holy or unholy must be done modestly and tentatively. It is relatively easy to categorize particular acts as more or less holy; much less so to categorize particular persons in that way.

• • •

Israel's particular holiness, the holiness of Synagogue and Church together, is given her by the god. It is not something she has of herself and is then recognized, praised, and chosen by the god for having. Neither is it something she obtains by effort. She does not self-burnish in the same way and for the same reasons that she does not self-create. No. She receives a kiss and a caress from her god, and when things go well (it is rare that they do) she turns her face eagerly to the giver and asks for more. *Osculetur me osculo oris sui!*, she says, at the beginning of the Song of Songs; and, when the god's kisses and caresses appear to have been withdrawn, she goes on, *in lectulo meo per noctes quaesivi, quem diligit anima mea*—"I looked for him by night, in my bed, the one in whom my soul delighted." Israel is eager for her god and her god is eager for her. That is one way of interpreting the god's choice of and love for Israel, Church and Synagogue both. The god lies between them, kissing and caressing each and both together, in a perfect ménage à trois that moves Synagogue and Church toward embracing one another as well as the god, in order to please the god, and in order to resolve the fugal flight into a fugal harmony. The kisses the god gives Israel do for her what the seraph's scalding of Isaiah's lips with the burning coal did for him: they make it possible for Israel to kiss the god back by providing her the holiness that makes such kisses acceptable. Israel is anointed, and so she can make love with the god; she is spoken to, and so she can converse with the god; she has her eyes opened, and so she can look at the god; she has her ears opened, and so she can hear the god. She is inflamed by those gifts with desire for more. And, again when things go well, she looks first to the god and acts as a beloved does, seeking above all to delight the god. That is her holiness. It is what she shows the world, and it is by showing it that the gentile world and the rest of the animate and inanimate world are moved toward holiness. If glory is the evidence of holiness, then Israel is glorious and the world is radiant with her glory.

Israel's passion for the god is shown to the world and to the god most fully in her liturgical life. That life, since Israel's complication, has a double form: synagogal and ecclesial. The particulars of each form differ widely, but they share a common formal feature: they are Israel's holiness enacted. They do not effect holiness, which is without remainder the god's gift. They are, rather, evidence of holiness: a monstrance in which the consecrated wafer of Israel herself is set. The liturgical aspect of Israel's life is her explicit, public acknowledgment of and service to the god, whether corporately or individually. Its forms are varied and elaborate, often requiring considerable habituated skill for performance, but they are all characterizable at root as the giving of glory to the god. Glory (radiance, fire, wind, and so on; the tropes are many) is how the god's holiness appears in the world; to give glory to the god, then, is to return what has already been given. Often, the word "glory," in Latin (*gloria*) or in the vernaculars, figures explicitly in the Western Church's liturgies (*gloria patri . . . gloria deo . . .* and so on), but even when the word is not in play, glorification, the giving of glory, is what is being performed in Israel's liturgies, whether in the form of praising the god, confessing Israel's unworthiness and gratitude, remembering this or that event in Israel's life with the god, celebrating or lamenting this or that occurrence in the life of some Jew or some Christian, making a sacrificial offering to the god, and so on. Some Israelites live this liturgical life both acutely and chronically; others, Jews and Christians both, not at all; and many somewhere between, engaging it occasionally, perhaps. Those who do not live a liturgical life at all are not the less Jewish or Christian for that lack; they are deficient, rather, in the mode of life most characteristic of Israel. They are like those who no longer memorialize their parents' or children's or siblings' birthdays; or like writers who no longer write, musicians who no longer play, painters who no longer paint. They remain what they were, but their actions no longer show their condition to the world.

An objection warrants mention here. It is that the way in which liturgical life has been presented here suggests a unity, even a monolithic unity, in Israel's liturgical life—that Israel's liturgies are all of a piece and all of a kind. But there is no such suggestion. What unity there is does not descend much from the stratosphere: Israel's liturgical life glorifies (when things go well) the god and shows holiness to the world. That is true of the liturgies of the Church and those of the Synagogue, though not identically and not necessarily equally. But that is compatible with enormous variation closer to the ground, both within the Church and the Synagogue, and across those lines. Eating and drinking are regulated differently; the god is acknowledged and described differently; funerals and weddings are performed differently in almost every particular; the balance between song and speech in glorifying the god is different; attitudes to and uses of translations, whether of Scripture or of other works, is different; initiation is performed differently; the degree to which and the purposes for which nonvocal musical instruments are used is different; and so on. Israel's liturgical observances have a shared and single origin (the god's gift) and purpose (glorification of the god by return of gift); but Israel's complication, particularly but not only evident in the fugue that separates and may yet bring together Church and Synagogue, has effected an array of particular differences, so many that, often, full engagement on the part of an individual in the liturgies of the Synagogue renders impossible full engagement in those of the Church, and full engagement in those of the Church renders impossible full engagement in those of the Synagogue.

• • •

Israel, in her ecclesial as well as her synagogal form, has a halakhic and a theological life as well as a liturgical one, each of which is an element of her holiness. The three are, for some analytical purposes, very different from one another and properly to be distinguished.

Halakhah, for example, can be understood as the body of implicit norms and explicit regulations that order Israel's life in the world, and a halakhic life as one responsive to and articulated with those norms and regulations. In that sense, both the Church and the Synagogue have a halakhic life, with a rich literary deposit. There is, for instance, the Synagogue's *responsa* literature; and there is the Church's body of canon law. Halakhah may order such things as sartorial, gastronomic, sexual, artistic, and political life; it may be highly codified, or minimally so; it may aspire to cover every significant aspect of the life, or content itself with a few, leaving those it does not codify to local gentile norms; it typically has in some part to do with the difference between Israelites and gentiles and what that difference implies for Israelite life in the world; and, since Israel's complication, there are, as there must be, halakhic particularities concerned with Jewish behavior toward and with Christians, and with Christian behavior toward and with Jews. Halakhic life, like liturgical life, shows, when properly ordered, Israel's holiness to the gentile world, and although they may differ in the degree to which they explicitly invoke the god, and in the degree to which they are evident to gentiles, halakhic and liturgical life can nevertheless be treated together for the purpose of depicting Israel's holiness as this appears to the Church.

Israel also has a theological life. It is her thoughtful response to the god, and to the god's gifts to her. Its literary deposit is large, and it ranges from treatises on difficult conceptual questions (the god's nature; the god's name; the god's triunity; the god's relation to Scripture; the god's giving of law; and so on), to guides for the composition of prayers and chants and hymns addressed to the god, to exegeses of Scripture and other authoritative texts—and much more. Both the Church and the Synagogue need and have a flourishing theological life; but it is a minority interest within Israel. Most Israelites have no need of it, and few engage in it. It, too, glorifies the god when it is well done (it rarely is: theology seems, more than other disciplines, to attract to itself those who are confused about how to do it and about what it is to do it), and so it too can be understood as a kind of liturgy (this writing, whether well or ill done, is an instance of the Church's theological life, and also, therefore, a species of liturgical act).

Each of these three aspects of Israel's life, liturgical, halakhic, and theological, is, since the complication, bifurcated. That is, each has a synagogal form or forms, and an ecclesial form or forms. For the last sixteen hundred years or so it has been possible, even usual, for Christians with a liturgical and halakhic life in the Church to have no direct acquaintance with synagogal liturgies and halakhah; and for at least that long the Synagogue's practices in these connections have had no normative significance for the Church. Representations of Jews are, of course, everywhere in the Church's life; and, sometimes, Jewish bodies have been present in Christian liturgies, as willing or unwilling baptizands, participants in marriage with Christians, and so on. Christians have also interacted halakhically with Jewish bodies, by ghettoizing them, marking them, and killing them, and, much more rarely, by succoring and nurturing them. And there is a large body of Christian theologizing about Jews and about the Synagogue, mostly in the service of elaborating a view of the Church as not-Synagogue, and of the ways in which the Church, *fides nostra* as Christian theologians sometimes say when distinguishing her from the Synagogue, *fides vestra*, is closer to the god than the Synagogue. There are traces of the Synagogue's liturgical and halakhic life everywhere in the Church (there are also traces of the Church's life in the Synagogue, but they are, probably, less extensive), sometimes unrecognized, and sometimes framed and interpreted as what-we-don't-do-and-don't-like. But, still, the Synagogue's liturgical and halakhic holiness is, in its detail and texture, by now so different in practice from its ecclesial counterpart that observant Catholics who participate in synagogal liturgy for the first time are likely to be as puzzled as monoglot English speakers would be were they taken to a Portuguese village and asked to participate in a conversation with locals at the bar. They might recognize some words; they might hear that the language has some Latinate roots, and some syntax that makes intuitive sense; but they would not be able to go on, and would not be able to participate in the conversation; they would retreat into the silence of the interested but puzzled observer.

Among the significant implications of the depiction of holiness given here is that it elevates the holiness of Israel above that of the gentiles. This may reasonably be objected to. Are there not holy gentiles, even by Israel's standards of holiness? Are there not gentiles who exhibit a deeper, more radiant, more nuanced and elegant holiness than any in Israel? Are there not corrupt, violent, and murderous Israelites? And if so, does this not call into question the view that Israel's holiness is different from, more elevated than, gentile holiness?

It is true that from an ecclesial point of view (perhaps also from a synagogal one) there are individual gentiles whose holiness is deep, broad, beautiful, and instructive to the Church. It is also true that many individual Israelites, Christian and Jewish, do not live holy lives, and may live lives so corrupt and so violent, so opposed to the god's gift, that they make much ordinary gentile viciousness seem amateurish. The line that separates Israel from the gentiles is not one that corrals holiness on only one side of it. Rather: Israel is a form of life constituted by the god with holiness as its point and purpose, and as the form of life in which holiness can find its proper culmination; a lack of holiness on the part of individual Jews and Christians, the absence, that is, of a well-ordered halakhic and liturgical life, is a falling away from what they are. This happens frequently, and for many reasons; Israel is not exempt from the world's damage. Gentiles, by contrast, are not called to the evangelical holiness of particular intimacy with the god. Their task is not the world's repair. When they are holy according to the Church's understanding of what it is to be holy, that is due to a particular gift of the god to them, often with a purpose inscrutable to Christians and Jews, and it points holy gentiles, proleptically, toward Israel as the place in which their holiness can find its fulfilment. Holiness among gentiles is like perfect pitch among baseball players: surprising and beautiful, but extrinsic to the vocation. Baseball players seduced by perfect pitch may end as opera singers; gentiles dazzled by holiness may end as Israelites. There is, then, no deep tension between the claim that, according to Israel's own criteria of holiness, some gentiles are holier than some Israelites; and the claim that Israel is the form of life in which holiness is most fully established, and in which it will, eventually, find its proper fulfilment. Similarly, it might be said that the university is the form of life established for the living and perfection of the intellectual life (no longer a plausible claim, but perhaps it can be allowed for the purpose of illustration); that is compatible with saying that there are some outside the university whose intellectual lives are fuller and more perfect than those of any in it.

There is a more fundamental objection. It is that gentiles have no reason to accept Israel's form of life—her holiness, imperfect as it is—as a desirable one in the first place. We, the gentiles might say, can show you a better life than that: a democratic life, perhaps; or one whose god is the market; or a pagan life whose gods are exclusively local and whose horizon is entirely this-worldly; or one characterized by freedom from all constraint. You may call your liturgical and halalakhic life holy, and commend it to us, but so far as we can see, they might say, it is a tissue of implausibility and the form of life it yields unattractive or worse. To this there is no answer at the level of argument. Gentiles do lack reason to conclude that Israel is desirable. Desirability is not, at root, something reason discerns but rather something to which the passions are drawn. Israel's task—a task only by courtesy; the god both gives it and makes it possible, and so it is not in the ordinary sense a task—is to become most fully what she already is. Her hope, a hope shared, as the Church sees it, by herself and the Synagogue, is that as she approaches this by becoming more holy, her radiance will bedazzle and seduce the gentiles, and they will come to see the mode of life she is as what they too want. But that end is not to be reached by reasoning.

• • •

Israel's holiness is both synagogal and ecclesial; the former, because of the thickness and detail of the Synagogue's halakhic life, is the most fully orbed of the two, the most fully reflective of the god's gift; ecclesial holiness, because of its tendency to dissolve into local gentile mores, is easier, slighter, more transparent, more ductile, more suited to neophytes. Both, however, are essential to Israel if she is to fulfill her evangelical mission, which is to empty the world of gentiles by bringing them to Zion, which is also to say into the arms of the triune god, and in that way to repair the world's damage. Israel's holiness is therefore evangelical. It is not, however, demanding as it may seem, a matter of effort. To be holy as Israel is called to be is, first, a delighted response to a gift of love, the kind that a beloved gives to a lover's kiss; and then, second, a matter of habit and reflex, as a beloved settles thoughtlessly into the company of the lover, responding with a pattern or form of life every element of which is responsive to the lover's presence. That form of life, Israel's form of life, synagogal and ecclesial, is far from what it should be; it too is damaged, incomplete, and inadequate, cracked, at times almost shattered, by its own characteristic flaws, chief among which is the violence of the fugal flight. The repair of that damage, a further gift of the god, will gradually make Israel what she should be, and when that happens she will seem so beautiful to the gentiles that they will be eager to dissolve themselves into her.

6

ISRAEL'S PROPINQUITIES

PROPINQUITY IS CLOSENESS, proximity, nearness. It might be spatial (I'm closer to Chicago than you are), or temporal (you're closer to death than you were), or relational (I'm closer to her than anyone else is), or teleological (we're closer to a solution than we were), and so on. To have propinquity to something is to be related to it in a certain way, and it comes in degrees: there is no absolute propinquity, just as there is no absolute distance; there is only more or less propinquity, and that is why *propinquitas* in Latin, like its kin and derivatives in English, finds its ordinary uses in comparative sentences like the examples canvassed, and like this one: *Fides nostra propinquior est deo quam iudaica*, which is a sentence from one of Anselm of Canterbury's letters (no. 380 according to the enumeration in Schmitt's edition). Propinquity is always of something to something else in some respect and to some degree.

Anselm's sentence might be rendered into English like this: "Our [Christian] faith is closer to the god than [your] Jewish [faith]." It has the usual comparative form: something—the Christian faith—is closer than something else—the Jewish faith—to the god (*deus*), which in the context of Christian talk and writing, to which Anselm firmly belongs, is best taken as the god of Israel, which is to say, in the terms used here, the LORD of the Synagogue and of the Church. Both, Anselm may be read to say, have some propinquity to the god, but the Church has more of it than does the Synagogue. Perhaps using the descriptor *fides* of both Synagogue (*fides vestra*, *fides iudaica*) and Church (*fides nostra*, *fides christiana*) already carries this sense: to be a form of life appropriately so called is already and necessarily to have some proximity to the god because *fides* is a gift of that god and directs those given it to that god. So, anyway, Anselm may be read to say—which is not a claim about what he meant but instead one provoked by what he wrote.

Anselm's sentence specifies neither the respect in which the Church is closer to the god than the Synagogue, nor the degree of difference between them in that respect. But it is not difficult to do this. The respect in question is loving intimacy given by call and promise. It is the intimacy of the embrace: of Jacob's wrestling match at the Jabbok, or of the intimacies exchanged by the lovers in the Song of Songs. Other kinds of proximity to Israel's god are possible: hatred and rebellious opposition, for instance, provides a kind of intimacy, and one unavailable to those embraced by the call and the promise (the demons have it, we might suppose); and it is possible to know things about Israel's god by way of distanced contemplation or precise conceptual analysis that those embraced by love need not know and often do not know (there are skilled gentile theologians, while many faithful Christians exhibit theological confusion). But for those writing and speaking within the bounds of the Church's doctrine and discipline (and, I suppose, for those doing the same within the Synagogue's—but that is for them to affirm or deny), to speak of propinquity to the god is paradigmatically to speak of elected intimacy, of an embrace by the god given unconditionally and opaquely to some (Israelites) rather than to others (gentiles).

As here, in words from the scriptural part of Israel's archive (many other examples of equal intensity could be provided)—it is the prophet Isaiah who speaks as proxy for the god:

You will no longer be called Abandoned,
nor your land Desolate;
but you will be called My Pleasure Is in Her,
and your land Married
because the Lord is pleased with you,
and your land will be Married.

For as a young man brings a virgin home
in the same way your offspring bring you home;
as one spouse delights in another
so your God will delight in you.

(*Isaiah 62:4–5*)

The second person directly addressed is Israel-the-people, the descendants of Jacob, and she is closely paired with Israel-the-land. The god delights in both, and in doing so marries them as a bridegroom does his bride. Neither people nor land can any longer be said to be abandoned or desolate; they are, rather, now wedded to the god, and that intimacy extends down the generations: future Israelites (*filii tui*) will partake of the god's intimacy with and delight in Israel-the-people and Israel-the-land, here barely to be distinguished. That participation is what makes Israel. It is, in short, holiness, and it is the respect in which propinquity to the god is possible. The degree of anyone's propinquity to the god is their degree of holiness.

Anselm's claim then comes to this: the Church is holier than the Synagogue, and is so in the only way possible, which is by the god's call and promise. The god delights in the Church more than in the Synagogue, and it is her mode of being in the world (her *terra*, her form of life) of which it may now be said, *Beneplacitum meum in ea.* It is not, so Anselm's sentence suggests, that the god takes no delight in the Synagogue. It is that the god takes less delight in her than in the Church, and that is why *propinquior deo* can be said of the Church when compared with the Synagogue.

On this reading of Anselm's sentence, it provides an instance of what seems at first blush to be an entirely standard element of the grammar of Christian speech: whatever might be said about the degree of the Synagogue's closeness to the god now, since Israel's complication (it ranges, Christians have said, from none at all—desolation and abandonment—to some real but undetermined degree), it is less than that given to the Church. The syntactical principle in question—whatever degree of propinquity to the god the Synagogue is permitted is exceeded by the degree allowed the Church—seems sufficiently obvious to most Christians that it is scarcely seen to need justification or explanation. Were explanation to be requested, the answer given would be in terms of Jesus. The Church has been embraced by the god, Christians are likely to say, as the body here below of the second person of the Trinity the god is, and it is that embrace that provides her the holiness, the propinquity, to the god she has. Since propinquity to Jesus is propinquity to the incarnate one, to the very flesh of the god by the birth, death, resurrection, and ascension of which the damaged world is repaired, it can neither be matched nor exceeded by any other form or mode of closeness to the god; they recede before it as does the handshake before the kiss, the relic before the body, the paraphrase before the poem. So far a typical, if atypically technical, Christian explanation of *propinquior deo*.

The claims about Jesus that inform the explanation are intrinsic to Christian speech and writing. Jesus is the god incarnate, the only begotten; the Church is the body of the same; Christians are cleaved to Jesus's flesh by baptism; and the baptism-created body, as the complex and beautiful, though damaged, form of life it is, partakes of the call and promise that makes Israel as a whole what she is. The abandonment of these claims would be the abandonment of Christian discourse; their significant alteration would be the significant alteration of Christian discourse. I do not recommend to the Church that this way of talking should be abandoned: this is what Christians say, and, so long as they continue to talk as Christians, this is what they should say.

Saying such things does not, however, require Anselm's conclusion, that the Church is *propinquior deo* than is the Synagogue. Explicit intimacy with Jesus does not have to be taken as definitive, much less as exhaustive, of what closeness to the god is. Anselm's sentence takes the grammar of election, the grammar that distinguishes Israelites from gentiles, and uses it to distinguish Christians from Jews, or, more exactly, the Christian form of life, which is the Church, from the Jewish form of life, which is the Synagogue. Just as all Israelites are closer to the god than all gentiles, so, on this reading of Anselm, all Christians are closer to the god than all Jews. But the claims about Jesus just canvassed, though they permit this move and can be made to support it, do not require it.

• • •

There are three ways in which these Jesus-claims may be related to the question of the Church's and Israel's relative propinquity to the god, and this Anselmian version is only one among them, even if the one to have found most support among Christians during the long course of the tradition. Each of the three ways assumes that Israel now contains both Jews and Christians (Anselm's sentence also assumes this), and that the question about propinquity is therefore, for Christians, a question about the internal economy of Israel, a question, that is, internal to the life of the god's beloveds. (What the question may be for the Synagogue is not here at issue.) It is not a question about the gentiles; and it does not entertain the possibility that the Synagogue is no longer of Israel. Anselm's formulation is naturally read in this way: the word *fides* applies to both the Christian and the Jewish forms of life. And the developments in Christian doctrine about Israel, the Synagogue, and the Jews at and since Vatican II require such an assumption. The question, therefore, is this: Within Israel, is there a hierarchy of holiness, of intimacy with the god, that separates Christians from Jews, the Church from the Synagogue?

The first answer, following Anselm, is to say that anyone close to Jesus—anyone baptized, perhaps—is ipso facto closer to the god, *propinquior deo*, than anyone who is not, which entails that, within Israel, the Church is, simpliciter, closer to the god than the Synagogue. The second answer is to say that there is no hierarchy of holiness distinguishing Church from Synagogue; if some Israelites are *propinquior deo* than others, that need have nothing to do with whether they are Jews or Christians; and there is no pressing reason—and perhaps no reason at all—to think the Church collectively closer to the god than the Synagogue, or the other way around. And the third way is to say that the Synagogue's mode of intimacy with the god within Israel places her, simpliciter, closer to the god than is the Church. Each of these answers can be subdivided and modalized in various ways, most obviously by distinguishing their versions in the order of knowing (Christians have reason to believe one or another of them) from their versions in the order of being (one or another of them is the case). But I shall not pursue those niceties here. Each answer is, so far as I can see, possible for Christians in the sense that it does not immediately or obviously call into question other Christian essentials. And it is certainly the case that the first answer has long been, and probably still remains, the standard or dominant Christian answer. The second answer, too, has its adherents among Christians, and there is something to be said for it. So far as I can see, however, the third answer, rarely given by Christians, is the right one, the one that says how things are; it is also the one that Christians, now, have the most reason to take to be true. At the very least, it is the answer the Church should now seriously entertain.

Suppose we consider propinquity to a sovereign state as an analogy. The USA is such a sovereign state, and, like most (perhaps all), it has geographic boundaries, which demarcate territory over which it is sovereign. Within those boundaries at any particular time are people, some of whom will have been there for a long time and some for a short. The analogical question: Are there, among those present within the boundaries at some time, some who are *propinquior columbiae* than others? If so, who are they? It might be said that the citizens among the populace have greater propinquity to the USA than do the noncitizens, because closeness to her, intimacy with her, is located paradigmatically in the civic intimacies that citizenship makes possible and its absence rules out. Paradigmatic among these, perhaps, are voting and traveling under the protection of a US passport. Those who can do these things are, so this answer to the question goes, necessarily *propinquior columbiae* than those who cannot. This answer is like Anselm's about Israel. Being a citizen substitutes for being baptized.

But, as with Anselm's answer, this is merely stipulative. Answering the question in this way diverts attention from, and in extreme cases renders invisible, modes of intimacy with the USA that noncitizens may and do have, and that some or all citizens cannot have. One of these is military service, which in its purest form involves martyrdom, the laying down of life for the sake of one to whom the giver is close. Numerous noncitizens have had and have this kind of closeness to the USA, and it is barred in principle to some citizens (the young, the old, the infirm), while others who could have it never will. There are also people resident within the territories over which the USA is sovereign, in some cases for generations, who, although citizens, lack access to some of the civic intimacies granted, for example, to those recently naturalized (consider the limitations on voting for residents of the District of Columbia and Puerto Rico). They lack intimacies new citizens have; new citizens also lack, as recently-off-the-boat immigrants, intimacies that long-term citizen-residents of Washington, DC or Puerto Rico have. The conclusion that every citizen is *propinquior columbiae* than every noncitizen is one that may be held, therefore; but, like its equivalent about the Church and the god, can be held only stipulatively and brings particular blindnesses with it.

The second answer, that there is no evident hierarchy of propinquity to the USA among those present in her territory at a time, and perhaps no such hierarchy at all, is equally possible, as with the case of Israel, and it, as in that case, comes with the advantage that it permits, and even promotes, attention to the various modes of intimacy with the beloved which are in fact present within her borders. It is possible that there are, for instance, noncitizens within those borders whose understanding of her politics, economics, and history exceeds those of any citizen; and it seems certain that there are noncitizens whose attunement to and resonance with her mores exceeds those possessed by some of her citizens, and is flavored in a way theirs cannot be by the fact of noncitizenship. The second answer to the question about propinquity is therefore also possible, and opens some conceptual and attitudinal doors closed to those who affirm the first.

The third answer to the question under the analogy—that noncitizens are *propinquior columbiae* than citizens—is also possible, and the way in which it is possible sheds some useful light upon its churchly equivalent. Suppose we take one of the constitutive elements of the polity of the USA to be the promise of democratic self-government to any among the world's poor who seek it. Suppose, further, that this promise is prior to and among the conditions of the possibility of the body politic it offers: that the recipients of the promise are the principal reason for the being of, the *conditio sine qua non* for, the body politic promised. And suppose, lastly, that citizens within the sovereign territories of the USA have for a long time (centuries perhaps) forgotten the shape of the promise that provides their reason for being what they are, and have as a result condescended to, bullied, and violently oppressed, to the point of torture and killing, noncitizens within the sovereign territories—particularly the poor seeking to breathe free. Then, if all this is seen clearly, it is reasonable, and perhaps more, for citizens seriously to entertain the thought that noncitizens are *propinquior columbiae* than they are because noncitizens—or at least those who are being persecuted now—are those for whom the USA has been constituted and for whom it now exists. They are the beloveds, and collectively they constitute the beloved community. Such serious entertainment might lead to a shift in the frame of vision and a concomitant alteration in conduct. Citizenship might come to be seen as instituted for, constituted by, even exhausted by, the service of noncitizens, which would include the extension of citizenship to all so that, in the end, the distinction between citizens and noncitizens would fall away. That falling away would not be because everyone would now be a citizen; it would be because the distinction between citizens and noncitizens would no longer have purchase. The end of that distinction would be the telos of the USA, and it would not be the making of everyone into an American. It would be, rather, the dissolution of America into the flourishing of all.

I don't offer this analogy as a convincing reading of what the USA is and is for (though there is something in it); neither do I offer it as a perfect parallel to the *propinquior deo* question within Israel (though there is something in it in this respect, too). I mean it only suggestively, as a stimulus for Christian thinking about that question.

In more detail: How might the Church's thinking about the Synagogue go were she to adopt as her frame of reference the obverse of Anselm's claim—the thought, that is, that *fides iudaica propinquior deo est quam christiana*? What would that thought suggest that she look at, and what might she then see?

• • •

There is, first, the question of fleshly propinquity to the god.

What is this like for Christians, and what is it like for Jews? More exactly: What is it like for Christians, and how might Christians imagine it to be for Jews? That second way of putting the question is to be preferred because, again, Christians have standing to say how things are with the god for themselves (which does not mean that they always get it right; only that they might), but lack it for claims about how things are with the god for the Jews. The Jews in what follows are creatures of the Christian imagination first; whether that imagination accords with their own is not for Christians to say, as also is how the question appears *sub specie dei*. The answer provided here is a speculative position only, though one which is, so far as I can tell, concordant with what the Church has come to teach about Israel.

A Christian stripped naked is not recognizable as a Christian, whether to other Christians, to non-Christian Jews, or to gentiles. Christian flesh is not visibly marked as such by baptism, which is the means by which non-Christian flesh, Jewish or gentile, is made intimate with Jesus. Baptism does something to the flesh, but what it does is invisible. That is not accidental. The embrace Christians are given by the god leaves and is intended to leave no mark on them. The god's kiss does not reshape Christian lips by leaving them swollen; the god's hug leaves no finger bruises on the back or the buttocks or the thighs; baptizands rising out of the waters of baptism look just as they did when they went in, and the Church does not feel called to mark the fact of baptism by branding: no tattoos, no scars, no surgical alterations—particularly, no circumcision. Christian bodies may be marked in any of these ways, and many are; but when they are, those marks do not identify them as Christian. Such markings are, so far as the Church is concerned, adiaphoric—to be taken or left, of no intrinsic interest one way or another.

There are, it is true, some marks on Christian bodies of interest to the Church, and this interest is evident in the broad ecclesial consensus that some such marks remain on resurrected bodies. The five wounds of Jesus are the paradigmatic case. They were inflicted on his flesh at the crucifixion, and they remain evident, no longer bleeding or painful, on his resurrected and ascended flesh. In similar fashion, the wounds on the bodies of Christian martyrs remain on their resurrected bodies—that, anyway, is the position usually taken in the Christian archive, and devotion responsive to the wounds of Jesus and to those of the martyrs has from time to time been an important element of Christian life. There are, too, cases of living Christians showing the depth of their participation in the sufferings of Jesus by bearing the stigmata on their bodies, or so it is said. There is, so far as I am aware, little discussion in the archive of whether marks such as those continue to adorn the resurrected bodies of those who have suffered them in life; it would seem concordant with the consensus already sketched that they should.

The marks on the flesh of Christians which the Church does value and attend to have two features in common: they are wounds produced by Christian interaction with a violent gentile (and occasionally Israelite) world; and they are participant in the wounds of Jesus, which also have the first feature. They are not produced by the god's embraces, and they are not, therefore, marks of Christian identity, as is also evident from the fact that they are vanishingly rare among Christians. To repeat: the god's love for and embrace of non-Jewish Christians, which is what makes them Israelites, leaves their flesh unmarked.

A second point about Christian fleshly propinquity to the god: nothing about it can be transmitted procreatively. The wombs of Christian women are not places in which Christians can come to be, and the seminal fluids of Christian men are not capable of fertilizing eggs in such a way as to bring Christians into being, whether in the wombs of Christian women or elsewhere. This is concordant with the absence of baptismal marking: Christian flesh is not reconfigured in those ways by baptism. Non-Jewish Christian men and women beget, and can beget, only gentiles. This state of affairs explains why the children of Christian couples need baptism in order themselves to become Christian. It also explains, even if less directly and more disputably, the tensive relation the Church has had to fleshly families. Baptism provides something, the Church has typically taught, which is not only incapable of being provided procreatively but is of greater importance than anything capable of provision in that way. When families of the flesh come into conflict with the Church about this or that, they can be set aside. One sign of that, among many, is that godparents need not be, and preferably should not be, from the fleshly family according to Catholic canon law. Another is the elevation of the vocation to celibacy over that to marriage. What can be effected by marriage and procreation is, so far as fundamental ecclesial grammar is concerned, somewhere between an irrelevance and an obstruction to becoming a Christian and living as one. The god of Israel, it seems, though warmly concerned with Christians and delighted to welcome them into Israel, has no interest in marking their flesh as Israelite, and no interest, so far as the perpetuation and spread of the Church are concerned, in their procreativity.

The Church in recent years has put a good deal of energy into affirming the importance of the fleshly family—into downplaying, for example, the hierarchical distinction separating the celibate from the married life, and playing up, for instance, the value of the fleshly family as a means of handing on the faith. But these changes of emphasis do not go deep, and do not, so far as I can see, call into question the grammatical fundamentals just set out. It remains the case that the god of Israel, the god of the Church, shows no interest in marking the flesh of the Christian beloved as such; and that nothing Christians can do in their flesh can make, or contribute to the making of, new Christians.

What significance has this view of Christian fleshly intimacy with the god for the question of comparative propinquity?

A tentative answer to that requires comparison with Jewish fleshly intimacy with the god, and any attempt on the part of a non-Jewish Christian to describe such a thing demands the usual caveats. First among these is that no Christian since the complication has standing to offer a normative construal of the Synagogue's life with the god. What follows is therefore not that. It is also not a nuanced historical description, being very largely insulated from study of what the Synagogue's archive has to say about these matters, and almost entirely so from what historians write about such sayings. It is certain (the word is not too strong) that there is variance and disagreement among Jews about matters such as circumcision and the significance of procreation in making new Jews. It is also certain that contemporary historiography undertaken by those who understand themselves to be doing something other than writing in the service of Synagogue or Church pays attention to particulars in such a way as to call into question almost any generalization about the Synagogue and circumcision, or the Synagogue and procreation. The account that follows is of a different order. It is a hypothetical act of the ecclesial imagination: suppose it's like this for the Jews with respect to these matters, the account will say; what does, or might, considering that it might be like that for the Jews suggest to the Church about what she might then write or say, specifically about the question of fleshly propinquity?

Suppose, then, that the call of Abraham brought into being a beloved community whose principal mode of recruitment is procreation following the mother's line. That is: Israelite women from Sarah onward are such that their wombs are capable of bearing Israelite children, both female and male. Suppose, further, that Israelite men from Abraham on are required by the god to have their condition as such marked on their bodies by circumcision. There are exceptions and special cases and difficulties; but these—the gift to Israelite women to bear and birth Israelites; the gift to Israelite men to be marked by circumcision as such—are among the principal ways in which Israel, subsequent to the call, is close in the flesh to the god. Such propinquity is close indeed. It involves all the loveliness and bloodiness and pain of human procreation: the god grants to all that the capacity to perpetuate the beloved community, and is concerned to mark that intimacy on male flesh by circumcision—as, perhaps (this is sheerly speculative, with, so far as I know, little grounding in the archive, synagogal or ecclesial; it has, however, some *convenientia*, and perhaps even some persuasive force), a consolation to men, a mark of their lesser fleshly intimacy with the god than has been given to Israelite women, who can bear and nourish Israelite children in their wombs. These gifts by the god to Israelites are, like all such, not unambiguously (and perhaps not at all) pleasing to those who receive them; they are likely to seem burdensome and painful—again, recall Jacob wrestling at the river ford. They are, however, still gifts, freely granted without respect to merit or desert.

So far Israel prior to the fugal complication that issued eventually in the decisive institutional separation of Church from Synagogue. That separation eventually brought into being two kinds of Israelite. One, the Jews, continued and continues to have the kind of fleshly intimacy with the god common to all Israelites before the complication. The other, the Christians, was given and continues to have a mode of fleshly intimacy with the god, and specifically with the second person of the Trinity the god is, which is invisible. That invisibility goes beyond the absence of marks on the body, and the impossibility that the condition of being a Christian can be transmitted procreatively. It extends also, by and large, to the refusal by Christians to adopt distinctive modes of dress or distinctive patterns of eating and drinking. Jews are much more likely than Christians to have a mode of life that does demarcate them from the local gentiles and from the local Christians, and not only because such marking has often been forced upon them by Christians and gentiles. The halakhic life of Israel after the complication is therefore bifurcated: its synagogal mode is visible, highly ramified, and particular; its Christian mode is invisible, minimally ramified, and general—indistinguishable, largely, from whatever the local gentile habits happen to be. Observant Jews find many, perhaps most, aspects of quotidian life explicitly ordered by halakhah; observant Christians find fewer such orderings, and those they do find tend toward the publicly invisible.

This is a grossly generalized picture to which there are many exceptions. The very offering of it by a Christian for Christian-theological purposes raises difficulties to be addressed shortly. The picture does, however, permit a more pointed asking and answering of the question that prompted it. What might the Church reasonably say now about the respective fleshly propinquity of Jews and Christians, Israelites both, to the god who loves them? The short answer is that the Synagogue appears to be more intimate in the flesh with the god than does the Church—*propinquior deo* in that sense; and that the Church ought affirm that claim as a regulative principle in her speech and writing about Israel and her own place in it. Those two positions—the claim itself and the affirmation that it ought be regulatively affirmed by the Church—are distinguishable and capable of separate justification.

As to the first. It is an ordinary aspect of human thinking about fleshly intimacy that it involves care for the particulars of the flesh, and that the degree of that care is a close index of intimacy. Parental care for the flesh of their children is close and deep: they are carried in the womb and then in the arms or on the back; they are fed and washed and cuddled; their diet, their defecation, their urination, their clothes, their gait, their speech—all these, all matters of the flesh, are attended to and shaped and cared for. There is in many fleshly family settings, it seems reasonable to say, halakhah (even if usually uncodified) for all these things, and it is an ordinary index of fleshly intimacy that there should be. Correspondingly, the absence of such care, or its presence in lesser degree, is an index of the absence of such intimacy. Similar things can be said about the fleshly intimacies shared by spouses or lovers. A person you never touch, and for the modes of whose touch you have no concern, is a person with whom you have vanishingly little fleshly intimacy. You may have abundant intimacies of other kinds with them; but of fleshly intimacy you have little.

It follows easily from this pattern of thought that the god of Israel shows considerably more care for the flesh of Jews than for the flesh of Christians, and that, therefore, the Synagogue, so far as the flesh goes, is *propinquior deo* than is the Church. The flesh of Jews lies close in the god's arms, while that of Christians is across the room out of reach. It is as though, with respect to the flesh, the god beds the Synagogue and offers an air kiss to the Church; or that the god cooks meals for Jews while providing Christians with a gift certificate to an all-you-can-eat smorgasbord; or clothes and adorns the bodies of Jews while authorizing Christians to wear whatever the locals do; or procreates with Jews and adopts Christians. None of these is more than an analogy, which is also to say that each misleads if pressed. But each underscores and perhaps illuminates the claim that the Synagogue is, *carnaliter*, closer to the god than the Church. That claim is, of course, because Synagogue and Church are both of Israel, compatible with the claim that the Church's call and promise are as irrevocable as the Synagogue's. The Synagogue's greater propinquity in the flesh establishes a hierarchy of holiness within Israel in respect of the flesh, but calls into question neither the distinction between Israel and the gentiles, nor the claim that Synagogue and Church together constitute Israel.

As to the second. The commonsensical application of ordinary patterns of speech and writing about fleshly intimacy to the question of fleshly propinquity to the god is not the only reason why the Church should seriously entertain the claim that *fides iudaica propinquior deo est quam christiana*, at least in terms of the flesh. There is also the resonant affinity such a claim has with the Church's need for penitence and penance before the Synagogue as a result of the damage done by the fugue. Whether or not it turns out to be true that the Synagogue is, in the flesh, closer to the god than is the Church, affirming (with reason) that it is so will serve the Church in the penance she needs to perform. Coming to see herself as at arm's length from the god while the Synagogue is closely held should provoke humility, and help the Church to see that holiness has a fleshly aspect to which she has sometimes been blind.

There are, however, two difficulties with the line just taken pressing enough to note even if not especially difficult to rebut.

The first is that the preceding several paragraphs reinscribe an ancient ecclesial claim about the Synagogue, which is that she is of the flesh, fleshly, while the Church is of the spirit, spiritual. That claim, in its usual form, has been a weapon: it has been taken by those churchly thinkers who have made it as an indication of the Synagogue's inferiority to the Church, and of the Church's greater intimacy with the god—who is, after all, so the grammar of the position goes, a spirit, and who values spiritual intimacy more than mere fleshly intimacy. Given the difficult and largely noxious history of this ecclesial way of speaking and writing about the Synagogue, might it not be better to avoid reinscribing the position? Perhaps so. I am acutely and chronically aware of the difficult echo. But there is a defense. The first element in it is that the valence of the position is here reversed. I depict, as the Church in her right mind also should, fleshly intimacy with the god as a desideratum for Israel, not a problem for her. Christian doctrine strongly suggests that this is the case: Jesus, the second person of the Trinity the god is, is enfleshed; Christians are cleaved to that flesh in baptism, they eat that flesh eucharistically; and the very flesh of Christians is promised resurrection for eternal life in the flesh with the god, whose own flesh will then be present to Israel in the person of Jesus in his ascended flesh. Intimacy with the god is a matter of the flesh from beginning to end, at least for persons enfleshed (perhaps, though I find it unlikely, there are fleshless persons, and if there are the modifier is necessary). It can therefore be no criticism of the Synagogue to note the depth of ingression of fleshly intimacy with the god into her life. Rather the reverse. The second element in the defense is that, so far as I can see, in matters of the flesh, as discussed, the Synagogue's life just is more consistently and fully articulated with the life of the god than is the life of the Church. This may turn out not to be so; but it is certainly worth the Church's while to entertain it, even if, and perhaps just because, such confused uses have been made of claims like this in the past. Much about the fleshly life of Christians is judged by the Church to be adiaphoric—rightly so, so far as I can see; extending the realm of the adiaphoric here below is an important part of what it means to be a Christian. But then it is not difficult to see that it is possible, within Israel, to have a fleshly life the particulars of which are mostly not adiaphoric. And that is the life of the Synagogue.

A second difficulty: it might be said that Christians have a mode of fleshly intimacy with the god altogether lacking in the Synagogue, and that noting this requires at least modification of the position just argued, and perhaps its abandonment.

In slightly more detail: the god has flesh; it is the flesh of Jesus; intimacy with, participation in, cleaving to (other metaphors are possible) that flesh provides a kind, as well as a degree, of fleshly intimacy with the god in principle not available to those who are not baptized and, consequently, do not receive the eucharist; Christians—the baptized—have just that kind of fleshly intimacy with the god, and this means that, *carnaliter*, the Church is *propinquior deo* than the Synagogue. There is something right here. The Synagogue is not cleaved to Jesus's flesh; the Church is. And Jesus's flesh is the very flesh of the god—also, of course, Israelite flesh, or, as we would now say, post-complication, Jewish flesh. Yes. But it still remains that the Church's mode of fleshly intimacy with the god is unmarked, and separated from the possibility of procreative transmission. As argued. It is to our flesh (blood, bone, semen, eggs, the integument of skin, the dark-centered pupil of the eye) just as a chalice of wine is to a cup of blood: capable of transfiguration, transubstantiation, transmutation, but even when so transubstantiated not, so far as our tongues can tell us, salty enough, iron-tangy enough, to count as blood—not, to extend the analogy, bloody enough to be transfused into a vein. There is a distance, a diastolically extended breath-pause, between the sense of flesh in play in this objection and the sense of flesh in play in the position argued for. That is consistent with, even another aspect of, the Church's refusal to allow the wombs of Christian women to hold Christian children: a pause is needed there, too, between conception and labor and birth, an inbreath within which baptism can happen. Christian fleshly intimacy with the god is, though real, though fundamentally important, though with a locus not shared explicitly by the Synagogue, still more distant (it seems the most appropriate word) than the kind the Synagogue has. Christian carnal intimacy with the god is both fleshly and not. Jewish carnal intimacy with the god is fully fleshly.

• • •

Propinquity does not have only to do with the flesh. There is also closeness and distance in language. And in this matter, too, the Synagogue appears to the Church, or should so appear, ***propinquior deo*** than she is herself. The Synagogue is Israel's poem, while the Church is Israel's paraphrase. So it may be, and so the Church should teach.

This is a thesis about language. A poem, because of the condensed intensity of its language, is among the most difficult of verbal artifacts to translate without significant loss—of rhyme, meter, assonance, echo, diction, and more. When a poem is translated it is typically rendered, melted down, that is, for its juicy and translucent essence, as fat is made from pork or ghee from butter. Rendering may give clarity; it may provide something that can be seen through and easily digested. But it does that at the cost of removing the nourishing opacities of the thing rendered. A poem translated is typically transfigured from something that needs a good deal of chewing into something that goes down smoothly. When this is not so, it is because the translator has made a poem in the target language rather than rendering one from the source language. That is difficult and rare. It is more common, and easier, to render: to look for the glassy essence of the poem, to attend to it, to remove from it its local contingencies and give to it whatever seems necessary to make it viable in its new place. That process, the rendering process, has paraphrase as its telos: it provides in other words the heart of what it paraphrases, but not its poetry.

The clearest indication that the Church is Israel in paraphrase, the one that the Church should take to heart, is that she has, and has always had, translation as a central concern. To exaggerate only slightly: the Church has, and should have, little interest in the *ipsissima verba*, the very words, that Jesus spoke to Israel in the time of his flesh; or in the very words the god has spoken to Israel since the call of Abraham. She has, and should have, great interest in what these words say: in what they may be rendered to show. But for her, no natural language (not Hebrew, not Aramaic, not Greek, not Latin) has privilege in this respect. The gospel is as fully available in English, Xhosa, Farsi, and Japanese as in any of the languages in which the canon of Scripture was composed; what Jesus has to say to the Church need not be said in Aramaic. The Church preserves almost nothing of what Jesus said in that language (*ephthatha*; *talitha cumi*; *eloi, eloi, lama sabachthani*; *abba*—and a few other words and phrases), and, since it is unlikely, though not impossible, that Jesus spoke any Greek, the upshot is that the Church has to hand only renderings of Jesus's poetry. That alone is striking enough; still more so is that the Church has rarely shown any sense that this absence is a lack. She has been and remains, properly so, concerned with the content of Jesus's speech, a content that can be rendered without loss so far as her purposes are concerned in any and every natural language. The Church does not yearn for Jesus's Aramaic voice.

The same is true of the Church's attitude to and use of the works that make up the canon of Scripture. These were composed in Hebrew, Aramaic, and Greek, and have, mostly by Christians or at Christian urging, been rendered into almost all of the world's languages. What counts, for the ecclesial part of Israel, is that the baptized be able to hear and read what the god has to say to them in their local language. After Scripture is read at an ecclesial liturgy, a concluding formula such as "the word of the LORD," or "the gospel of the LORD" is used; the Church does not say, "This is a translation of the word of the LORD," and that is significant. What the god says is fully available, without remainder or reservation, in whatever has just been read. The Greek or Hebrew or Aramaic from which a vernacular version has been made is not, from the Church's point of view, a better or fuller or more adequate presence of *locutio divina*.

The grammar of the ecclesial position about language in general, and the god's use of language in particular, is straightforward enough. Linguistic difference was introduced at Babel, as the account in the Genesis has it. Before that, *erat autem universa terra labii unius et sermonem eorundem*, and so communication among human creatures was without obstacle, and they were able to aspire to make a single name for themselves—that is, to act as one, and to seek the civilizational achievements that division would make difficult. They began to build a tower that would reach to the heavens. The god was displeased, and decided to make it so that *non intellegat unusquisque vocem proximi sui*. Confusion and division resulted.

This is a just-so story about the origins of linguistic diversity, and that difference, or more particularly the mutual incomprehensibility it involves, is presented as a curse. Translation, for the Church, is salve to this wound, a move toward heavenly existence in which there will be no linguistic barriers, and perhaps no language at all. The Lord prefers none among the particular languages used by us; and, in particular, all human languages are on a par with respect to their intimacy with *locutio divina*. The story of Pentecost as told in the Book of Acts shows the grammar of the Church's position: those who hear the preaching of the apostles in Jerusalem after Jesus's ascension do not gain the ability to understand that preaching in a single language; rather, each hears it and understands it in their own language: . . . *audiebat unusquisque lingua sua illos loquentes*. Babel is recapitulated and proleptically overcome by Pentecost (the verbal echoes within the canon of Scripture on this matter show this very clearly), and this is fundamental to the Church's eagerness to translate. Christians do not need to hear Jesus in Aramaic, to read or hear Genesis in Hebrew, to read or hear Paul in Greek, but rather to hear and read in whatever language is most comprehensible to them.

It is not that the Church fails to recognize a certain priority of the Hebrew and Aramaic and Greek texts over their renderings in other languages. She sees what is obviously true, which is that these renderings are just that, renderings, while the texts they render are, instead, compositions. This is a real difference, and it is a significant one for some purposes, particularly scholarly and historical ones. But the difference is not significant for the liturgical life of the Church, and particularly not for the presence and use of the canon of Scripture in that life. The god can, and does, address and inspire Christians in the vernacular; the gospel is fully present as gospel in the vernacular; and those understandings, together with the practices of translation and interpretation that accompany them, place every natural language at an identical distance from the god—or, what is the same, gives every natural language the same degree of intimacy with the god. The linguistic rough places are in this way made smooth.

As the Church sees her (and perhaps as she is) the Synagogue has another view about these matters, and a correspondingly different set of practices. She sees one natural language, Hebrew, as particularly intimate with what the god says. There are metaphysically developed and subtle versions of this view, according to which the syllables or letters of the Hebrew language are the ordering principles of creation, such that the world, everything that is the case, is supported by them and ordered by and to them. Less elaborately, it may be thought that the text of the Torah (perhaps also of the entire Tanakh) as written and spoken (there can be various views about the relations between the written and spoken text) is, in every particular (letters, syllables, words, spaces/silences, pronunciations/breathings, and so on), identical with what the god has said to Israel. These understandings can be modulated and developed in many directions; but for the question of linguistic intimacy with the god those particulars need not detain us. All the Church needs for considering that question is clarity about the central feature of this entire family of positions, and about how it differs from her own. And that central feature is clear: it is that Hebrew, in all its lexical, syntactical, and sonic particulars, is the language the god speaks, to all Israel first, and then to the Synagogue. From this it follows that when the *verbum domini* is read liturgically in the Synagogue, it should be read in Hebrew, and if instead a version of it in some other language is read, then that is not, *stricto sensu*, the god's speech. That is the first key difference between what the Church takes to be the Synagogue's view of language and the god. A second is close to it: although the Synagogue may sponsor and use translations of the Torah and the Tanakh (in fact she does), she does so with an understanding that what is produced is more distant from the god than is the Hebrew text.

There is a third difference, this one having to do with the use of versions of Scripture stored and handed on without being voiced. The Church is promiscuous here: so far as she can see, there is no important difference between a manuscript, a printed book, and electronic data coded for display. All these, in any natural language (and some nonnatural ones), can do the same work so far as the Church is concerned, which is to store what the god says and to make it available for reading or hearing. The means of making such artifacts, and the means of storing them, are adiaphoric for the Church. But the Synagogue, as the Church imagines her and perhaps as she is, has a different view. She values, above all other means of storing and handing on the Torah, a handcopied text, of course in Hebrew; and not only that, but one written on a parchment scroll rather than in a paper codex (it is likely that Christians invented codices, or were at least instrumental in their popularization in the early centuries of the Christian era, and that is another mark of the difference between Synagogue and Church on these linguistic questions), and in a stylized Hebrew script for the writing of which special training is necessary. That scroll may be kept in an ark within the edifice of the Synagogue, in something like the way that Catholic Christians keep the reserved sacrament in a tabernacle within the edifice of the Church (this is one of the deep family-resemblance currents within Israel as the Church sees things). And in many liturgical celebrations, Jews venerate the scroll: they stand as the ark is opened and the scroll taken out, and they touch and kiss it as it is paraded around the room. And then, when a portion of the Torah is read, that scroll is what is read from rather than from any other object in which the words of the Torah may be stored. It is, by contrast, commonplace in churches to see the gospel book elevated before the liturgical reading of the Gospel, and then set aside and the words read from something else—a paper bulletin, a screen, or what-have-you.

The synagogal practices, as the Church imagines them, establish and participate in a set of intimacies: between the god and the spoken Hebrew language; between Jews gathered for worship and the spoken Hebrew language; between the god and the Torah-scroll as a work of Jewish hands; and between Jews gathered for worship and that scroll as a material presence of the god's speech to them. None of these intimacies can properly belong to the Church's life. They have and can have no sense there. Even when some remote analogue to them is present in Christian life, what is being venerated is not a material object but rather something more distant, such as what the book makes it possible to say. And when, as sometimes happens, Christians begin to treat some or another natural-language version of Scripture as if it were the real thing—Catholics sometimes do this with the Latin Vulgate; Protestants sometimes with the seventeenth-century English of the King James Bible; Orthodox sometimes with the Greek New

Testament—from which all other versions are derived and for which god has special concern, they commit a solecism. There can, for Christians, be no such thing as that.

The contrasts sketched in the immediately preceding paragraphs are no doubt overdrawn. Not all Christians would agree with every element of the picture given of Christian attitudes to the god's relation to language; and there is, I expect, much more variety in synagogal practice than I know of or than might seem plausible in light of the sketch provided. (It is not, in any case, a sketch intended as an empirical description; it is an act of ecclesial imagination; only the Synagogue can say to what extent it is acceptable as a rendering of her understandings and practices.) And there are more questions to ask, for example about bibliomancy among Christians and Jews, and about the apotropaic use, among Christians, of printed Bibles for such things as keeping evil spirits at bay or preventing milk from curdling. But the contrast does permit a provisional answer to the question of linguistic intimacy with the god of Israel. That answer is that the Synagogue is linguistically *propinquior deo* than is the Church: all the evidence points in that direction. The Church is happy promiscuously to extend the set of words that constitute the canon of Scripture to all natural languages, which is the same as to say that she has no particular intimacy with any one of them, and that she takes Christian holiness to be capable of nurture and growth without any such particular intimacy. The Church's liturgical treatment of words is concordant with this: when the god speaks in the congregation it can be in any language, with any accent, from any written or printed artifact. All that is different for the Synagogue.

To return to the discussion of fleshly intimacy above: just as there the Church was shown to have a kind of fleshly intimacy with the god independent of bodily markings or the fertility of wombs, so here the Church appears as one who has a kind of linguistic intimacy with the god equally compatible with all natural languages, and independent of particular books. The Synagogue is a scrolled poem; the Church a codexed paraphrase. The Church should think of the Synagogue as *propinquior deo* with respect to language than herself.

An objection: Might it not be that the Church should take the Synagogue to be in error in her veneration and use of Hebrew, and herself to be correct in her advocacy of translation and her refusal to establish any natural language as closer to the god than any other? Might she not press her understanding of Pentecost as the right thing to think, and as an event that sweeps away linguistic particularity as it is understood and practiced by the Synagogue?

That can only be plausible as a response to the difference about language if coupled with the view that the Synagogue since the complication has been largely or entirely incapable of exchanging intimacies with the god—the view, that is, that her liturgies are not received by the god with delight. Catholic doctrine rules that out. Since the complication, both Synagogue and Church are liturgically intimate with the same god. Error and damage are present in each, but not error and damage of a kind that predicates the heart of their liturgical practice on error. The Church cannot avoid, and should not want to avoid, saying that when Jews venerate and read from the Torah scroll in the Synagogue they are exchanging words of love with the Church's god. The complementarity of the Synagogue and the Church within Israel suggests, rather, the claim that Israel as a whole needs both ways of responding to and deploying the canon of Scripture.

A better ecclesial response to the question of linguistic intimacy has two parts. The first is to affirm that the Synagogue is indeed linguistically closer to the god than she is herself, and to honor her for it. The second is to affirm her own practice with respect to language as asked of her by the god, and as necessary for the flourishing of Israel. Saying both things suggests that the Synagogue's tasks and the Church's, though both proper to Israel, are not the same. The Church's linguistic promiscuity is of a piece with the fact that she can perpetuate herself only by recruitment, and with the fact that recruitment therefore has a central place in her life. Effective large-scale recruitment (the Church has been good at this) sits well with a Pentecostal answer to Babel: get everyone to hear the gospel in their own language. Christians are baptized; they love Jesus; they hear the gospel in English and Farsi and Xhosa and so on; they are, the Church can reasonably say, intimate with the god, yes, Israelite, yes, but so far as both the flesh and language go, in an anteroom; the holy of holies, where the flesh is marked and the *verbum domini* is spoken and heard without paraphrase—that is the Synagogue. If you want the poetry, the Jews have it; if the paraphrase is what you can manage, the Christians have it. Israel needs them both, but Israel needs, now, the Church to acknowledge her relative distance from what the god says and the Synagogue's relative intimacy with it. Here, as in the case of the flesh, the Synagogue is emphatically *propinquior deo* than is the Church. So the Church should say, and so it may be.

• • •

Propinquity can be spatial as well as fleshly and linguistic, and here too it seems that the Synagogue is *propinquior deo* than the Church—and that the Church should say so.

The Synagogue has a home here below, but is largely exiled from it; she has *heimweh*, homesickness, the longing of an exile for a home whose location is known. The Church has no home here below, and is therefore a wanderer; she has *fernweh*, farsickness, the longing of the homeless for a distant place not yet found, which might become a home. Israel, therefore, is as a whole both placed and placeless, located and dislocated, and this difference between Synagogue and Church is another instance of a possible difference between them in propinquity to the god here below, prior to the end.

The Church can be seen as without holy places, and as constituted within Israel by the god exactly by the absence of such places. This sounds, on its face, absurd; it can, however, be given sense by considering the intrinsic portability of everything of significance to the Church's life, together with the necessary transience, evident in abandonability, of the nonportable things (land, buildings) the Church uses for its purposes.

The Church's life is lived in relation to, and as the outflow of, an absence: its god is enfleshed but unavailable in the god's very flesh: Jesus, after his resurrection, ascends to a place in which he is, for the most part, inaccessible to the senses of Christians. The Church then lives with, and as, a sacramental economy the precise point of which is to make the sensorially unavailable present *in figura* to the senses at call, anywhere and anywhen. The flesh and blood of the risen and ascended Jesus are given to Christians as food and drink crosswise to the griddable and measurable extensions of timespace. That is clear from the fact that they are available, and consumed, simultaneously in widely separated places. There is no difficulty in the baptized consuming that flesh and blood simultaneously in London, Tokyo, Kinshasa, and Tasmania, and that is because the body and blood are not located in the ordinary sense of that word. They are, rather, indexically available: available, that is, wherever the faithful are and wherever the appropriate liturgy is performed. They are here, but also there . . . and there, and there, and there. Another way to say this is to say that the flesh and blood are portable, not only in the sense that they can be carried about by us, though this can be done, but also in the sense that their here-now-ness is transverse to ordinary location. There is no particular place sanctified by their presence, and because the conditions necessary for their presence (the god's free gift; the congregation; the priest; the liturgy) are themselves portable—they can be assembled anywhere, at any time—it makes no sense to say that they can be tied to a place. There is no place locatable on a map or capable of identification by a global positioning satellite closer than any other to the sacramental presence of Jesus. A similar account can be given of the other sacraments: of the presence of the Holy Spirit at baptism, say, or at ordination. In every instance of the Church's sacramental life in action the components are the same: the god's grace; the baptized assembled; the liturgical celebrant(s); and the material means of grace (bread, wine, water, oil, and so on). Nothing nonportable, no piece of ground and no building, lends additional holiness or makes the sacraments more sacramental. To say so is incoherent, an incomprehensible solecism so far as the Church's grammar is concerned.

But, it may be objected, there are other material things of importance to the Church's life in Israel. There are, for example, relics: the material remains of saints; and there has always been, as there still is, a desire on the part of Christians, endorsed (even if sometimes with reservations) by the teaching Church, for close physical intimacy with these remains. Burial *ad sanctos*, for example, burial close to the place where a saint's body, or a part of one, is to be found, is an old Christian practice entirely accommodatable to orthodoxy. Relics, too, are incorporated into altars in church buildings, or interred in the walls or crypts of the same. And the places where such things are, or are imagined to be, have often, and rightly, become places of pilgrimage, places, that is, to which Christians are eager to go because they are holy, and by going to which they can amass merit. Why not call these sites, the places where holy things are, holy places? And if they may be so called, why are there not holy places in the life of the Church?

It is correct, unimpeachably so, that the practices mentioned in this objection are a proper part of the Church's life. But it is less clear that the right thing to say about the presence of a relic in a place is that it makes that place holy. The holiness is not in the place, but rather exhaustively in the relic, as can be seen by the translatability of relics: they can be moved from place to place, and often are. When a relic is moved—and they are all portable—the place where the relic was but is no longer ceases to be holy. Holiness is not, for the Church, transmissible from bodies to spatiotemporal locations in this way. Just as a tabernacle in a church building ceases to be a locus of holiness when the reserved sacrament is not in it (it would be a mistake to genuflect toward it when it's empty), so the ground in which a relic was buried ceases to be holy when the relic is removed from it (it would be a mistake to want to be buried next to an absent relic). That this is, by and large, the way Christians intuitively understand this matter is clear from the intensity of argument, often of a strictly political kind, about the location of relics: when a relic goes from one place to another, the power of holiness goes with it. The place where it no longer is has been stripped of that power. The holiness of bodily relics is without remainder a matter of the flesh. And that is also to say that it is portable, transportable, translatable. The semantic echo between the translatability of texts and the translatability of relics is significant here. The Church's practice with respect to the one is resonant and homologous with its practice with respect to the other.

There is a difficulty here to which I cannot immediately see a clear answer. It is that the Church, in its doctrine and canon law, recognizes relics other than bodies: lower-class relics, that is, which have been intimate with the bodies of holy people (clothing, implements, ornaments), but which are not parts of their bodies. These are less holy, less significant as loci for and containers of holiness, than body parts. But they are not understood by the Church as stripped of holiness by their separation from the bodies of those who used or wore them. Does this suggest that holiness can be transmitted from animate bodies to inanimate ones? And if so, why not to pieces of land or buildings? It is instructive in considering this to think about ecclesial practice with respect to the blessing of inanimate things. Water is the obvious example—the stoup of holy water is a fixture in most church buildings, or was before epidemiological worries emptied or removed them—but also, sometimes, soil, or household implements, or baby carriages, or rosaries, or cars, or ships, or dresses. Papal audiences in St. Peter's Square in Rome typically involve the blessing of almost anything transportable there by the faithful. And that is one part of the answer: all the things the Church blesses in contexts such as that are portable, even when inanimate. The act of blessing is a quasi-sacramental act, then, extended as those acts are typically to portable things, animate or inanimate. Lower-class relics might be understood in this way. They might be said to have been blessed by their contact with the saint's body, and to be usable by the faithful in the same way that holy water or a blessed rosary is. The holiness of such things, on this account (other accounts are possible within the grammar of the faith), lasts as long as the things do, as is also the case with the reserved sacrament. (It may of course often be difficult to discern the line dividing continuing existence of a thing from its ceasing to be.)

The exception to the limitation of holiness to portable objects (it is apparent rather than real) has to do with buildings. Some of these are not in any practicable sense portable, being too large or too fragile to be moved, and yet it seems that they can be, and are certainly treated as, loci of holiness. There are, for Catholics, liturgies for the consecration of a building (or a room within a building) for use as a place of worship. These, however, involve principally the placement and blessing of particular portable objects within the building—a relic in the altar, for instance—so that it becomes suitable for worship. Deconsecration reverses the process by removing all the portable things that made the building a church. Once deconsecration has occurred, what was a church building is stripped of holiness, so that it can now be used as a bank, a brothel, or a sports stadium. In this case too, the locus of holiness reduces to portable objects, with bodies as the paradigm cases.

A further objection. Christians make pilgrimages to holy places, only some of which contain relics. There are, for example, the sites of Marian apparitions (Lourdes, Fatima, Medjugorje), some of them formally acknowledged as such by ecclesial authorities. Might it not be the case that these places, because of what happened there rather than because of any objects still to be found there, are repositories of holiness? And might they then not serve as exceptions to the general rule in play here? It is possible. An account of that sort can be given of them. But it is avoidable. Suppose we assume that these sites are as they seem to many Christians to be, which is appropriate for pilgrimage and occasions for healing and other particular graces. It may be that Mary, or the god, choose to act there from time to time for their own reasons, rather than that the place where they once acted remains holy in a way that makes seemingly miraculous events possible. The rival explanations deal with the available data equally well; and the one that reserves holiness to bodies and persons and portable objects for as long as they last sits better with fundamental ecclesial grammar than the one that makes particular sites capable of holiness.

Were there a home for the Church, a place from which she could be exiled, it could only be a holy place given to her by the god for that purpose. And if, for her, holiness of place is always temporary and has portable objects as its paradigmatic possessors, there is no such place. Not Jerusalem, even though Jesus in the flesh walked there; not Rome, even though the Bishop of Rome has his *cathedra* there; not Constantinople as was (Istanbul as is), to which the charism of the Western empire was perhaps temporarily transferred; and certainly not more recent candidates (St. Petersburg, Salt Lake City, others). The Church may have long residence in some of these places, but she is, or should be, always aware of their transience, and of the fact that the god's promise to her that she will endure does not come with any gift of place. She is definitively homeless; her life here is entirely portable; and while individual Christians may have more or less deep attachments to particular places, those attachments have no bearing on their life as Christians—or, more exactly, only the bearing that any gentile practice may have—and are always, and properly, called into question by that life. A constant signal in the Church's liturgies is that her heart is not here, and that the hearts of Christians may never be fully here either.

The Church's lack of intimacy with particular places is concordant with her lack of intimacy with particular languages, as well as with her incapacity to perpetuate herself in the flesh. These conditions are concordant, too, with the fact that her deepest connection with the god, the connection to be had in her sacramental life, is with the god's flesh as present in its absence. It is this structural condition of the Church's life with her god that provides these distances.

What, now, about the Synagogue and place? She appears in Israel, so far as the Church can see, as given by the god not only a particular language, and not only the capacity to perpetuate herself procreatively coupled with the duty to mark her fleshly identity by circumcision, but also a particular place in which to be holy and show her holiness, which is the god's holiness, to the gentiles. That place is the tract of land also called Israel. Israel's archive, both synagogal and ecclesial, is abundant in its witness to the gift of the land; it is almost equally abundant, and unsparing, in its witness to the bloodshed and suffering caused by that gift, to the Israelites prior to the complication, to the Jews after it, and to the gentiles displaced from the land by Israel's laying claim to it, or killed by Israel while resisting that claim. That story is clear in the scriptural book of Judges, as much as in the history of the State of Israel since its establishment in 1948 following the great slaughter of Jews in Europe during the preceding decade. It is a story of blood from beginning to end, and its end is not yet.

The violence of the story does not by itself, however, so far as the Church can see, call the god's gift of the land to Israel into question. If there is a home, a place, for any part of Israel, however, it cannot also be one for the Church, for the reasons just canvassed, and this entails that if the gift of land still has purchase on Israel's life it can only be for the Synagogue. And there is, so far as the Church can tell, a good deal about the life of the Synagogue to suggest that the gift still does have purchase. Some Jews have, and show, a kind of *heimweh* for the land, even if not one strong enough to make them move there. And there are indications in Jewish liturgy (next year in Jerusalem . . .) that the thought of the land, and of its promise, is vital in the Synagogue's life. There is also Zionism, here understood in the broadest possible way as a thread of thought and action among Jews eager for a synagogal life in the land, and perhaps, too, for the recovery of liturgies in a (rebuilt? new?—the details are not for the Church to comment on or speculate about) temple in Jerusalem.

There are some difficulties for the Church in thinking about and depicting the Synagogue's intimacy with the land as a gift of the god. One, the most pressing grammatically, is that the Synagogue appears to the Church as her counterpart within Israel—the emergence of the Church and that of the Synagogue cannot be separated from one another, that is, and there is no telling of the Church's story which is not also a telling of the Synagogue's. This is also to say that there is no depiction of Jews that is not also a depiction of Christians, and vice versa (certainty about that is at the heart of this book). And, as it seems to the Church, the single story of Israel since her complication into Synagogue and Church is, at least until 1948 (and perhaps still), one of a wandering people. Wanderers can be exiles (the Synagogue) or definitively homeless (the Church), but all of them share the sense that wherever they find themselves now, this Easter, this Passover, is a temporary halt. The passport is always to hand (should the secular authorities not have confiscated it), the bag always packed, the shoes always by the door; and the conviction that all the necessities of ecclesial and synagogal life can be regathered or remade anywhere at all is ever present. This condition is proper to the Church. It has never been otherwise for her, and never can be; it is among the most characteristic deformities of the Church to forget it by identifying some or another place as the Church's home (this deformity is an exact analogue to that produced by identifying some or another language as the language of the Church).

But how should the Church imagine the Synagogue's condition of exile? Should she see the Synagogue now, since Israel's complication, as irremediably and constitutively exiled, a condition that will continue, like her own homelessness, until the end of things? Or should she see the Synagogue's exile as remediable here below by the relocation of the Synagogue in the land? That is one way, an ecclesial way, of putting the question of Zion and the difficulty of Zionism. An index of the depth of this difficulty for the Church can be had by observing how hard it appears to have been for the Vatican to decide, after 1948, to give full recognition to the sovereign State of Israel, and how long it took for her to do that.

Consideration of these questions is constrained by the hard boundary of standing. The Church can make no recommendations to the Synagogue about the economy of her life, and that limit is perhaps especially important in this case, which is deeply implicated with violence done to Jews (no State of Israel without the Shoah) and violence done by Jews (principally to those who have come to be called Palestinians, and who have been variously killed, dispossessed, and ghettoized by Jews since 1948). Any picture the Church might paint of the Synagogue's exile must contain the following elements, so far as I can see; but they are limited in scope and provide no definitive image of the possibilities for the Synagogue in the land.

First: the gift of the land to Israel has not been rescinded. The god does not take back gifts given, and this one, like the gift of particular intimacy, is *sine paenitentia* on the god's part. Second: since Israel's complication, the gift of the land, like those of circumcision and procreative continuity, is given only to the Synagogue; Jesus has removed the Church from those gifts by making her, for the sake of the gentiles, capable of homelessness and in need of baptism. Third: the Synagogue's relation to, hopes for, and shaping of the post-1948 State of Israel are hers to engage with; the Church lacks even the capacity to imagine that relation, those hopes, and those political shapings, much less to stipulate, guide, or otherwise interfere in them. Any ecclesial picture of the Synagogue's place in the world that includes these elements shows the Synagogue as fully capable of a liturgical, halakhic, and theological life with the god, whether that life is lived within or without the borders of the sovereign state of Israel; as nonetheless exiled, in large part, from that land, which state of affairs provides one of the distinctives of the Synagogue's life with the god; and as more intimate with the god (*propinquior deo*) with respect to place, therefore, than is the Church, who is definitively placeless and homeless. That last is so exactly because the Synagogue has been given a place that the god has hallowed for her, and that she hallows by her presence in it. There is no equivalent for the Church.

One further point needs to be made on this kind of propinquity, for which there is no analogue in the cases of the fleshly and linguistic kind. It is that the Church's particular love for the Synagogue—her greater concern, that is, for the well-being of Jews than of gentiles—has special application here, and that the Church ought not avoid prudentially and provisionally thinking through what that particular love might mean for her consideration of the State of Israel. Suppose, for example, that the Synagogue is reasonably understood by the Church to be under constant threat of violence done to her members, and of violence directed at herself with the purpose of her erasure (with, of course, the accompanying awareness and acknowledgment that much of that violence has been done by Christians, and that some continues to be). Suppose, further, that the Church comes to think, as, again, she reasonably might, that given the political order of our corrupt and violent late modernity, an essential bulwark against murderous and genocidal violence directed at Jews is the existence of a sovereign state ordered and administered by Jews for Jews, as a bolt hole if needed for those Jews who do not live there, and as a place of safety for those who do—then, the Church might reasonably become an advocate for and supporter of the State of Israel with a degree of enthusiasm she shows for no other sovereign state. That would be an appropriate corrective for the Church's approach to the State of Israel since 1948, and an appropriate penance for her complicity in and occasional active support of and engagement in anti-Jewish violence during the years leading up to that foundation. Such advocacy and support would be predicated on no ecclesial judgment about the place the land should have in the Synagogue's life with the god. It could be a set of prudential judgments articulated with a particular love.

7

ISRAEL'S END

THE GOD BROUGHT Israel into being principally as a remedy. She was to repair the world's damage by making holiness attractive to the world and thereby returning the world to the god from whom sin had separated it. At the end of things, that repair will have been effected. Then everything will be as it should be, the distinction between fact and value will have been removed, the god's purposes will have been fulfilled as it was always the case that they would have been, and all creatures will be rightly and indefectibly related to the god. In such a situation there can be no more remedies because there is nothing to be remedied. Therefore, if Israel, Synagogue and Church together, is to continue at the end of things, in the heavenly paradise, it cannot be as a remedy. If Israel was and is nothing other than a remedy, then the conclusion that she at last ceases to be is unavoidable. Where there are no sick people there are no hospitals; buildings in which the sick were once cared for may remain, but they will have been repurposed and will therefore no longer be hospitals. Is this what should be said of Israel at the end? That as the world was once, before Abraham, without Israel, so the world will once again be, when repaired, without Israel?

This is a possible view for the Church, but it depends on understanding Israel as remedial only, a device in the god's hand with a single purpose. It is clear that the world's repair is Israel's principal purpose; it is clear, too, that had the world not been devastated it would not have needed repair, and that therefore if, counterfactually, Israel had existed in an undamaged world, she would have been unrecognizably (to human creatures) different from what she has in fact been. But it is not necessary to conclude from this that Israel is only a remedy. There is another theme evident in Israel's archive, and it is that the god loves Israel noninstrumentally, for herself alone, as well as for what she can do for the world. That love is inscrutable, certainly; neither the Church nor the Synagogue is depicted in such a way as to show why the god loves them, or what it is about them the god loves. But inscrutability is an ordinary feature of particular loves, especially of noninstrumental loves, focused as they are upon the particulars of the beloved without calculation of what the beloved might do for the lover or for anyone else. Jesus loves the Church in this way, both in the persons of its individual members, those cleaved to him in baptism, and in the person of her collective self, his beloved and bride and mother—this last when the Church is personified as Mary, to whom her son is devoted just because she is his mother. And the god, the triune LORD, the god of Israel, has the Synagogue as beloved in similar fashion: she is, severally and collectively, marked as the god's bride, and her life with the god delights the god for itself; for the god, the Synagogue is like a lily when all others are thorns whether or not the Synagogue behaves as she should, and whether or not, therefore, she contributes to the repair of the world as she should.

There are devices the god uses for the world's repair, and for the life of Israel, which are best understood as purely instrumental, and therefore as ceasing to be once their purpose has been achieved. Human procreation is perhaps one. This is, among other things, instrumental in and essential to Israel's endurance through time; it is one of the ways in which new Israelites come into being (there are other goods connected with it as well). But procreation is, without remainder, a response to death. In the absence of death it has no purpose and no sense, and since, as the Church sees it, death is the principal mark of the fall and the heavenly paradise is entirely without it, procreation has no place there. Israel continues in the heavenly paradise without it, as also without the instruments of liturgical recruitment (baptism, mikvah) she uses now. As there is no novelty in paradise (paradise is the *novissimum*, the condition than which there can be no newer, which rules out the possibility of novelties), so there are no new Israelites. Perhaps, too, Scripture is a device whose purpose will have been exhausted in paradise. Since creatures there will see the god face to face and know as they are known, hear as they are heard, touch as they are touched, and so on, there is no need for the kinds of intimacy with the god and knowledge of the god prompted by hearing and reading the words of Scripture.

These positions are arguable so far as the Church is concerned; a case can be made, though not a convincing one, for the continued existence and use of the canon of Scripture in paradise, and even, perhaps, for the continuation of human procreation there. I mention these speculative positions not to show their correctness but only as contrastive cases, instances that show a fundamental and standard pattern of reasoning in the ecclesial archive about what does and what does not continue in the life of the world to come. That pattern is this: anything that does not contribute to the well-being of creatures in paradise (death provides an instance) is absent there; anything that does contribute to the well-being of creatures in paradise (flesh provides an instance) is present there. Scripture and human procreation arguably belong to the first category because the real contributions they make to creaturely well-being in the devastated world have no purchase upon the world to come; Israel, in a limited and transfigured sense, may belong to the second category. How so?

The paradisial life of the world to come has a clear formal delineation. It is a life centered upon the three-personed god, including Jesus, who is present there in his ascended flesh. Every creature living that life participates in and is intimate with the god as completely as its kind and its history permit. The participatory intimacy with the god in which all such creatures live has no terminus: the life itself, seeing and being seen, knowing and being known, touching and being touched, hearing and being heard, smelling and being smelled, tasting and being tasted, is the terminus—the appropriate and delightful end beyond which there is nothing further, no new thing—of creaturely life, and it is, without remainder, ecstatic delight. That is paradisial, the good we were made for.

Most human creatures (all except the saints), including most Jews and most Christians, are not, at death, ready for the life of the world to come. They are too malformed to be as capable of participatory intimacy as they can be, and as they will be. They need purging, purifying, reconfiguring, transfiguring: a remaking that removes all extrinsic and contingent obstacles that would prevent them from receiving the god's love as completely as they might, and delighting in it as fully as they ought and can. Even what they take to be their virtues will need, more often than not, to be burned away. They need purgation, at the heart of which is surprise at what needs to be removed and what needs to be received in order to become as fully capable of the god as may be. Exactly how this happens—its details and texture—needs no further comment here, in part because those details and that texture are neither known nor knowable, and in part because this is not a treatise in eschatology. The Church knows, formally, what our end is; the Church also knows, formally, that she has little imaginative grasp on the particulars of how, postmortem, human creatures arrive at their end; and she knows, and in her better moments finds herself able to say, that the tarnished mirrors in which we now see the god mean that radical surprise is inevitable when we see the god directly. It is not only that we will then understand more about the god, and be able to respond more fully to the god, than is possible now; it is also that a good deal that we take ourselves to see and know about the god will then show itself to have been mistaken. If there is a formal addition to make to the characterization of the life of the world to come just given, it is that all those who enter that life will find the god they encounter there stranger than the one they expect. That applies as much to Israelites as to gentiles; and as much to Christians as to Jews.

This proviso, that we will learn how ignorant and mistaken we have been, provides the first thing of importance to say about the internal economy of Israel at the end.

According to it, the Synagogue will see Jesus, and will learn, in seeing him, something previously unknown to and sometimes denied by the Synagogue. An ignorance and a mistake will then be corrected, and the correction will be a delight for the Synagogue. This is not the place to set out in detail what the Synagogue will learn about Jesus; that would require a treatise in christology, and even were a summary one to be offered here, it would not elucidate the central point at issue, which is that the Church does not now know, and cannot now know, how what the Synagogue then learns to see will seem to her. That is for at least two reasons. The first is that the Church's own Christology will turn out, then, to have been inadequate and in some particulars (I do not know what they are) erroneous—if not literally, then at least as standardly interpreted in the Church. The second is that the Church's understanding of how the god now seems to the Synagogue is inadequate (the word is too weak), which means that she is in no position to tell how it will seem to her when she is faced with something new. It may be, which means that it also may not be, that the Synagogue's knowledge and imagination of the god is already sufficiently capacious to have little difficulty in accommodating what Christians, including this one, ordinarily imagine to be the chief difficulties—I mean the claim that the god has taken human flesh, and the claim that the god is triune.

The Synagogue will not be alone in finding her ignorance exposed and her errors corrected when she takes her preeminent place in the creaturely array before the god. The Church will be in the same condition. She will learn, as it seems to me, what has so far been largely beyond her grasp, and often denied, which is that the Synagogue's form of life here below has been *propinquior deo* than her own, and that the Synagogue is, collectively and individually, closer to the god and more beloved by the god than she is herself, both then and now. The Church will see and know that her love of Jesus has turned her face toward the gentiles, and has therefore required of her a form of life less holy, and therefore less reflective of the glory of the god she now sees, than the

Synagogue's. She will find herself, therefore, placed in paradise close to the gentiles, whom she has been instrumental in bringing in to Israel, and further, therefore, from the god than the Synagogue, who has, more steadfastly than she, turned her face to the god.

These corrections will be occasions for nothing but celebration on the part of both Jews and Christians (nothing other than celebration is possible in the life of the world to come). Jews will celebrate who they have been and who they have become; Christians will do likewise; and an element integral to the celebration of each will be understanding of what Israel has been and now is, which is also to say of how Christians and Jews have together constituted her and continue to do so in the life of the world to come.

Israel does, then, continue in the life of the world to come, and continues as what she has always been, which is the god's principal and most intimate beloved. The marks of the wounds of Israel's fugal complication will remain, and most especially the marks of the wounds on the bodies of Jews put there by Christians. But those marks will no longer be painful. They will be cicatrices that commemorate and remind, and will serve the same function in the heavenly paradise as the scars on the bodies of Christian martyrs and the marks of the five wounds on the ascended flesh of Jesus.

• • •

The life of the world to come in the heavenly paradise, as this appears to the Church, is formally identical for all creatures, as described; but it is substantively different for different creatures because their capacities and histories differ, and these differences are not erased in paradise. These substantive differences have many aspects; one among them, of central significance for this discussion, is of capacity for intimacy with the god. Those within Israel have a greater capacity for this than those without because of their peculiar history of election and promise with its concomitant form of life. Because of this history, Israelites have been made capable of greater intimacy with the god than have gentiles, and they are therefore closer to the god in paradise than are gentiles. This is the sense in which Israel continues in paradise. She remains what she has been since Abraham, which is the god's chosen bride, bedded and loved and marked and placed and charmed and endeared by the god with a closeness and specificity and care not given to the gentiles. In spatial metaphor: within the array of creatures around the ascended flesh of Jesus in paradise, the resurrected Israelites are closest to him (except, perhaps, for the angels), with Mary, his mother, closest of all, and with the other Jews close to her; Christians are more distant: they are the bridge between the circle of the gentiles and that of the Jews, and so their assembly is the next concentric circle, with the assembly of the gentiles beyond them, clinging to them as Adam and Eve clung to Jesus's finger ends when brought up out of the tomb by him on Holy Saturday. In sonic metaphor: Jews in the resurrection vibrate bodily to the music of Jesus's voice, reproducing its essence in their flesh, their heartstrings ready-tuned for it, while Christians hear the music and sing it back in a variety of voices harmoniously blended (Pentecost thus represented and transfigured), and the gentiles read the score, seeing into its depths and hearing its melody in their minds' eyes. Every individual human creature contributes in its own way to heaven's harmony, and each is fully delighted to do so, aware in doing so that others are contributing differently, some more fully and others less, but each fully itself and fully aware of itself in its relation to others. In this way Israel remains at the end, internally differentiated; and the surprise and delight of the Jews in finding Jesus is matched and reciprocated by the surprise and delight of the Christians in acknowledging the Jews as more capable of the god than themselves.

8

PROSELYTIZING IN ISRAEL

PROSELYTES ARE STRANGERS, sojourners, people from elsewhere. That is the core meaning of the Greek word *proseluthos*, from which the English remotely comes. Exemplary proselytes, the clearest cases, have left a familiar form of life with its habits and norms and begun a new one. They lack the habits belonging to the new, find its norms opaque, and are, at least when neophytes, recognizable to indigenes as people from elsewhere. They have exchanged something familiar, bred in the bone, for something alien, strange, and difficult; and while they may learn this new form of life, even to the point of becoming as fluent as indigenes, they are always proselytes. That is true even if they forget it themselves. A second language may come to be spoken and written with native fluency, and may altogether displace the first; habits of intimacy with a new beloved may overwrite those shared with an old, without apparent remainder; but still such speakers and such lovers remain proselytes. It is still the case that they once lived otherwise, that they are immigrants from elsewhere; this differentiates them from indigenes, who have never not lived in the form of life they now inhabit.

Proselytizers seek proselytes, and use proselytism to do it. What they want, in the ideal-typical case, is to estrange those they address from the form of life they now live by bringing them, as strangers, into a different one, new to the proselyte. Proselytizers may do what they do because they think the new life they offer, estranging though it is, good for those to whom they offer it. In extreme cases, it may seem to them that what they proselytize for (democracy, temperance, truth telling, the free market, transvestism) is so good for everyone that all those not yet brought in should be forced in: *compelle, intrare* is an appropriate motto for such proselytizers as that. But most lack that degree of conviction about the goodness of what they proselytize for; and some, tormentors, try to persuade, or force, others into forms of life that will, even as the proselytizer sees it, damage them.

Some proselytizers are effective in making proselytes. But there is no necessary link between proselytizers and proselytes. Many who become proselytes have no proselytizer, and many proselytizers make no proselytes. Proselytes often become so by their own decision, or are pressganged by circumstance, or lured by happenstance. The presence of proselytes and the work of prosleytizers are distinct, therefore, and should be so treated.

The exemplary case of proselytism involves effortful and explicit action aimed principally, or at least directly, at making proselytes. I proselytize you in this sense if, having discovered the delights of going to the opera, I encourage you to accompany me, to learn about the repertoire, to study librettos and scores, to come to know the powers and limitations of the virtuoso singers currently working, to listen to old recordings and new, and so on. I may or may not succeed in making a proselyte of you; but when I try, as described, I proselytize overtly.

By contrast: I might, on my daily walk around the neighborhood, pass a garden that impresses me with its beauty, with the unusual range of flowers and shrubs and trees it contains, with the careful impression of spontaneity it provides, and with its seasonal effects. I never meet the gardener, but I look closely at the garden every time I pass it, take occasional surreptitious photographs so that I might later identify its plantings, and work, over time, to replicate some of its patterns and effects in my own garden. I have become a proselyte, but I have not been overtly proselytized: the gardener has had nothing directly to do with me, and I have no reason to think that she gardens proselytically. Even if she does, even if among the motives of her gardening is to show beauty to passersby with the hope that they will go and do likewise, she is still far from the ideal-typical proselytizer. The gardener brings something lovely into the world, and lets what she has made do what work it can. She does not stand at her gate encouraging those who pass the garden to go and make one like it. This, if it is proselytizing at all, is the proselytism of the monstrance: something is displayed, shown, made evident; those who see might be delighted and moved to enter the form of life in which such things are done and made; they might be left cold and unimpressed; they might be repelled, and pass by as quickly as they can on the other side; and they might scarcely notice (that is the most common case: few of us notice anything much about the world in which we find ourselves). In all these cases, they respond not to what the gardener explicitly encourages or urges them to do, but only to what the gardener has made.

There are many shades and gradations both within overt proselytizing and within the proselytism of the monstrance, and there is no bright line between the two kinds. There are many cases in which it is unclear which classification fits best. My concern is only with clear cases of overt proselytizing, cases in which Israel, whether as Church or Synagogue, is intentional and explicit in her attempt to make proselytes. Both Church and Synagogue show themselves to the world in various ways, and sometimes those showings, those placings of themselves within a monstrance at the crossroads, make proselytes. Gentiles, for example, might come across this or that activity on Israel's part, done because it is what Christians or Jews do (parading relics through the streets of the city; davening in the ruins; pausing the quotidian in favor of the Sabbath; writing with passion and precision for and about the god; offering food and clothes and care to the destitute; gathering for liturgical service of the god; living a halakhic life crosswise to local norms; and so on), and be moved toward the form of life that contains those things, even to the point of seeking entry. They may also, and with as much likelihood, happen across Israel's doings and find them uninteresting or repellent.

It is clear that the Church inevitably will, and properly should, show herself to the world by what she does and what she makes, and that when proselytes are made as a result there is no in-principle difficulty for an ecclesial grammar of Israel. If an unbaptized Jew or a gentile is moved toward, or away from, the Church by seeing her at work in the world, that is epiphenomenal to the work, and not something the Church needs to consider further as part of her thinking about Israel's ecclesial grammar. She must consider what to do next should an unbaptized Jew be attracted by what she does and move toward her; questions of interest for her grammar of Israel arise that point, but there are no such questions about showing herself to the world, as in a monstrance. The same is true for the Synagogue as she appears to the Church: to the degree that she shows herself to the world, the world may find her beautiful—or, of course, not.

• • •

In Israel, there are both indigenes and proselytes, in varying proportions at different times. Proselytism has always been, as it remains, the principal means by which Israel recruits gentiles to herself. Abraham, the first Israelite (not, according to the account given here, the first Jew), was a proselyte, recruited by the god, and asked to leave his homeland and go to a new place to live a new life. Jews and Christians both identify a wandering Aramean as their father. There are scriptural accounts of recruiting gentiles into Israel by marriage, some of them coupled with ambivalence about the practice; and the Synagogue, since Israel's complication, has maintained means, usually liturgical, for recruitment of both gentiles and Christians, even as she has also sometimes made these burdensome and been reluctant to encourage their use. The Synagogue can afford to make proselytism relatively marginal to her life because most Jews are indigenes, and so neither her survival nor her growth depend on proselytes; those occur principally by way of conception in Jewish wombs. Proselytism always remains a possibility for her, however, because she is of Israel, and Israel, by definition, has recruitment of gentiles as an unavoidable aspect of her vocation. What the Synagogue does or does not do by way of overt proselytism is her business; the Church may observe it and learn from it, but she lacks standing to comment normatively on it, or to intervene in it.

Proselytism is central to the Church's life in a way that it is not to the Synagogue's. That is most obviously because there are no Christian indigenes: every Christian is a proselyte, and that encourages proselytism because without proselytes the world would rapidly empty of Christians. Whenever baptism occurs, someone who was previously either a gentile or a Jew becomes a Christian, in the former case by erasure of *gentilitas* and its replacement by being a Christian, and in the latter by establishing an additional mode of being an Israelite, the Christian one, alongside the one already there, the Jewish one. Ordinarily, too, baptism involves proselytism on the Church's part: parents and godparents of infant baptizands are encouraged (catechized, persuaded, threatened by appeal to dire consequence, and so on) to submit infants to baptism, and instructed in what baptism is and does; adults may be persuaded of the delights and blessings and advantages of life as a Christian, and sometimes threatened or forced into it (though the Church has now renounced those modes of proselytizing); and the Church has at times made efforts to preach the gospel to entire populations among which it had previously been unknown, with the intention and hope that they will receive baptism. All these practices involve active and overt proselytism.

The Church must proselytize if she is to survive, and that is a significant contrast between her and the Synagogue. But the ordinary ecclesial way of explaining why the Church seeks proselytes does not involve appeal to her need for it in order to survive. Rather, the explanation involves, typically and first, appeal to the instructions and commands about this given by Jesus, as for example at the end of the Gospel of Matthew, when Jesus tells his followers to teach and baptize all gentiles in the triune name of the god, Father-Son-Spirit: *Euntes ergo docete omnes gentes, baptizantes eos in nomine Patris et Filii et Spiritus Sancti* . . . (Go, then, and teach all peoples, baptizing them in the name of the Father and the Son and the Holy Spirit). This command,

and others like it, not all of them so unambiguous in restricting proselytism to the gentiles (assuming that *omnes gentes* should be so interpreted), have been taken by the Church to provide sufficient reason for proselytizing. The Church has often spoken as though what she wants is the baptism of everyone, which would result (it has never been approached: at no time, probably, since Jesus's ascension has the baptized portion of this planet's population of human creatures exceeded one-fourth of the whole) in the elimination of gentiles, as well as the elimination of unbaptized Jews (not the elimination of Jews simpliciter, which cannot be done by baptism or in any other way).

Need for survival and obedience to the god's command: those are two principal causes of the Church's eagerness to proselytize, and of her energy and ingenuity in doing it. Informing both is the thought that knowing and being cleaved to Jesus are desiderata for everyone. Everyone should want them, and they would be good for everyone. One way of putting this is to say that salvation—the final and indefectible repair of damage by way of intimacy with the god—depends upon them; another is to say that damnation, irretrievable and final separation from the god, is the inevitable result of their absence; a third is to say that they are necessary conditions for human flourishing, both collective and individual; and yet another is to say that since the work of the god always and without exception involves Jesus (the god is triune), knowing and being cleaved to Jesus brings those who enjoy it to a degree of intimacy with the god otherwise unattainable. There are many other possible justifications and explanations of the Church's concern to proselytize, not all compatible with one another, and this family of ways of thinking about the world's need for baptism came fairly early in the Church's history to be taken to imply that the fundamental division among human creatures is that between the baptized and the unbaptized, and that every other distinction should be subsumed into it and construed in its terms.

These patterns of thought require and justify proselytism of the unbaptized. They have often been taken by Christians to apply straightforwardly to unbaptized Jews, and when that is done, Jews vanish as a separate category with respect to the question about proselytism. Because of this, the Church has sometimes proselytized and baptized Jews using all the same devices (persuasion, encouragement, threats, compulsion, violence) she has applied to gentiles.

But often, too, the Church has distinguished Jews from gentiles, and has shown reluctance to proselytize them. That has most commonly been because the Church has thought of the Synagogue's continued existence, at least until Jesus's return, as required and guaranteed by the god as an independent witness to the truth of what the Church teaches about Jesus, at least to the extent that the Jews preserve the corpus of texts that Christians call the Old Testament independently of the Church, and in that way show that Jesus was prophesied and prepared for long before the time of the Church. That complex of views (it comes in many kinds) was most often used to discourage the Church, or this or that secular power, from killing Jews, and in that way removing from them the capacity to witness to the Church; but it could be, and sometimes was, also used to discourage the Church from proselytizing and baptizing Jews. The god, according to this line of thought, intends the Jews not only to be preserved until the end, but also to be preserved as observant, with all the particulars of their liturgical, halakhic, and theological lives.

The god, on this view, does not permit the world to be emptied of Jews, ensuring instead their preservation and scattering throughout the world so that the Church might have them present as witness wherever she finds herself—which, ideally, is everywhere. Both the Synagogue and the Church are scattered, though in different ways, and this line of thought makes that state of things, since Israel's complication, proper to both of them.

This is hardly an exalted view of the place of the Synagogue in the god's economy, though its correlation of the Synagogue's geographic scattering with the Church's bears further thought; but it did, to some degree, preserve the Synagogue from erasure by the Church and constrain the Church from baptizing Jews; and it may sometimes have motivated her to protect the Synagogue from gentiles bent on her removal for their own reasons.

Advocating ecclesial restraint in proselytizing Jews was rarely, however, until recent times, connected, as it is here, with the claim that Israel comprises the Church and the Synagogue together, without any claim of identity between them, and with differences between them that make a hierarchical ordering of them with respect to intimacy with the god not straightforward, but which suggest that the Church should, on the whole, take the Synagogue to be *propinquior deo* than she is herself. Considering Christian proselytism of Jews with this as backdrop makes possible some new avenues of speech and writing about it.

There has also been a long tradition in the Church of worrying about the propriety of Christian participation in the liturgical and halakhic life of the Synagogue. Those who encourage this have, already in Scripture and throughout the long tradition, been said to engage in judaizing. That word covers many things: the thought that baptized Jews may, or should, live according to some or all of the Synagogue's liturgical and halakhic norms; the thought that Christians who are not also Jews may or should do those things; the thought that a life lived in accord with those norms is permitted or required of anyone (unbaptized Jew, baptized Jew, non-Jewish Christian, gentile sympathizer with the Synagogue) since the ascension of Jesus; the thought that any of the Synagogue's practices, liturgical, halakhic, or theological, may or should, since Israel's complication, be adopted or adapted into the Church's life; and so on.

There is also, lastly, the question of the Synagogue's direct proselytism of Christians who are not also Jewish. This is not, so far as I can tell, a prominent object of concern or discussion by the Church during most of its history, but there is no doubt that it has sometimes occurred, just as there is no doubt that in most times and places there have been some non-Jewish Christians who have been recruited into the Synagogue by way of her usual liturgical means. The Church has certainly sometimes worried that close connection with Jews, as in marriage, may tempt Christians to live as Jews; and has sometimes even shown concern that, because the Jews have the law and the prophets, they are more likely than gentiles to be able to subvert Christians.

In sum: it is clear that there are proselytes in Israel as she is now constituted, and that there is also proselytizing. The proselytes are of four kinds: ex-gentile Christians; ex-gentile Jews; Jewish Christians (Jews who have received baptism); and Christian Jews (Christians who have been recruited liturgically into the Synagogue). Both the Church and the Synagogue, though with great variation as to frequency and intensity, proselytize gentiles; and there is some, though less, proselytism of Jews by Christians and Christians by Jews. There are also questions within Israel, certainly for the Church and perhaps also for the Synagogue, about the degree to which the liturgical and halakhic life proper to each is possible or appropriate for members of the other, questions that in one direction have to do with judaizing, and in the other with what may be called christianizing. It seems clear, for example, that some aspects of Jewish liturgical practice in the USA were self-consciously borrowed from Christians, usually of the Protestant variety. Proselytism directed at gentiles, whether by the Synagogue or the Church, faces outward: its concern is to augment Israel in one way or the other. Proselytism directed at Jews by Christians, or at Christians by Jews, faces inward: its concern (not typically under this description by those who practice it) is to bring into being people who have a double mode of intimacy with Israel's god, rather than to increase or decrease the number of Israelites. Questions about judaizing and christianizing have to do with the nature and porousness of the boundaries that separate the ecclesial from the synagogal form of life.

• • •

With these distinctions in mind, what does the ecclesial grammar of Israel suggest about Israel's overt proselytisms, and about the condition of proselytes within Israel?

First, there is the Synagogue's overt proselytizing, whether of gentiles or of non-Jewish Christians. The Church's history with the

Synagogue has removed from her any standing to intervene in the Synagogue's life, or to comment normatively upon it, from which it follows that should the Synagogue wish to proselytize gentiles, or Christians, that is her business. The Church can, however, say how these activities, should they occur, seem to her on the basis of her understanding of Israel, and that is a relatively straightforward matter. Israel comprises the Synagogue and the Church, and is separated from the gentiles by a bright line. Proselytization of gentiles by the Synagogue, then, is aimed at recruiting them into Israel. The Church celebrates this because she understands it to be an element of Israel's reason for being and a contribution to the world's repair: all the gentiles are eventually to be brought in, and whatever proselytization of them the Synagogue undertakes is aimed at a goal the Church shares with the Synagogue.

Synagogal proselytization of non-Jewish Christians is barely more complicated (it seems now not much to occur, but at various points within Israel's history it has been more frequent). This is an activity only possible consequent upon Israel's complication into Church and Synagogue, and from the Church's point of view it is aimed at supplementing a Christian mode of intimacy with the god with the possibility of a Jewish one. When such proselytisms are successful, they bring into being Christian Jews, and the Church ought now regard such complex and difficult creatures with a mixture of regret, puzzlement, and envy. The regret has to do with loss of explicit intimacy with Jesus, as well as distance from the sacramental life of the Church, which might be consequent upon successful proselytisms of this kind; the Church loves her own, wishes them close, and is saddened by any distance of her own from herself. They remain, from her viewpoint, cleaved to Jesus by way of their baptisms—nothing the Synagogue does can change that—but the Church acknowledges, or ought, that a Jewish liturgical and halakhic life is at least as intimate with the god as her own, and seems in most respects to be more so; she celebrates the new and different intimacies with the god that such proselytes might develop; and she sees that such complex creatures as Christian Jews are inevitable concomitants of Israel's own complication. Their coming into being brings felicities as well as losses, as has that complication itself. And since the Church has, because of her history with the Synagogue, now a penitential commitment to the Synagogue's flourishing greater than that to her own, she celebrates the coming into being of Christian Jews as a contribution to that flourishing, even if it also seems in some ways to be to her own detriment. She does not, however, seek it for her own non-Jewish members, or commend it to them. They are already Israelites; they are cleaved to Jesus; and they have, already, a form of life which makes them intimate with Israel's god. Non-Jewish Christians have no need to become Jews, and the Church should freely and energetically point this out to any who think of entering the Synagogue. When a non-Jewish Christian does become a Jew, the Church should make it her pastoral practice to say, it ought be for particular, non-generalizable reasons (marriage to a Jew; a particular movement of the Spirit; others). And it remains the Synagogue's business to decide how to think about and treat Christians who seek to enter the Synagogue.

Equally little need be said about the Church's proselytizing of gentiles. This, like the Synagogue's version of the same, belongs properly to Israel. It aims to augment the population of the god's beloveds by way of liturgical recruitment, and so to contribute to the repair of the world that is Israel's first and last reason for being. Gentile baptism, therefore, is a good like in kind to the Synagogue's liturgical recruitment of gentiles; it is a straightforward fact that produces a straightforward account. There are better and worse ways of doing it (the use of force or threat is always to be ruled out); the Church should attend to the disruptions and losses that gentile proselytes often undergo as a result of their baptisms (no good, in a devastated world, is without attendant lacks and losses); and the Church may reasonably conclude that in some locales and in light of some particular histories overt proselytism even of gentiles might need to be abjured for a time. But these complexities raise no particular difficulties for the Church's grammar of Israel. Proselytism is intrinsic to the god's call and choice of Israel, and both the Church's and the Synagogue's proselytizing of gentiles belongs to that vocation.

There is also the Church's proselytization of Jews. This is the Church's explicit encouragement or persuasion of Jews to receive baptism, and in receiving it to be cleaved to Jesus, which is to say to the god to whom they are already cleaved because they are Jews.

There is no principled reason for the Church to do this. Her own grammar of Israel, once properly configured, tells her that Christians have no closer intimacy with the god than do Jews, but rather the reverse, and therefore that encouraging Jews toward baptism cannot be justified on that ground. Jews are already the god's beloveds, already within Israel, already in the Father's arms; and if, as is the case, the principal reason for ecclesial proselytism is to augment Israel for the world's repair, telling Jews that they should be baptized is without reason. Doing it is like encouraging citizens of North Carolina to become citizens of South Carolina on the ground that South Carolina is a better state, one whose citizens can more completely fulfill the vocation of American citizenship.

The analogy is suggestive. Even if, as it should be, the thought that North Carolina is a better (or a worse) sovereign state than South Carolina is rejected, and even if the working hypothesis is adopted that the citizens of each are equally, even if not identically, intimate with the goods of citizenship, there might still be other reasons in particular contexts to advocate the exchange of one citizenship for the other. If North Carolina is about to suffer a disaster (plague, famine, invasion, flood, violent revolution) from which it seems that South Carolina is secure, and if the two states are in other respects equally well ordered, equally intimate with the goods of citizenship, it might be reasonable to offer particular North Carolinians, or North Carolinians en bloc, security and citizenship under the protection of the constitution of South Carolina. Similarly, perhaps, it might be possible for the Church to offer Jews her baptismal embrace if it seemed to her that doing so might protect Jews from other dangers and threats. According to her own grammar of Israel, that baptismal embrace neither removes Jews who receive it from Israel, nor cancels their Jewishness; why not then offer it, proselytize for it, in cases where it might provide security and protection for them?

The weight of history provides the answer to this, as perhaps it also does in the imagined Carolinian case. The Church, because of her history of violence and misrepresentation directed at the Synagogue for the last millennium and a half or so, altogether lacks standing to proselytize Jews, in something of the same way that the US military lacks standing to proselytize for democracy in sovereign states it has devastated with violence (recently, Iraq, Libya, and Afghanistan). Even were it the case that Jews could be protected from disaster by being baptized, as some Jews and Christians in Europe thought in the nineteenth and twentieth centuries, and as some may now be thinking again as overt violence against Jews by Christians and gentiles increases there, offering it to Jews is no longer a defensible act for the Church. When it is a question of defending the Synagogue against the violence offered her—which is something the Church is rightly interested in because she and the Church are both of Israel, and she therefore has concern for Jews that precedes and exceeds her concern for gentiles, and, now, for Christians—the Church must find other means. She might, for example, offer her church buildings and abbeys and monasteries as sanctuary; and she might work to support the local civil power in providing protection for Jews against violence and other unpleasantnesses.

But there is, according to the ecclesial grammar of Israel, no situation in which the Church, or any individual Christian, has reason overtly to proselytize any Jew. Renunciation of that for the foreseeable future is a part of the Church's penance for her past offences. It is an element in the movement of Israel's still discordant fugal condition toward harmonic resolution, as it is also an aspect of the Church's self-diminishment in favor of the Synagogue's increase. Showing Jesus to unbaptized Jews now requires the Church, not paradoxically, to refrain from speaking his name to them so that they might be supported in coming to closer intimacy with the god Jesus is without the use of that name. These are temporary measures, but it is possible that they will last as long as distended linear time itself; they should certainly last as long in the life of the Church as did the pattern of confusion and violence and contempt, which is to say at least a millennium and a half.

It is not that overt proselytism of Jews should be placed under the ban for the Church. Prohibiting an activity that seems attractive and desirable is among the least effective ways of discouraging it. Better to offer something more attractive. A vision of the Synagogue and the Church as complementarily constitutive of Israel might be that offer. To the degree that the offer comes to seem attractive to the Church, it will begin to seem unattractive to her to proselytize Jews directly and overtly. She will want, instead, to observe, admire, wonder at, and learn from the Synagogue's love and knowledge of the god; and to offer the Synagogue herself, in a monstrance disfigured as she is by her misunderstandings of and violence toward the Synagogue and conformed in her sufferings to those of Jesus.

• • •

Judaizing raises more complex questions. When directed toward non-Jewish Christians, it is a kind of proselytism. But it differs from those so far considered in that it does not propose a wholesale shift from one form of life to another, but rather adoption, by borrowing that involves mimicry, of some element or elements of the Synagogue's liturgical or halakhic life. The extreme case of this would be urging the adoption by the Church of every element of the Synagogue's life in one or another of its varieties or local flavors, and in that way the replacement of ecclesial life with a simulacrum of synagogal life. More moderate examples would encourage the adoption of this or that synagogal practice (sabbath observance, keeping kosher, sitting shiva, and so on) into the life of some non-Jewish Christians, or into the life of the Church more universally. Proselytism in favor of mimicked borrowings like these might also encourage or require the replacement of approximately equivalent ecclesial practices by the borrowings.

Borrowings of this kind all involve mimicry of what Jews do, or are imagined by Christians to do or to once have done, and they produce simulacra rather than new tokens of the imitated type because they are, by definition, done not by Jews but by non-Jewish Christians. They intentionally render the shape and detail of a form of life, or of a particular practice, which has a synagogal context in which it is done by Jews; but they advocate that it should be, or may be, done by Christians without recruitment into the Synagogue. There are many variants of this kind of judaizing, including some that commend imagined versions of what Jews might have done at this or that past time; or recommendations that the Church should adopt this or that liturgical or halakhic practice that belonged to Israel before her decisive fugal separation into Synagogue and Church.

Judaizings of one kind or another come and go in the Church's history; they are usually products of Christian rather than Jewish imagination, and some are lively now. Although they differ considerably in scope, detail, and purpose, there are some general principles that apply to them all.

First, no non-Jewish Christian now needs, or can properly participate in, simulacra of the Synagogue's postcomplication life. The Synagogue's life of intimacy with the god as it has developed since the complication is closed to the Church, which also means to individual non-Jewish Christians (different things will need to be said about Jewish Christians). The Church can study that life, learn from it, admire it, even participate in this or that element of it when invited by Jews to do so. But she can no longer interfere with it, and making simulacra of it, whether in whole or in part, for the use or amusement of her non-Jewish members, is a mode of interference. A seder banquet, modeled on the Synagogue's liturgy for the first evening of Pesach and undertaken by non-Jewish Christians in a church basement or private house, is an offense and an abomination. Such performances arrogate to the Church the right to do what she likes with the Synagogue's liturgies, and they are spectacles that cannot be what they look like because their participants are not what their words and actions show them to be—which is Jews. A Christian seder, as things now are and have for long been, is the acting of a play: as if a Eucharist were to be celebrated on stage in full form and detail by someone not a priest for a congregation not Christians. There might be a place for such a thing; I can imagine a satirical performance of that kind done by gentiles, and would have nothing principled to say against it. But there is no place for such performances within the form of life that is the Church. Any remotely adequate ecclesial grammar of Israel takes the Synagogue's life seriously enough to see it as a mode of intimacy with the Church's god proper, now, only for Jews, and therefore allots no space for making that life, in whole or in part, a spectacle or an entertainment. When Christians attempt this kind of thing, they act as gentiles perhaps may, but as they themselves certainly may not without performative contradiction.

Suppose that you and I have a mutual friend, and I observe the two of you at dinner together one evening, exchanging verbal intimacies and reminiscences (stories, jokes, allusions, catchwords) rooted in your history together. May I, at my next meal with our mutual friend, talk to him as I have seen you do, using the same stories and allusions? It would be absurd and improper; it would take neither of our particular histories with this friend seriously; it would be baffling to our friend; it would be an offensive charade. My history with him is not yours, and the endearments and allusions I have to share with him are also not yours, just as yours are not mine. It makes no sense for me to start talking to him as if I were you. To do so shows disrespect, even contempt, for both him and you. So, with appropriate changes, and with allowances for the limitations of the analogy, for the kinds of judaizing that commend liturgical and halakhic simulacra of these kinds to non-Jewish Christians.

There are even difficulties, as it seems to me, with non-Jewish Christians participating as invited guests in this or that Jewish liturgy. These are not set up by the Church as simulacra, and so they do not involve the absurdities and improprieties just canvassed. But elements of them require or encourage participants to speak as Jews, out of a particular history with the god (and with the Church). "Next year in Jerusalem," for example: for a Christian to say this in a seder requires either that the words be moved from use to mention, as when I say "I love you" in illustration of a grammatical form in English without thereby confessing love for you; or, again, the words make a spectacle, a simulacrum that has no place in a liturgy. Not every element of every liturgical guest performance is like this, but some are; the Church needs to develop prudence with respect to these matters, and to apply it in counseling Christians as to what they are doing when they participate in synagogal liturgies. There are, no doubt, parallel difficulties for the Synagogue and for Jews in the reverse direction.

Another instance illuminates a different aspect of the problems that judaizing can involve. I take it to be an important aspect of the liturgical lives of most Jewish congregations to have, read from, and in various ways venerate a Torah scroll written by hand in Hebrew using very particular and precise methods, specified halakhically. These scrolls are holy objects, as it seems to me: they are a mode of the god's presence to the congregation, and their use is among the congregation's caresses responsive to the god's manifest love of them. Christian congregations, these days, have no equivalent. When, as they of course do, they read from the canon of Scripture in liturgical celebrations, they do so from printed books or from electronic texts displayed on screens, and most commonly not from a copy, printed or electronic, of Scripture, but from a lectionary, which is a florilegium of excerpts from Scripture arranged for liturgical reading. They read, too, not in Hebrew or Aramaic or Greek, the languages in which Scripture was composed, but in whatever the local vernacular happens to be. A judaizing proselytizer might recommend the adoption of the Synagogue's practice in churches. This might include the development of principles and practices for making handwritten copies of Scripture in the original languages, and the treatment of these as holy objects, the very words of the god on paper or vellum or whatever the approved material might be. But this practice is not accommodatable by the Church for reasons additional to those canvassed in the case of the Seder. The Synagogue's practice in this matter exhibits a reverence for the Hebrew original of the god's words, and for the numinous presence of those words when written by human hands without mechanical intermediary. The Church's practice suggests, and perhaps entails, that the god speaks as directly to the congregation in English or Xhosa as in Hebrew or Greek; and that there is no independent significance to the material objects from which those words are read. The Church, unlike the Synagogue, is careless about the preservation and disposal of her books; and she is promiscuous and unreserved about translating the god's words, again unlike the Synagogue (it is not that the Synagogue refuses to translate, but that doing so appears to be, for her, *faute de mieux*; not so for the Church). Israel would be impoverished by replacing the Church's practice in these matters by the Synagogue's. It is not that the Church's practice is correct and the Synagogue's incorrect; neither is it that the Synagogue's is correct and the Church's not so; but they are noncompossible in the sense that no liturgical community can accommodate both; the introduction of one moves the other in the direction of extinction, and Israel as now constituted needs both modes of speaking and responding to the god's words. The Church cannot, therefore, judaize with respect to this matter without impoverishing Israel. I should think, too, that the Synagogue cannot christianize on this without the same effect, though that is for her to say.

These instances (many more could be canvassed) do not suggest that no elements or versions of what Jews do may be done by non-Jewish Christians. Some of what the Synagogue and the Church do, halakhically and liturgically, are similar in any case, without need of judaizing recommendations to get the Church to do them. And even when this is not the case, as, for example, it is not with dietary practices, Christians might, I suppose, eat as observant Jews do to one degree or another; they might make use of synagogal music; they might make liturgical use of words written by Jews; and so on. What the instances do suggest is that there is no need or reason for non-Jewish Christians to judaize, and that there are many not to do so when such borrowings involve mimicry and simulacra.

• • •

A reasonable objection to the line taken here about judaizing is that it hermetically seals the Church's form of life from the Synagogue's. Surely, the objection may run, there is more porosity between the two forms of life than seems here permitted? Hasn't there been much back-and-forth borrowing? Is all of it mistaken?

It is true that the seal is far from hermetic, and it is true that elements of each form of life have been borrowed from the other, even since Israel's fugal complication. It is remarkable, for instance, that most Protestant Christian Old Testaments contain the books they contain because of what is in the Synagogue's Masoretic text of the Tanakh; remarkable, too, that the Masoretic text is itself what it is in part because of reaction against earlier Christian Old Testaments; more remarkable still that early printed editions of the Talmud, and many that remain in use in the Synagogue, contain emendations required or recommended by Christian censors. There has been and continues to be a good deal of porosity and reciprocity, even if much of it has been occluded and has involved conflict. The point here is neither to deny the porosity, nor to commend policing by the Church of all future borrowings and back-and-forth flows. It is rather to commend to the Church serious consideration and deployment of the following principle with respect to judaizing proposals as they concern non-Jewish Christians: that the extent to which a proposal for the adoption of synagogal practices into the life of the Church requires non-Jews to speak and act as if they were Jews is the extent to which the Church should oppose it. It may often be difficult to decide whether some practice is properly thought of as synagogal, and whether some practice requires non-Jews to speak and act as if they were Jews; but there are clear cases, and when such a case shows itself, the Church's task with respect to it is equally clear. Adopting and using the principle shows awareness of what Israel now is, and of how she has become what she now is—of, that is, the creases and folds produced by her postfugal complication.

A final and interesting difficulty here, on which I can arrive at no clarity, has to do with hospitality. If I, as a non-Jewish Christian, am a guest in a Jewish household, or in a Synagogue, and am assured by my hosts that I may participate, even that they are eager for me to participate, in this or that synagogal liturgy even though I am not a Jew, should I not do so? Does not the task of being a good, responsive, accommodating guest require that I should, even if it seems to me that what I would do were I to participate would involve playacting or some other kind of dubious pretense? Are not my hosts better judges of these matters than I? Have they not standing to make judgments about these matters, while I lack it? Would it not be appropriately penitential for me to do what I'm being encouraged to do—isn't it, after all, the offer of a gift?—even if it seems to me that I shouldn't? Does not scrupulosity here show its face, which is an unattractive one, as always? Perhaps. I don't know the answers to these questions. I can say only that the principle stated in the immediately preceding paragraph and the delightful duty of guesthood can seem in tension, and that it is a difficult task of practical reason to resolve the tension in particular cases. It would always be a mistake, however, to fail to take the difficulty seriously.

• • •

The final instance of judaizing to be addressed here concerns Christians who are also Jews. Some of these—the baptized who have subsequently been received into the Synagogue—are likely to be living synagogally, and while it is clear that their baptisms are not rescinded by their having become Jews, the Church ought celebrate the form of life within Israel they now live, and ought relinquish, penitentially, any jurisdiction over them to the Synagogue, while also mourning any loss of explicit intimacy with Jesus and Mary and the Christian saints they may have suffered as a result of their undertaking a Jewish liturgical and halakhic life.

More pressing questions are raised for the Church by those who, Jews already whether by birth or reception, are subsequently baptized.

The principle in such cases is clear enough, though its application to cases is difficult. The principle is that so far as the Church is concerned any and every aspect of the Synagogue's life, halakhic, liturgical, and theological, is licit for Christians who are also Jews; and that the necessity for the Church's penitence before and service of the Synagogue provided by the history between them gives the Church the pastoral duty of instructing Jewish baptizands that the form of life with the god of Israel offered them by the Synagogue is preferable for them, and instructing the Jewish baptized that the Church encourages and supports them in whatever degree of synagogal life they might seek, including a return to life as a Jew simpliciter.

There are two ancillary constraints upon this principle. One has to do with the Synagogue: she will have her own, doubtless internally disputed, views about and requirements of Jews who seek or receive baptism, and the Church must attend and defer to those even when they conflict with her own judgments and recommendations. The other has to do with noncompossibility: synagogal and ecclesial life have by now diverged enough that some aspects of the one cannot be practiced together with some aspects of the other by any single person. It is hard, for example, to see how one person could fully engage the liturgies of the Easter triduum while also fully engaging those of Passover when these coincide calendrically; and it is hard to see how one person could engage the text of the Tanakh as the Synagogue would while also engaging the text of the Old Testament as the Church would.

Even without considering either of these ancillary constraints, the Church will, and should, find particular persons and particular situations difficult to assess. That difficulty is proper to the monstrosity of Israel's current condition, and there will be no resolution of that until the end. The Church's response to a baptized Jew asking whether it is licit for her to observe synagogal dietary laws (why not?) will be different from her response to a baptized Jew asking whether he may install a Torah scroll in a church building and read from it during Christian worship (certainly not), and different again from her response to a baptized Jew ordained as a priest who then seeks to become a rabbi (no, not even if the Synagogue allows it, which surely she won't), and perhaps different again from what she might say to a baptized Jew who wants to hang a mezuzah on her doorpost (perhaps, but let's first ask the local rabbi how that seems). But the principle remains intact in spite of many intractabilities of this kind, and it is important: it recognizes the oddity and distinctiveness of the place of baptized Jews within the Church, and acknowledges that what is possible and desirable for them with respect to the Synagogue's form of life differs very largely from what is possible and desirable in this respect for non-Jewish Christians.

There is a last point to make about baptized Jews, and it is the most difficult of all. It is that they may prompt wistful envy in non-Jewish Christians. I find that they do this for me. That is because, so far as I can tell, they have a double blessing. They are, of all the god's intimates, the closest and most beloved. They are cleaved to Jesus in their baptisms, and they are embraced by the Father in their Jewishness; they are, like all Christians, turned evangelically toward the gentiles, and they are, like all Jews, given halakhah for closeness to the Father in flesh and language and place. It may be difficult for them to know what to do with this double blessing given Israel's complication. But it remains a double blessing, and one not available to most Israelites. At the end, in the end, they will be closer than any others to the triune Lord in the heavenly paradise.

9

BAPTIZING JEWS

WHAT IS THE proper place of Jewish bodies in the Christian liturgical performance of baptism?

In the generations immediately following Jesus, both Israelites and gentiles were baptized in Jesus's name; and when Synagogue and Church had come to be distinct bodies, the Church continued to baptize Jews—sometimes many and sometimes few; sometimes children and sometimes adults; sometimes by compulsion and sometimes because Jews freely sought it. The Church has renounced the practice of baptizing adults without their consent; and when she baptizes infants or children, she requires the consent and participation of parents, or other proxies. So there is no longer any question of baptizing Jews who would rather not be baptized, or who, without proper proxies, are not in a position to know what is being done to them. It is important that these developments have occurred, because it was often otherwise; a commonplace view in Europe once was that the secular power may properly force baptism upon Jews, on the principal ground that even if they did not want it, it was likely that their descendants would become sincere Christians. The question is rather about the willing participation of Jews, as baptizands in the liturgy of baptism performed by the Church. The Church now treats the baptism of willing Jews as if it were in no liturgically or theologically significant way different from the baptism of gentiles. But should she? What pressure does the Christian grammar of Israel put on the act of baptizing Jews? To begin to answer this question, some consideration of what baptism effects is necessary.

• • •

Negatively, baptism does not and cannot effect the removal of a Jew's Jewishness. Nothing can do that: the condition is irrevocable, just as is a Christian's Christianness. Baptized Jews remain Jews according to the axiom that the god's promises are not revocable: once a Jew, whether by birth or liturgical reception, always a Jew, and so a baptized Jew is just that—a Jewish Christian or a Christian Jew. This is a fundamental difference between baptized Jews and baptized gentiles. The *gentilitas* of the latter is removed without remainder by baptism because that condition is no particular gift of the god; it is nothing more than the condition not-of-Israel, and so it can be wiped away; among Israel's purposes is that it should, for each and every gentile, be wiped away. Baptism does wipe it away, as does whatever liturgical means the Synagogue authorizes to recruit gentiles into herself. But the same cannot be said of baptism's effect on Jews, as it also cannot of the effect of the Synagogue's liturgies of initiation on Christians.

Positively, baptism effects three things.

First is washing. Whatever damage baptizands have undergone—however corrupt they are (like wasp-bored apples fallen from a tree), however habituated to vice they are (like Napoleon on Elba, imagining, still, world dominion), however grimed they are (like diamonds encrusted with mud), however consumingly self-regarding they are (like worms eating their own tails), however world-emptyingly envious they are (like those no longer handsome who wish everyone ugly if they must be so themselves)—is repaired. They come out of the baptismal bath new-made, new creations, ready for the unalloyed and unobstructed service of the god. That immaculacy (*maculae* are dirt stains), shown by the white baptismal garment and the new-lit baptismal candle, does not prevent the newly baptized from damaging themselves by sin as soon as they get the chance; neither does it prevent them from being damaged by others and by the entropic chaos and violence of the world. Baptism is not a prophylactic. It is an effective bath. While baptismal immaculacy lasts (seconds? minutes at most), it is real, and it is the first thing that baptism effects.

Second is incorporation into Jesus. Baptism cleaves the flesh of the baptized to that of the god enfleshed; the baptized are claimed for Jesus, and the Spirit comes to them to confirm that claim. The liturgy deploys invocations of the god's triune name as well as invocations of the name of Jesus, and at the rite's culminating moment the celebrant immerses, or pours water upon, the baptizand three times in order to reflect the triune name, saying, "I baptize you in the name of the Father, and of the Son, and of the Holy Spirit." This incorporation by way of the ritual use of the name, and of water, is in one sense the same as the washing: one might say that it is the incorporation that gives the wash its full effect, or, alternatively, that it is the incorporation—the use of the triune name, with the water—that does the washing. Suppose the latter view. Then it is the liturgical use of the name of the god, together with water, that washes those who suffer baptism by incorporating them into the triune god—which is the same as to say that they are cleaved to Jesus (the Trinity's second person) and inbreathed by the Spirit (the Trinity's third person); and also the same as to say that the newly baptized are now Christians. (It is noteworthy, however, that baptism's culmination, the point at which it takes full effect, contains no mention of the name of Jesus. The name used is the name of the triune LORD, which is the name of Israel's god as Christians speak it.)

Third is initiation into a particular community of which baptizands were not previously members. That community has a universal aspect (it is Catholic) and a particular, local form (typically a parish). Baptism initiates into both. The local community has a liturgical, halakhic, and theological life, which also means that it has particular ways of speaking and otherwise acting; it has a particular mode of being in the world; it is a form of life. Baptism marks the beginning, for baptizands, of learning to live in accord with that form of life's norms and habits. It also provides a place in that community for them: it makes them visible there, and known there by name.

Baptism is, however, not necessary for initiation so understood. The Church has other means for that, as is evident in the case of those who seek full communion with the Church and who have already been baptized in other ecclesial communities. They are received into the Church, both universal and particular, without baptism because they have already been baptized (they are called candidates rather than catechumens, which latter is the term applied to the unbaptized). They, too, need initiation, but they get it without baptism.

Baptism also does not suffice for life in the Church. This is in large part for sheerly practical reasons. No neophytes are capable of exercising all the skills, rights, privileges, duties, burdens, and habits of the forms of life they have just entered. When I was married at the age of twenty I scarcely knew my wife, and did not at all know how to live with her. When I was sworn in as a new citizen of the USA at the age of thirty-eight, I did not yet know how to live as an American (in some respects I still do not, almost three decades later). The appropriate skills and habits had to be learned, and this is also true for the newly baptized, whether they are baptized as infants or adults. They need mystagogy: to be led into the mysteries whose neophytes baptism has made them. The Church recognizes, formally and liturgically, that baptism, while it does wash and incorporate and initiate, does not suffice for full participation in the community. Stages toward that condition are marked liturgically (first communion; confirmation), and each of those requires mystagogic instruction and formation and habituation.

Washing, incorporation, and initiation: these three effects of baptism are real in the order of being as the Church understands the matter. That is, they are what the rites of the baptismal liturgy effect, whether or not the baptizand knows or can say that they do, and no matter who the baptizand is (with caveats to be entered in a moment). In this the three effects are like the immunity a vaccination provides against a viral infection (the vaccine does what it does no matter what its recipients know or can say about what it does), or like the habits of speech produced by exposure to a particular linguistic community during the first five years of life (those habits are what they are no matter what those formed by them know or can say about them). Baptism need have no effects in the order of knowing, at least for the baptizand. That is obvious enough in the case of infant baptism. But it is true also for the baptism of adults: some, when baptized, can say little about what happened; others say a lot, most of it confused or otherwise mistaken; it is rare that the account a recently baptized adult gives of what happened is accurate so far as it goes; and it is impossible that any such account be complete (the Church corporately lacks a complete account of this or any other sacrament).

Nevertheless, baptism does what it does. To ask, then, about the Church's practice of baptizing Jews—about the propriety of Jews undergoing that liturgy, and about what it is that happens to them when they do—is not to ask about what Jewish baptizands know or need to know; it is, at first, to ask about what happens to them in the order of being, and the question is not easy to answer.

• • •

A first and simple answer to the question, one that the Church now ordinarily assumes, is that what happens to Jews in baptism is just what happens to gentiles when they are baptized. Everyone not already baptized, without exception or reservation, is washed, incorporated, and initiated. That assumption is evident in the fact that the Church has no baptismal rite especially for Jews, and takes no notice, in the form of the rite, of whether a baptizand is a Jew or a gentile. But when the Church and the Synagogue are understood jointly and complementarily to constitute Israel, and when the Synagogue, with her liturgies, is understood to be gracefully intimate with her god who is also the Church's god, there are immediate questions about that assumption.

First, as to washing, and the associated question of rebaptism. Baptism's cleansing is, as the Church sees it, distinct from subsequent cleansings. Sins performed and damage suffered after baptism also need to be cleansed, but that is not done by another baptism; there are other means for it, the particulars of which need not here detain us.

Baptism's washing, or, to alter the metaphor, the rectification (setting right, setting straight) effected by it, is singular and fundamental in ways that subsequent cleansings and rectifications are not. By it, baptizands are removed from a condition otherwise unavoidable, of distance from the god and concomitant saturation by and distention into the world. Otherwise put (the Christian archive provides many ways to put the matter): the unbaptized are incurved upon themselves while also spread thin in the world; they cannot, because of the damage they have suffered and the sins they have performed, receive or return the god's kisses. Their lips are sealed. Baptism opens those lips, and makes it possible for the baptized to receive the god's gifts and to return them to the god with a synergy that brings light and love and joy and holiness. All this is grammatical, by Christian lights, about gentiles. It is consonant and coincident with standard Christian accounts of the fall, and of damage, and of sin. But when these things are said about Israelites, they begin to sound like solecisms. Israel is, obviously (for Christians) in the case of the Church, but also in the case of the Synagogue, already set apart from the gentiles, already intimate with the god, already involved in exchange of gifts with the god. That holiness is Israel's reason for being. It is why the god called Abraham. And it remains the reason for being of both the Synagogue and the Church since both are in and of Israel. The lips of Jews are not sealed, and therefore baptism cannot be required to open them. Jews are already washed, rectified, removed from the gentiles' incurvation into self and absorption into the world. They therefore do not need baptism's washing. That is a direct implication of the grammar of Israel here in play. If the relevant line of division is not between the unbaptized and the baptized, but rather between Israelites and gentiles, then baptism becomes a rite proper for making gentiles into Christians, but not for making Jews into Christians. If that second thing is to be done, there should be other ways to do it.

The essential grammatical rule about baptismal washing and Israel can be put briefly: whatever is appropriately said about the condition of the newly baptized with respect to sin and damage is also appropriately said about the condition of newly minted Jews with respect to sin and damage. (Jews, according to the account given here, which may also be acceptable to the Synagogue, come to be either in the amniotic fluids of the wombs of Jewish mothers, or in the waters of the mikvah. Those fluids, according to the grammar in play here, do the washing that the waters of the baptismal font also do.) That rule, if taken seriously, would provide the Church with means to recognize and correct theological and liturgical error in this connection. It is also, ecclesially speaking, a revolutionary rule while at the same time a traditional one: the revolution lies in the rule's implication that it is improper to baptize Jews in the same way as gentiles are baptized; the traditionalism lies in the attention the rule requires to the identity of Israel's god as the god of both Synagogue and Church, which requires that Jews are already, because they are in Israel, intimate in holiness with the Church's god—already, that is, washed.

A corresponding account might be given of what the Synagogue does when she recruits, liturgically, members from outside herself. Perhaps in that case too her liturgies of recruitment are fundamentally predicated upon a distinction between Israelites and gentiles (not a distinction between Jews and gentiles), and perhaps in that case too the initiatory ritual bath, the mikvah, has as its point and purpose the making of gentiles into Israelites. Such a view is attractive to Christians in part because it makes the cleansing waters of baptism and those of the mikvah strictly analogous, at least so far as the washing goes: each washing rectifies gentiles by bringing them into Israel, and each makes it possible for the gentiles so cleansed, so set right, to begin to return the god's kisses liturgically, halakhically, and even, when so gifted, theologically. Such a view is also consonant with the thought that Church and Synagogue have each come to be what they are in considerable part by understanding themselves to be not the other, and, therefore, each understanding themselves to the sole bearer of the burden of being Israel, whether or not under that name. The Church's version of this assimilates Jews to gentiles, and requires them, just like gentiles, to be baptized in order to enter the beloved community. That is an error, and a damaging one.

The Synagogue's version perhaps does the same in reverse: Christians become gentiles, and therefore need to be recruited liturgically in order to enter the beloved community. If the lines are instead drawn as here suggested, then these positions can be seen as what they are, which is instances of fugal flight; the adjustments here entertained, according to which the Church would not need to baptize Jews in order to make it possible for them enter the Church, and the Synagogue, correspondingly, would not need to wash Christians in order to make it possible for them to enter the Synagogue, belong to the reharmonized version of the fugue, in which subject and counter-subject begin to interweave. But since the Church altogether lacks standing to intervene in and rule on matters internal to the Synagogue's life, the suggestion that she might come to see that her ways of recruiting Christians into herself ought be distinct from her ways of recruiting gentiles into herself can only be, for the time being, a statement of how things seem to the Church, not a recommendation to the Synagogue.

• • •

Nothing written here so far suggests that Jews do not need baptism at all. It suggests only that they do not need the first thing baptism effects, which is washing. What about the second thing baptism effects, which is incorporation into Jesus, cleaving to the flesh of that particular person, an Israelite—we might now say, though anachronistically, a Jew—who is also the second of the god's three persons? Here too, perhaps, though with more hesitation, it can reasonably be suggested that Jews do not need this because they already have it. How might that counterintuitive position be elaborated?

Being an Israelite, Jew or Christian, is in part a matter of the flesh. That is obvious in the case of being born a Jew; it is almost equally so in the case of the liturgies used by Synagogue and Church to remake gentiles into Israelites. In those rites, the flesh is washed, transfigured, and cleaved to the flesh of Israel. New fleshly observances, both liturgical and halakhic, become possible and proper. The standard Christian-theological account of this has already been given: baptism incorporates, which might better be said enfleshes, those baptized into Jesus's flesh. They become his limbs, his body; and, later, by way of the Eucharist, they deepen and enrich this cleaving by eating and drinking the flesh and blood of the one to whose flesh they have been cleaved, eating and drinking what they already are. A new liturgical and halakhic life of intimacy with the god is articulated with this transfigured flesh, and explained by the Church for the most part in terms of it. And further: the flesh of Jesus is the flesh of the god, the flesh the god took and continues to take. It is the archetype and paradigm of all human flesh, therefore, in virtue of its taking up by the god. And it is this flesh that baptism enfleshes the baptized with. It is Israelite flesh.

What then, and in this light, is unbaptized Jewish flesh? It is Israelite flesh, as the flesh of Jesus also was and is. When the Church eats and drinks Jesus, it eats and drinks Israel; it eats and drinks what Jews, whether born or made, already are in the flesh. Israelite flesh is the flesh the god called, via Abraham, for particular intimacy; and since—again from a Christian point of view—what the god was is also what the god is, atemporally (the god is outside the temporal economy, even though related to us within that economy), the flesh of Israel always, atemporally, is the flesh of Jesus. The offspring of Abraham and Sarah participate already in the flesh of Jesus because the flesh of Jesus is, archetypally, the flesh of Israel. That is all in the order of being; Abraham and Sarah did not know it to be the case, as most Jews now do not know it to be the case, and would deny it if the claim were offered them. But that does not alter the flesh they already belong to, which is Jesus's flesh. Unbaptized Jewish flesh, then, is already incorporated into the flesh that baptism would incorporate it into were it baptized. On this understanding, Jews do not need the incorporative aspects of baptism because they already have them. Baptism cannot provide a condition already present, which is among the reasons why the Church came to see that rebaptism makes no sense. As for washing, so for incorporation: what baptism offers is what Jews already have. The condition of the flesh of the newly made Jew is not, in the order of being, distinct from the condition of the flesh of the newly baptized Christian. That is the correlate in the order of being of the grammatical rule about baptismal washing given already.

It is worth returning to a point already made, which is that although the baptismal liturgy is deeply Jesus-centered, it culminates not with the name of Jesus, but with the name of the god—the triune name, of course, but still the god's name. That culminating invocation, and its reflection in the triple immersion, shows that for the Church, the rite reaches its crescendo in a reminder that what the god does to and for us, in the created order, even when that doing is done by Jesus, is in fact done by the triune god in all three persons: to be incorporated into Jesus just is to be incorporated into the god of Israel. This buttresses and makes more comprehensible the picture sketched in the immediately preceding paragraphs. What baptism incorporates into is the flesh of the god; the god is the god of Israel; Jews are already incorporated into that flesh because of the flesh they bear as Jews; they are therefore already in the condition, as regards the flesh, that baptism would provide them. Baptism's incorporative aspect is therefore appropriate for gentiles, and of no effect for Jews.

And this makes it reasonable for the Church to say, as in the case of the baptismal washing, that the Synagogue's liturgies for bringing gentiles into herself incorporate those who suffer them into the god's flesh. That is why Jews can exchange kisses with the god in their liturgies and their halakhah and their theology. The claim here is not that this is a construal of, say, the mikvah, that the Synagogue will or should accept; it is that this is how that liturgy can reasonably appear on the stage of the Church's theological speculation.

A final point about this incorporative aspect of baptism. The baptismal liturgy is entirely explicit about Jesus: it declares Jesus, claims baptizands for Jesus, and makes them, explicitly, members of his body. From the Church's point of view, these are truths about baptism unknown to or denied by the Synagogue, and they are truths of fundamental significance to the liturgy, and to the life of Israel—to that of the Church explicitly, and to that of the Synagogue implicitly. Baptism therefore declares something that the Synagogue's liturgies do not declare: the enfleshment of the god, and the triunity of the god. But saying that, as I do and as the Church does, is entirely compatible with saying that the Synagogue's liturgies declare things about the god and the god's relation to Israel that the Church's liturgies do not; and with saying that two liturgies can have the same effect upon those who undergo them even when what they declare is not identical. The grammar of Israel at play here, and especially the metaphor of the fugue to illuminate Israel's complexity, make this situation both predictable and comprehensible. If one beloved community is addressed by and responds to the god in poetry, while another is addressed by and responds to the god in paraphrase, and if each mode of address and response is intimate, desired, and revelatory, then what each community says to and about the god will be different—different in style, in rhetoric, in lexicon, and in the mode of intimacy with the god established by its utterance. In such a situation, such differences, such presences and absences in what each community has to say about the god, about itself, and in its liturgies, are not occasions for hierarchical orderings, for claims about greater or lesser propinquity; they are occasions, rather, for admiring, if puzzled, interest in what the other community has to say, coupled with steadfastness in saying what one's own community has to say.

• • •

Perhaps, then, Jews do not need the incorporative aspect of baptism, either, just as they do not need to be washed by it. (I have marginally less confidence in the rightness of the suggestion about incorporation than in that about washing, though I have it still to a high degree.) But even this does not yield the conclusion that they do not need baptism at all. There is still a third thing that baptism effects, which is initiation into a particular form of life, which is the ecclesial life.

This, it seems clear, Jews do not already have. They are already washed; they are already incorporated into the triune god, even if not under that description; but they are not already initiated into ecclesial life. They have not begun the process of learning the skills and habits proper to that life, and insofar as baptism is necessary for mystagogy, it is necessary also for Jews if they are to have an ecclesial life. Being born a Jew, or received into the Synagogue by the appropriate liturgical means, is no gateway into the Church, any more than being born in England and educated and acculturated there into something like the same language and something like the same form of political life available in the USA is a gateway to citizenship in the latter sovereign state. That was my condition, and it meant that I already had most of what the USA could offer; but I had neither citizenship, nor the local knowledge and local habits that accompany life in the USA. For all that I had to be initiated, by way of naturalization, and then to live in the USA, as I have done these past four decades, almost twice as long as I lived in England.

This third effect of baptism seems the clearest case, then, of provision of a condition that Jews do not already have. If so, then baptism effects something for Jews that otherwise they cannot get.

But even here reservations are in order, as the distinction between initiation and mystagogy suggests. A rite of initiation marks an *initium*, a beginning, and it does that by removing obstacles to mystagogy, which is the inculcation of the habits, attitudes, and practices that make a form of life what it is. I could not become habituated to and therefore skilled in the practice of voting in the USA without beginning to engage in it, and I could not begin to engage in it without removing the obstruction of not being a citizen. Hence my need for the initiatory rite of naturalization, which made me a citizen, and permitted (but did not provide) the rest. I was, until naturalization in 1994, a gentile with respect to the USA, and thereafter an Israelite within it—in very much the same way, as a matter of form, that I was a gentile to the Church until my baptism in 1977, and thereafter an Israelite, specifically a Christian, within her. But had I been (I was not) a Jew in 1977 rather than a gentile, I would have been with respect to the Church somewhat more as a child born to American parents in, say, Togo, and, without ever setting foot in the USA, raised by non-American aunts and uncles—without need of naturalization, that is, but in deep need of mystagogy should I wish to be in the USA as a citizen of it.

That is an approximate (both with respect to US law and with respect to ecclesial doctrine and discipline) analogy of the condition of Jews with respect to this third and last effect of baptism. They need baptism's initiation only if they are unwashed and unincorporated; otherwise, because there are no other barriers to a life in the Church, they do not need baptism's initiation, but, rather, a mystagogy that permits them to learn what they need to know and how to do what they need to do. The Church has a liturgical model already to hand for this—for, that is, the initiation of those who need mystagogy rather than baptism: the Rite of Christian Initiation for Adults. That rite distinguishes, both conceptually and liturgically, between catechumens and candidates. The former, gentiles according to the taxonomy in play here, need baptism in order to be led further into the mysteries, and so they are prepared for that and moved toward it. The latter are already baptized in the triune name (Orthodox, Protestants, others), and so are prepared for and accorded a rite of reception as the first stage of mystagogy. Jews, a well-ordered grammar of Israel suggests, are more like candidates than catechumens. They are in some important respects different from candidates as well, but that difference extends neither to the degree of their intimacy with the god, nor to their well-washedness before the god.

• • •

The provisional conclusion is that Jews who freely seek full communion with the Church do not need baptism. And further: they ought not be granted it. Instead, an ecclesial rite should be developed for the reception of Jews, one kind of Israelite, into the Church, another part of Israel with habits and practices distinct from those of the Synagogue. The move is lateral, not upward, or out: it involves the exchange of one kind of intimacy for another, and it can and should be marked liturgically for what it is. Such moves, given the fugal history between Church and Synagogue, are likely now to be comparatively rare; but they might, together with corresponding moves in the other direction, from Church to Synagogue, be an element in the future harmonic resolution of the fugue's theme and countertheme. This state of affairs places those with pastoral authority in the Church who might have care of Jews seeking a Christian life in a delicate position, but it is beyond the scope of this study to make recommendations about how to deal with those difficulties. One thing can be said with directness and precision, and without fear of reasonable contradiction: it is that for the Church to treat Jews who seek a Christian life as if they were gentiles seeking a Christian life is to commit a solecism: an offence against her own grammar of Israel.

• • •

There is an obvious objection to the claim that baptizing Jews is a solecism. It is that the Church has done it from her beginning, and continues to do it now. Were not most of the first Christians baptized Jews? Are not some among the Christians of greatest exemplary significance for the Church (martyrs, saints, *doctores eclesiae*, and so on) baptized Jews? Has the Church been committing solecisms in all these case? This objection assumes that if the Church has once rightly done something, then it may always rightly do that thing. Such a pattern of thought makes the Church's history accidental to her, and that claim is itself a solecism. Better to say, and to see, that what was once reasonable, desirable, even beautiful, may cease to be so when circumstances change. There are two relevant changes to consider here.

The first has to do with Israel's complication. That complication, rooted in the enfleshment of the god as Jesus of Nazareth, provoked the fugal flight of the Church and the Synagogue from one another. That flight issued eventually in the formal institutional separation of Church from Synagogue. Before that, whenever exactly it is to be dated (at different times in different places, no doubt), Israel's territory was differently configured. Baptizing Israelite followers of Jesus then was not initiation into a new and distinct form of life. Neither was it the relinquishment of an already-extant form of life. Church and Synagogue were not then sufficiently distinct to make those reasonable construals. Baptisms, then, were part of a complex, internally differentiated stream of Israelite life, still reasonably construable as single, even if not simple (it was never simple). There was, then, no solecism in baptizing Jews. Baptisms done then are not even best described as "of Jews," for the existence of Jews as the word is here used is contingent upon and defined in terms of the existence of Christians, as is also true in the reverse direction.

The second change, following from the first, has to do with the Church's corrupt and violent history, once the complication had arisen and proliferated, of using baptism as an instrument of oppression and manipulation of Jews. Baptisms were sometimes forced upon them, and often used in the service of trying to remake the Synagogue in the Church's image. That history cannot be unwritten. It can only be repented, and among the instruments of that repentance is clarity on the Church's part about the fundamental ill-formedness of baptizing Jews as if they were gentiles. It is possible, in the future, that things will change again, and in such a way as to make baptizing Jews proper. But at the moment, as things are, baptizing Jews remains a Christian solecism.

The Jewish body has no place in the Christian baptismal liturgy; that liturgy can do nothing to it and nothing for it because it is already where baptism would place it: in the god's arms, ready to return the god's caress. Any particular Jew might still want to know the name of Jesus, and to live a Christian life. But these wants (they are not needs) can be met by mystagogy. This position has obvious effects upon the appropriateness of Jewish participation in the Church's other sacraments, and in her life more broadly: Jews can, without baptism, participate in the other sacraments under the same conditions and with the same degree of preparation as the ex-gentile baptized. They can, validly and licitly, the Church might learn to say, be confirmed, receive the Eucharist, be ordained, confess their sins and receive absolution for them, be anointed as preparation for death and be sacramentally married—that last, however, raises particular and suggestive difficulties, to be treated immediately below.

Before doing so, it remains only to note that nothing here written suggests that Jews ought seek, or ought not seek, a Christian life; it sketches rather what it means for them to do so as the Church might come to see the matter. It is also clear, I should think, that the suggestions made here about baptizing Jews are radical. They have little chance of being adopted by the Church in the foreseeable future. In order for her to move any distance toward them, she will have first to take seriously the implications of her own current insistence that the Synagogue remains intimate with the god, and has had a sixteen- or seventeen-hundred-year exchange with and formation by the god the particulars and meanings of which are largely hidden from the Church. The first, and unavoidable, implication of that insistence is that baptizing a Jew cannot be the same as baptizing a gentile. The last several dozen paragraphs amount to a suggestion about how the difference might be taken. The suggestions are grammatical in kind.

10

MARRYING JEWS

AS WITH BAPTISM, so with marriage: the Church at the moment makes no distinction between unbaptized Jews and gentiles with respect to their eligibility for marriage with Catholics, whether themselves Jewish or gentile. But the distinction is necessary: the commitment of the Church to the deep and continuing intimacy of unbaptized Jews with the Church's god, a condition different in kind from that of gentiles, makes its lack at least puzzling and at most incomprehensible. To write in that way is to veil the fact that marriage between an unbaptized Jew and a non-Jewish Catholic is marriage between Israelites, which is, according to the Church's own grammar of Israel, marriage between two of the god's chosen beloveds. To occlude that state of affairs is to hide the most important thing about the persons in question.

How might the ecclesial grammar of marriage between an unbaptized Jew and a non-Jewish Catholic look were this veil to be drawn back?

Because *marriage* in English is a word with a wide semantic range, sufficiently so to darken counsel and confuse thought when a matter such as this is under discussion, some preliminary ground clearing is necessary.

First, marriage in this discussion denotes only the sacrament the Church calls by that name; if anything written here has bearing upon civil marriage contracts (I doubt that it does in anything but the most tenuous and distant ways), or upon common-law marriages recognized under that name by the Church or any civil power, such implications are not of interest here. This means that the use of *marriage* in what follows is close to that of *matrimonium* in, for example, the Catholic

Church's 1983 *Codex Iuris Canonici*, or *Code of Canon Law. Marriage* indicates the sacrament; *to marry* indicates its performance.

Second, at issue here is centrally what may be euphoniously (fittingly, appropriately, conveniently) said about marriages projected between unbaptized Jews and non-Jewish Catholics. Which conditions ought or might be placed upon such marriages? Which conditions ought or might be rejected? What can fittingly be said about the validity, licitness, and desirability of such marriages? There are further and interesting things to be written about marriages projected between gentiles and non-Jewish Catholics, and unbaptized Jews and baptized Jews, but these are treated here only to the extent that they provide useful comparisons with marriages projected between unbaptized Jews and non-Jewish Catholics. (The Synagogue has her own grammar of marriage, and therefore, I assume, her own things to say about marriages between Jews, baptized or not, and non-Jewish Christians, as well as about marriages between unbaptized Jews and gentiles. That discourse, and the practices associated with it, though of deep interest to the Church, are left aside here.)

With these restrictions in mind, what is the current state of ecclesial talk and writing about marriages projected between unbaptized Jews and non-Jewish Catholics?

• • •

There is almost no such talk and writing. In the entire corpus of canon law concerning marriage since the twentieth-century revisions, and of magisterial writing about marriage in and since the Second Vatican Council, Jews have no explicit place. That is because the categories into which persons are divided by the Church for the analysis of marriage have no place for them. Those categories are three: the baptized in full communion with the Bishop of Rome; the baptized not in full communion with the Bishop of Rome; and the unbaptized. Jews may belong to any of these categories, and the Church's doctrine and discipline of marriage does not consider the Jewishness of a Catholic's intended (or the Jewishness of a Catholic intending) to be of significance one way or the other. An unbaptized Jew is subsumed into the unbaptized; a Jew baptized into some ecclesial community other than the Catholic is subsumed into that group; and a Catholic Jew is subsumed into the group of Catholics. This absence of Jews is already a problem, already a solecism; but before addressing how these matters might better be spoken of, it is necessary to show how the Church's talk of and writing about marriage works when Jews are absent from it.

Marriage is, for the Church, a state of life in the Church. It joins two persons, a man and a woman, in a contract (a *foedus*, or *contractum*) that places them together as consorts and that has a dual purpose: the unity and holiness of the couple, and the conception and birth of children, each of which contributes, ideally, not only to the good of the couple, but also to that of the Church and of the world. The contract requires, and is constituted by, the consent of the parties to it; and when sacramentalized by being entered into by the baptized (Catholic or not), the contract is elevated (uplifted, upraised) to explicit participation in Jesus's love for the Church: the *coniuges christiani* are then filled with Jesus's spirit, and in that way it becomes possible for their state of life to image and participate in Jesus's love for the Church—as well as in the god's love for Israel—though the Church does not speak of Israel when speaking of marriage. As is written in a document from the Second Vatican Council,

> And so, Christian partners in marriage are sustained and in a sense consecrated by a particular sacrament for the duties and dignity proper to their condition. By the sacrament's power they fulfil their conjugal and marital obligations and are imbued with the spirit of Christ, who pervades their whole lives with faith, hope, and love so that they approach their own perfection, their mutual sanctification, and their glorification of God. (*Gaudium et Spes*, from §48)

That is far from a complete account of what marriage is, but it is enough for the purposes in play here. The Church, perhaps most especially in the writing of Karol Wojtyla (pope from 1978 to 2005) and Jorgé Bergoglio (pope from 2013 until the time of writing), has given considerable, sometimes lyrical, attention to the particular blessings and benefits and textures of married life, and to the elevation of its importance in the Church's life. But she is also realistic about the damage done to all marriages by sin, and about the extent to which they therefore fail. Her legal codes pay a good deal of attention to particular failings, and to the responses proper to them; and she is attentive to the impediments that prevent marriages from being validly entered into in the first place.

An invalid marriage is one that, though some of the proprieties may have been observed or be intended, including the liturgical ones, nonetheless suffers from some defect of form that impedes it by removing from it one or more of its requirements, or adding to it requirements it cannot bear. A diriment impediment to marriage does this: it breaks apart, or explodes, or dismembers (all possible renderings of the Latin *dirimere*, which underlies the barbarous English "diriment") the form of marriage. More exactly: a diriment impediment is a property or condition of a person that renders that person incapable of validly contracting marriage: *Impedimentum dirimens personam inhabilem reddit ad matrimonium valide contrahendum* (canon 1073).

Some such impediments (being too young; being a priest; being under compulsion—the Code shows a fetching concern for women who have been abducted for the purpose of marriage; being already married; standing in an inappropriate degree of consanguinity to the intended; and so on) prevent the person marrying anyone, baptized or not.

But some impediments prevent marriage only with Catholics, and among these is the one of interest here, which is the condition of being unbaptized. Should an unbaptized person marry a Catholic, the marriage is void of form because of disparity of cult, which means, roughly, that the couple have and engage in different and incompatible liturgies. The assumption is that all unbaptized persons have a liturgical life, which is a defensible-enough assumption: the world is full of gods, and it is hard, perhaps impossible, to imagine anyone with a life that includes no liturgical service of some or another god. The Church's principal concern about marriages with disparity of cult is that they make impossible the sacramentalizing of the marriage contract because of the obstacles they place in the way of the couple's shared attention to Jesus, in whom their marriage participates. A projected marriage between an unbaptized Jew and a non-Jewish Catholic fits here: it is clear that there is disparity of cult in such a case whether or not either spouse is observant, but evidently if both are.

It might seem that a sacramental marriage like this cannot occur: if one seems to have been celebrated, it is in fact invalid, and therefore null, because one of the partners is incapable of it—just as would be the case were a marriage performed when one or both of the partners is incapable of giving consent, or too young, or a priest, or a sibling of the intended, and so on. And that is in fact the Church's view, unless the impediment is dispensed, or made no longer a burden, by an authority competent to do that. That authority is ordinarily a bishop (there are complications here which need not detain us): he may, by removing the impediment, grant such a couple permission to marry, and his doing so makes the marriage valid, a sacramental marriage in proper form. A dispensation of this sort does not remove the condition in question: the unbaptized party to the marriage remains unbaptized. But it does remove the capacity of that condition to impede the marriage. How does it do that?

By placing additional conditions upon the marriage. The Catholic party must make a double promise: to do what is possible to remove the dangers of falling away from the faith inherent in such a marriage; and to do what is possible to have children of such a marriage baptized and raised in the Church. The unbaptized party must be informed that the Catholic party has made these promises. And both parties are to be instructed *de finibus et proprietatibus essentialibus matrimonii* (canon 1125.3) as these are understood by the Church. If these conditions are met, the impediment may be dispensed by the bishop. If it is, the marriage is, if all other conditions are in place, valid.

Unbaptized Jews have no special place in any of this: they are treated exactly as if they were unbaptized gentiles. Even the Church's recording of marriages (there are detailed canonical requirements about this) makes no notation as to whether an unbaptized spouse is a Jew or a gentile. Sacramental marriages between unbaptized Jews and Catholics therefore may, and of course do, occur. Such marriages are taken up into Jesus and become icons of his love for the Church.

It is instructive to contrast the Church's view of such marriages with her view of those between a Catholic and a person baptized but not in full communion with the Bishop of Rome (again, the Church shows no interest in whether such a person is a Jew or a gentile). These marriages are not impedimented, and, therefore, not invalid. There is nothing about the condition of the baptized non-Catholic party that calls into question the very form of a marriage; that person is, after all, baptized, cleaved to Jesus. The Church does not rebaptize, and so entering into marriage with a Catholic requires nothing of that sort: such a union builds upon the explicit relation with Jesus already in place for each party, and in that way is different from marriages involving disparity of cult. The Church has a different name for marriages of this kind: they are called mixed marriages (*matrimonii mixti*), and although they are not invalid, they are nonetheless prohibited and therefore illicit when they occur.

The distinction between invalidity and illicitness goes deep here, and there are many other instances of it. Suppose a mass is celebrated by a priest forbidden by his bishop to do such a thing. That is a valid mass: it is celebrated by someone who can do such a thing, and, assuming that the many other relevant conditions are in place, it is therefore, in form, a mass. A participant in it receives the body and blood. It is however an illicit mass: it should not have occurred, and if the bishop's diktat had been observed, it would not have occurred. Suppose, by contrast, a mass is celebrated by someone not a priest. That, too, is illicit (the bishop prefers, presumably, that such things not happen, and forbids them), but it is also invalid. Someone not a priest is not in a condition to celebrate masses at all, and even if all the proper liturgical forms are used, what happens is no mass. Participants in such an event receive only bread and wine. The same contrast applies to mixed marriages and marriages with disparity of cult: the former are illicit, but if they occur they are nonetheless marriages; the latter, unless dispensed as described, are not marriages at all because the impediment to them—the fact that one of the couple is unbaptized—remains effective, and makes defective the form of the marriage that apparently occurs.

Given this difference between mixed marriages and marriages with disparity of cult, it is surprising that the Code is explicit that the conditions that need to be in place in order for a bishop to remove the impediment of marriage to an unbaptized person, already described, are identical to those that need to be in place in order for a bishop to permit an otherwise forbidden mixed marriage. In mixed marriages, too, the Catholic party must make the promises, the non-Catholic party be informed of them, and both parties undergo instruction in the meaning of marriage as the Church understands it. This brings invalidity and illicitness close together in this instance. The remedy is the same in both cases, and yet the difference remains that in the one case the non-Catholic party is unbaptized and in the other baptized. This difference between the two kinds of marriage begins to be less clear: if a bishop's dispensation and his permission have the same conditions, then this suggests that the Church has the same problem with each kind of marriage, and that the unbaptized condition of the non-Catholic party in cases of disparity of cult is not, strictly speaking, that problem. The problem, rather, is precisely disparity of cult. Certainly, what the parties have to do in each case in order properly to marry is the same. The distinction would be cleaner and would carry more conviction were marriages with disparity of cult simply incapable of dispensation, and thus impossible in all circumstances, as is, for example, explicitly said to be the case for those in which the parties are too closely related to one another, as for example when it is written that *numquam datur dispensatio ab impedimento consanguinitatis in linea recta aut in secundo gradu lineae collateralis* (canon 1078.3).

However that difficulty is resolved (the prospects are not good that it can be), it is now clear that as things stand a projected marriage between an unbaptized Jew and a non-Jewish Catholic is invalid unless dispensed as described; and that if such a dispensation is given, the marriage is sacramental. It is clear, too, that in the case of sacramental marriage to a Catholic, an unbaptized Jewish body and an unbaptized gentile body are indistinguishable one from another so far as the Church's doctrine and discipline are concerned. And it is clear that it is irrelevant to that doctrine and discipline whether a Catholic party to marriage is Jewish or not. As with the doctrine and discipline of baptism, the fundamental division for the Church at the moment is between the unbaptized and the baptized, not between Israelites and gentiles.

• • •

According to the ecclesial grammar of Israel laid out here, these positions are ungrammatical. They are, indeed, appalling solecisms. They obscure the intimacy that unbaptized Jews have with the god; indeed, they erase it. If that intimacy, that holiness, becomes visible and is allowed its force, then Jews begin to look more like the baptized not in full communion with the Bishop of Rome than like the unbaptized—more like Lutherans or Baptists or Orthodox (Christians), that is, than like Buddhists or acolytes of the market or invokers of Krishna. Christians and Jews are both Israelites, and to construe their marriages as if they were not is to obscure what is most significant about them.

Fortunately, as is also the case with baptism, it would not be hard for the Church to adjust its doctrine and discipline. She has already developed and deployed a tertium quid: the non-Catholic baptized. Their baptisms have cleaved them to Jesus even when they are not fully sacramentally participant in the life of the Church, and that is why their marriages to Catholics are different, ecclesially speaking, from those of the unbaptized. It is a matter of how close they are to Jesus. Similarly, mutatis mutandis, for Jews: they are already intimate with the god, the god of the Church, that is, who is also the god of the Synagogue. Their names have already been spoken by the god as their flesh has already been embraced, washed in the amniotic waters of their Jewish mothers, or in those of the mikvah. These are facts about them similar (not identical) in significance in the order of being to those about what the waters of baptism have done to those who have been washed and incorporated and initiated by them. Disparity of cult, to return to the Church's preferred descriptor for marriages between Catholics and the unbaptized, cannot apply here. The same god is worshipped and acknowledged and named. The same god has called and blessed and embraced. There are of course deep-going liturgical and halakhic differences between what observant Jews do and what observant Catholics do; but these are not relevant to disparity of cult, for there are also deep-going differences between the liturgy and halakhah of observant hardshell Baptists and those of observant Catholics. The application (or denial) of the label has to do not with matters of that sort, but rather with how close in fact, in the order of being, a person is to the god. The Church's legal codes, in their consideration of marriage, show no interest in whether baptized non-Catholics are catechized or observant; only in whether they are baptized. The codes could attend to Jews in the same way.

If an unbaptized Jew and a Catholic project marriage, therefore, what they project is a marriage between Israelites, the god's beloveds. The Church might still reasonably categorize such marriages as illicit until explicitly permitted, and might still reasonably place conditions upon the giving of such permission, as she does in the case of mixed marriages. She might reasonably, too, call such marriages mixed, for in one sense they clearly are. But she cannot any longer reasonably or grammatically assimilate such marriages to those with disparity of cult: to do so is a solecism.

In the order of being the Church can celebrate such marriages without reservation. They bring Israelites together into a sacramental union that has the peculiar virtue of imaging and participating in Jesus's love for the Church (all sacramental marriages do that) by making one flesh of specifically Jewish and specifically Christian flesh, and in that way instantiating the reharmonization of the fugal separation of Church and Synagogue. Sacramentally blessed sexual intercourse between a non-Jewish Christian and an unbaptized Jew shows, therefore, not only Jesus's love for the Church in the universal sense, but also, more particularly, Jesus's love for Israel as she will be at the end, when there are, in Israel, no longer Jews and Christians, no longer Synagogue and Church, but only Israel in the flesh, gathered around the triune god. All this is so no matter the opinions about it of a Jewish or Christian spouse in such a marriage, and no matter whether either of them is observant of the liturgies or the halakhah of their respective communities.

The children of such marriages provide, for the Church (also for the Synagogue, I should think, but that is her business) a particular taxonomic problem. If, as is the working assumption here, Jewishness is passed on matrilineally (the Synagogue is the authority on this, so it can be no more than a working assumption for the Church), then, when the female partner in a Jewish-Christian marriage is a Jew, and children come of the marriage, those children will be Jews, and then all the considerations about baptizing Jews, discussed already, apply. If the Church does baptize such children, she ought do so after explicitly and urgently teaching the parents that this does not need to be done, and that doing it does not sit well with the Church's teaching about Israel. If such baptisms are ever performed, it should be *faute de mieux*, and with fear and trembling. When the Christian partner in such a marriage is female, children of the marriage will be gentiles, and in those cases decisions about baptizing them are easier, though still not easy. In no case, of course, can the children of such marriages be Christian without being baptized.

In the order of being, then, there is nothing about marriages between unbaptized Jews and non-Jewish Catholics to give the Church pause, and much to suggest that such marriages should be encouraged and supported. At this level, there is no reason why they should be understood as illicit until permitted, and thus also no reason why they should need permission at all, or prompt anything other than celebration and delight in the Church. But the Church does not, and should not, consider only what is the case in the order of being; she considers, too, the practical order, the order in which, for example, observant non-Jewish Catholic spouses married to observant unbaptized Jewish spouses must arrive at shared decisions about their own liturgical and halakhic lives, and about those of their children. And here matters are more complex in the case of Jewish-Christian marriages than in the case of mixed intra-Christian marriages.

There is, first, the burden of history, and associated with it the question of standing. The history of the Church with the Synagogue, once the effective separation between them had occurred, is mostly unedifying and often bloody. Sometimes Christians have advocated and sought a world in which all Jews are baptized, or, worse, one in which there are no more Jews. Christians confused about what it is to be a Jew have thought, as some still think, that achieving the former also brings about the latter; but there have also been some, a small minority but not vanishingly so, who have advocated a world without Jews in it simpliciter, a position brought to one kind of culmination by pagan Nazi theorists. The burden of that history is heavy, and it affects the grammar of the Church's position about marriages between unbaptized Jews and non-Jewish Catholics. The Church may not now participate in or advocate anything that attenuates the presence in the world of a liturgically and halakhically observant Synagogue. She lacks standing for that. Among her penances for her blood libels, her pogroms, and her complicity with pagan Jew-hatreds and Jew-slaughters ought be her renunciation for a millennium or so of anything that directly or indirectly threatens the observant lives of Jews. She ought configure her doctrine about and discipline of the marriages in question here in accord with this general principle, and this provides the Church with another reason for distancing these marriages even from what she now calls mixed marriages, and still more from what she calls marriages with disparity of cult.

Instead, the Church might do all she can to encourage both parties to a marriage between an unbaptized Jew and a non-Jewish Catholic to participate fully in the liturgical and halakhic lives of their respective communities, and to support one another in doing so. Second, she might encourage both parties to develop a shared liturgical and halakhic life to whatever extent is reasonably possible given the doctrine and discipline of their respective communities. On this the Church can speak directly to non-Jewish Catholic spouses, who could be instructed to take care to place no obstacles in the way of the liturgical and halakhic observances of their Jewish spouses; to themselves participate in those observances so far as the doctrine and discipline of the Church does not forbid, and so far as the doctrine and discipline of the Synagogue permits (some difficult prudential decisions are likely to be necessary in both directions); if the matter arises, actively to discourage their Jewish spouses from seeking baptism, or from entering more fully into a Catholic life than the Synagogue's doctrine and discipline permits or judges desirable; to themselves actively consider becoming Jewish in order more fully to enter into the Synagogue's life with the god; and, most especially if the marriage's children are Jews because born to a Jewish mother, but also if they are gentiles because the marriage's Jewish spouse is male, energetically to advocate that any children of their marriage not be baptized and be raised as observant Jews.

The last two recommendations are at the greatest distance from the Church's current doctrine and discipline of marriage. That doctrine and discipline has, in the case of marriages between Catholics and non-Catholics, baptized or not, as its principal desiderata the minimization of obstacles to a Catholic life for the Catholic spouse, and the minimization of obstacles to the baptism of children of such marriages. The last two recommendations above seem on their face to be directly opposed to those desiderata, for they ask a non-Jewish Catholic spouse seriously to consider becoming Jewish, and to seek to have the marriage's children be raised as Jews rather than as Catholics. The tension is real, but not beyond resolution. First, and most fundamentally, when non-Jewish Catholics become Jews, they do not cease to be Christians: their baptisms are not erased; they remain cleaved to Jesus. That is the firm doctrine of the Church, and nothing advocated here calls it into question. What the move does involve in the present state of things is the exchange of one form of life intimate with the god for another, also intimate (in fact more so), but sufficiently different in its particulars as to make the two forms of life largely noncompossible. The Synagogue's life and the Church's life may be, the ecclesial grammar of Israel suggests, placed differently in a hierarchy of intimacy with the god, with the synagogal form of life occupying a place closer to the god than the ecclesial one. Certainly, each is distinctive, enacting knowledge about the god and exchanging intimacies with the god lacking in the other. This means that new habits have to be learned that may both seem and be at odds with the old ones; old, explicit, and lovely intimacies (with Mary; with Jesus; with some among the Christian saints) may be gradually attenuated and eventually lost as they are replaced with new ones, equally lovely (I lack knowledge and standing to say what those might be in the case of an observant Jewish life, but not the confidence to assert that they are there: to say that they are there is a grammatical remark).

Such moves are difficult to make, and cannot be made often—life is not long enough. They are, perhaps, most like giving up one language and replacing it with another. There are some virtuoso instances of this in literature (Joseph Conrad, Vladimir Nabokov, Jhumpa Lahiri), but they are rare and remarkable and ordinarily not reversible—Nabokov, after he had attained virtuosic fluency in written English, did not subsequently return to writing novels or stories in Russian or French; probably he could not have done so. There is real loss as well as real gain in such moves, and the linguistic example is illuminating because it carries with it the thought of loss and gain without the thought of overall hierarchical ordering: it is odd to say that Russian is a better language than English, or English better than Russian; but almost self-evident to say that someone fluent in one who renounces reading and writing in it in favor of reading and writing in the other finds both loss and gain in doing so. So the Church can say, and so her grammar of Israel suggests she should say, about the condition of an observant ex-gentile Catholic who becomes an observant Jew, whether because of marriage or for any other reason.

The immediately preceding paragraphs show only that the Church has no in-principle reason to object to non-Jewish Catholics becoming Jews: she has no ground for calling such a move apostasy, or something equally unpleasant, because it leaves those who make it in a condition of elected intimacy with the Church's god. But the paragraphs do not show why, for example, a non-Jewish Catholic in a marriage to an unbaptized Jew should (rather than may) seriously consider becoming a Jew. There are two patterns of reasoning that suggest such a conclusion.

The first has to do with the greater intimacy of synagogal life with the god than ecclesial life. This is a real good that is not available to Christians in general, and that there is no general reason for them to seek. But for a non-Jewish Catholic married to, or considering marriage to, a Jew, this greater intimacy may provide a reason additional to and supportive of that provided by marriage alone.

But it is the weight of history that principally grounds the claim that a non-Jewish Catholic marrying a Jew should, rather than may, seriously consider becoming a Jew. Making such a recommendation to a non-Jewish Catholic entertaining marriage to an unbaptized Jew would be an act of penance on the part of the Church. It would involve the giving over of one of her own to the care of the Synagogue, which is to say to a form of life over which she has no control and of the particulars of which she has little understanding. It would be an enactment at once of her conviction (should she come to have it) that the Synagogue is more intimate with her god than she is herself, and that her history with the Synagogue of violence and misrepresentation requires renunciation of what might otherwise seem to be her own proper concerns and duties. That renunciation would be most clearly and dramatically evident in her recommendation, should the Church come to be able to make it, that the children of marriages between non-Jewish Catholics and unbaptized Jews are, now and for the foreseeable future, better raised as Jews than as Catholics. So saying would be a precise and elegant voluntary embrace of a Dantesque purgatorial *contrapasso* on the part of the Church. It would be a fully Christian act, responsive to a well-ordered ecclesial grammar of Israel, and properly demonstrative of regret, contrition, penitence, and penance.

The appeal to history also shows why the Church's understanding and regulation of marriages projected between non-Jewish Catholics and unbaptized Jews ought be different from her understanding and regulation of those projected between non-Jewish Catholics and baptized ex-gentiles not in full communion with the Bishop of Rome—what she currently calls mixed marriages. The history of the Catholic Church with separated ecclesial communities, Christians not in full communion with the Bishop of Rome, that is, is significantly different from her history with the Synagogue, especially in two ways.

The first is that, while the Church's history with separated ecclesial communities is strongly marked by violence (there were plenty of martyrs on both sides in Europe during the Protestant Reformation), the violence that disfigured those divisions was relatively short-lived and vastly less systematic in its application to the Church's self-understanding than has been the case with the violence that has marked the fugal separation of Church from Synagogue. The Church has never been not-Protestant (or not-Orthodox) with the same intensity and depth as that evident in her aspiration to be not-Synagogue. There is less to repent, and less to do penance for, in the case of the Church's responses to the separated ecclesial communities than in the case of her responses to the Synagogue.

The second is that the Church's doctrine with respect to her relations with the separated ecclesial communities is distinctively different from her doctrine with respect to her relations with the Synagogue. The Synagogue has a providential place within the god's economy of salvation: she is irrevocably called and appointed by the god for the repair of the devastated world, while the separated ecclesial communities, as the Church sees them, are not. There are no promises made by the god to them like those made by the god to the Synagogue; insofar as they are in receipt of promises, it is because of their participation, imperfect and damaged, in the sacramental economy of the Catholic Church. Although there are no doubt many goods present in the lives of the separated ecclesial communities, and many things there instructive for the Church, their existence is accidental in a sense impossible for the Synagogue; they could (not that this looks likely) be reabsorbed into the body of the Church Catholic at any time without offense to the economy of salvation. The Synagogue cannot be so absorbed.

There is no solecism, therefore, in the Church continuing to define and regulate mixed marriages as she currently does; her failure to differentiate marriages between non-Jewish Catholics and unbaptized Jews from those mixed marriages is, however, just such a solecism.

• • •

A complete ecclesial mapping of sacramental marriage, given all that has been written above, would require attention to six kinds of person rather than the three distinguished by the Church at the moment. The current three are Catholics, baptized non-Catholics, and the unbaptized; and since the Church's law codifies principally the duties and obligations of Catholics, which means in this case the conditions placed upon Catholic marriages, the result is that only three kinds of marriage are attended to: of Catholics with Catholics, of Catholics with baptized non-Catholics (mixed marriages), and of Catholics with the unbaptized (marriages with diversity of cult). The schema preferred here recognizes six kinds of person: unbaptized Jews; Jews baptized into a separated ecclesial community; Jewish Catholics; non-Jewish Catholics; unbaptized gentiles; and ex-gentiles baptized into a separated ecclesial community. Were Catholic doctrine and discipline amended in this direction, it would have to take account of eleven kinds of marriage, namely those of each kind of Catholic (Jewish and not) with each of the four kinds of non-Catholic (a total of eight possibilities), with each other (one more, bringing the total to nine), and with Catholics of their own stripe (two more, bringing the total to eleven). Of these eleven, three involve only Jews, three only gentiles or ex-gentiles, and five a gentile or ex-gentile party together with a Jew. The detailed discussion just given treats one of these ex-gentile/Jewish marriages, namely that between a non-Jewish Catholic and an unbaptized Jew. That case brings the issues into sharpest relief. But some light on the matter can also be shed by looking more briefly at another case: that of marriage between a Jewish Catholic and a non-Jewish Catholic. The other cases raise less immediately interesting questions, and conclusions about them can easily enough be extrapolated from the two discussed here.

In the case of a marriage between Catholics, one Jewish and one not, both are of course baptized, and both, let's assume, also confirmed. In the order of being, then, each is a Christian in full communion with the Bishop of Rome, and capable, therefore, of full participation in the liturgical and halakhic life of the Church. It is irrelevant to the discussion whether either is actually participant in that life, and if so to what degree; all that is needed is the assumption that they seek sacramental marriage with one another. From one angle, this is an easy case: the Church at the moment would take no account of the fact that one of the parties is a Jew, and would therefore treat the case without distinguishing it from any other intra-Catholic marriage. But were the Jewish status of one party to be recognized, an opportunity for catechesis and recommendation would also open, as well as an opportunity for amendment of the Church's law. The Church could remind the couple that in the eyes of the Church, who in this matter should be under the Synagogue's instruction, the Jewish party remains a Jew even when baptized, and that it is always possible, as the Church sees the matter, for Catholic Jews to assess, with the full support and cognizance of the Church, what this might mean for their overt engagement with the liturgical and halakhic life of the Synagogue. Undertaking marriage with a non-Jewish Catholic provides an opportunity for such an assessment, in part because children might come of the marriage, and the question of whether they should be baptized, and how they should be liturgically and halakhically formed, should be considered by the couple before any children are born, especially if the Jewish spouse is female, because then the children will be Jewish, and the decision as to whether they should be baptized differs in form from decisions about the baptism of gentile children. It belongs to the grammar of Israel here laid out to say that a Catholic Jew is an Israelite in a double sense, as Christian and as Jewish, and that the Church's predisposition in such cases, with proper attention to pastoral needs evident in particular cases, is to respond to the weight of history between the Church and the Synagogue by encouraging and supporting baptized Jews, and their offspring, and their non-Jewish Catholic spouses, to do all that is reasonably possible (what is reasonably possible will no doubt vary considerably from case to case) to have an overt and intimate relation with the Synagogue's liturgical and halakhic life. A maxim of the Code can usefully be applied here, even if in a sense not originally in play: *in re dubia privilegium fidei gaudet favore iuris* (in dubious cases the privilege of faith enjoys the favor of the law, canon 1150). The application in this case is: the privilege of being a Jew, whether in the case of a Catholic Jewish party to a marriage with a non-Jewish Catholic, or in the case of the offspring of such a marriage, should be recognized by Catholic canonists and by those who have the duty of providing counsel to those projecting sacramental marriages.

• • •

The upshot of the two cases just discussed can be generalized in a formal way. The ecclesial grammar of Israel, coupled with the weight of history, provides the Church a strong preference that Jewish parties, whether baptized or not, to marriage with non-Jewish Catholics, continue in or recover or begin a liturgical and halakhic life under the aegis of the Synagogue, whatever the current degree of their engagement with the liturgical and halakhic life of the Church; the same for Jewish offspring of such marriages, the baptism of whom is something approaching a solecism; and the same, even, for non-Jewish spouses of such marriages and non-Jewish offspring of such marriages, the liturgical recruitment of whom into the Synagogue providing a matter of rejoicing for the Church both because she recognizes such a life as one of intimacy with her god, and because she sees the need for penance in these matters on her own part. It is unlikely, so far as I can see, that any such amendments in the Church's doctrine and discipline will be made in the foreseeable future. That does not alter the seriousness of the suggestion, nor the claim that these amendments would be an appropriate response to what Israel is and to the Church's place within her.

11

REPRESENTING JEWS

THE CHURCH'S LACK of standing, and her history with the Synagogue that has produced it, has effects upon what she can properly do by way of representing and imagining the Synagogue and her Jews.

This matter has pressed the Church because differentiating herself from the Synagogue and the Jews, whether as imagined or as encountered, has been from the beginning, as it still remains, her principal device for coming to understand herself. She is not-Synagogue, and the Synagogue, as she appears in the Church's imagination, is not-Church. Christians, therefore, are not-Jews (and yet also, complicatedly, sometimes not-gentiles or not-Muslims), and the Church must try to say what this means. This has been a difficult task for her, and it remains so. She cannot ignore the Synagogue and the Jews because they are everywhere evident in her liturgical life: she acknowledges as her god's word, *verbum Domini*, many of the same texts that the Synagogue acknowledges as her god's word; the ecclesial archive is stuffed, from the beginning onwards, with depictions of the Synagogue and the Jews; she has always seen inchoately, and lately with increasing explicitness, that the Synagogue remains her god's beloved chosen; and she is clear that her god and the Synagogue's god are the same, even though not named and understood identically. The pressure of such acknowledgments is enormous, and has often squeezed bad theology and worse actions out of the Church. That fact does not, however, mean that the pressure can be avoided or the task of responding to it shirked. The Church must embrace the task of saying how she sees the Synagogue as at once like and different from herself. She must, that is, address the perplexity engendered in her by awareness that Israel contains both herself and the Synagogue—that Israel's inhabitants are both Christian and Jewish.

Since Israel is here treated as she seems to the Church, or at least to this Christian writing from within the Church, this entails address to the Synagogue's differences from the Church as they appear to the Church. What follows is therefore a contribution to the enterprise of the Church clarifying herself to herself by contrasting herself and her Christians with the Synagogue and her Jews. This ecclesial enterprise has mostly been done badly because churchly imaginings of the Synagogue have been predicated upon an assumption from which the activity itself can be separated. I mean the assumption that the differences in question are all of a kind that elevate the Church above the Synagogue. The differences, on this assumption, show the Synagogue to lack the goods the Church has. And so the Church, in indicating the Synagogue's lacks, shows her beauty and the Synagogue's ugliness, her truth and the Synagogue's lies, her leaping pirouettes and the Synagogue's heavy-footed stumbles, her benevolence and beneficence and the Synagogue's malevolence and maleficence, her delight in the embraces of the god and the Synagogue's weeping at her exclusion from them, her sleekly delighted participation in the god's feast and the Synagogue's dog-like begging for crumbs from that same god's table—and so, distressingly, on. Jews, in the Church's eyes, have mostly been paragons of vice and lack, while Christians have been, in their own eyes, paragons of virtue and abundance, their virtues being shown and defined principally by way of contrast with Jewish vices.

• • •

It will be useful as prelude to this topic to distinguish two kinds of Christian discourse about the Jews and the Synagogue. The first is constative: the making of apparently descriptive claims with the Jews or the Synagogue as their direct object. Anselm of Canterbury's sentence, earlier discussed, *fides nostra propinquior est deo quam iudaica* (Our faith—that is the faith of Christians—is closer to god than that of the Jews) can serve as an instance of this kind of thing. The second is predicative, typically in the form of an obiter dictum that some defect or vice or lack or other unpleasantness is Jewish, or characteristic of the Synagogue, or the like. George Herbert's lines, from his poem *Self-condemnation*, "He that doth love, and love amisse / This worlds delights before true Christian joy, / Hath made a Jewish choice," can serve as an instance of this second kind of discourse. These two kinds of discourse are each widespread in the Christian archive, and the distinction between them is not sharp and bright. They can and do shade and merge into one another. But they are nevertheless importantly different. The difference can be made clearer by exploring each instance in more detail.

The intentional object of Anselm's claim, as representative of the first, constative, kind of discourse, is the Jews; what the words claim, at first blush, is about the Jews, or the Jewish faith, and the claim made is about their propinquity to the god, which is said to be less than that of Christians, or the Christian faith. This particular claim, as already discussed, is not one that can reasonably be made by Christians: the Church lacks the knowledge she would need to make it, and has many counterindications ready to hand. But the point of quoting the example is not here to criticize it, but rather to show the kind of thing it is. It makes a direct claim about the Jewish faith, which is that it is less close to the god than its Christian counterpart. Like it is a claim already made many times in the course of this writing: *the Synagogue is loved and chosen by the god*, which has the advantage over Anselm's of abiding by the constraints of Christian grammar.

Christian discourse about the Jews and the Synagogue is full of this kind of claim about Jews, and a very great deal of it depicts its object negatively, whether simpliciter or by contrast with the Church and her Christians. Some of it is based upon direct acquaintance with Jews or Jewish artifacts and practices, while a very great deal of it is not. Christian constative discourse about the Jews and the Synagogue rapidly becomes, though at different rates in different situations, a self-replicating machine whose principal sources are other instances of the same rather than anything Jews write or do or say. It becomes, in the end, strictly doxographic: no Jews are required for its continuance, even though they are what it is putatively about. But whatever its degree of acquaintance with actual Jews, this kind of discourse has the same grammar: it depicts the Jews directly, usually negatively, and often as a way of building up the Church.

Herbert's lines, and the poem from which they are taken, are different. They are not principally about the Jews or the Synagogue; they do not directly depict either. Their concern is disordered love, love gone awry, love more involved with the world than with "true Christian joy." Those who love disorderedly, writes Herbert, love as Jews do: they make a Jewish choice. In writing this, Herbert does what I do when I write that an analogy limps, or that someone's words are bitter or their anger hot, or that they are snakes in the grass. I am not, in writing so, making claims about lame people, or the flavor of particular fruits, or the temperature of hot things, or snakes. I am, rather, using words that come to me when I want to categorize or depict or represent something as of a particular kind. These are dead, or almost dead, metaphors. Because they are that, they approach cliché: they are the kind of thing users of English typically say, a form of words that rolls off the tongue (no claim about spherical things there) without thought. For much of Christian history, though to varying degrees at different times and in different places, if Christians wanted to categorize some action or thought or tendency or habit negatively, calling it Jewish was commonplace. It is perhaps less so now, though only marginally so. Vices and defects and the like have not only been called Jewish by Christians; there is also a long and lively tradition of calling them pagan, and heretical, and Saracen, and (more recently) secular. But, probably, they were and are more often called Jewish than anything else. Herbert's categorization of love misdirected as Jewish is, then, best read as the application of a clichéd trope, and as such is different in kind from Anselm's direct claim about the Jewish faith.

These habits of representation can, and often do, work at a long remove from interaction with Jews in the flesh or on the page. People write of snakes and icebergs and whales, sometimes elaborately and poetically, without having seen or touched one, and without feeling the lack. A noun's use in a language may have little to do with its putative referent, and there is nothing wrong with that. The business of a grammarian is to observe and comment and taxonomize, not to police or regulate. If Christians commonly depict Jews as avaricious, blind, worldly, deceitful, cunning, and so on, then the grammarian observes that they do and may offer hypotheses about why, causally, that is the case. One such hypothesis in this instance is that Christians have found it convenient to elaborate their sense of themselves—to develop their ecclesiologies—by way of contrast with the Synagogue. If the Synagogue with her Jews is the negative image of the Church with her Christians, then the habits mentioned will develop almost of themselves: they will issue from the Church with the same regularity as excrement does from our bodies, and anything the Church finds good (Jesus, love, truthfulness, sacraments, images and icons, for example) will find its negation attributed to the Jews. All that belongs to the flight phase of the fugue.

But grammarians can do something else as well. They can point to other elements or aspects of a language, or a form of life, that stand in tension with the one currently under study; in juxtaposing them, and particularly in observing and commenting on the tension, the future direction of the language might be altered.

Laurel, for example, is redolent with victory: victors are crowned with it, and it is eagerly sought. Romantic love is something sweet on the tongue, like nectar, and beautiful to look at, like a rose: we want to savor it, and to look at it, and so we are moved toward it. English is strongly impelled in these directions when the words come up, and the positive clichés connected with laurels and love are many. But grammarians can point elsewhere, for example to these lines, from Swinburne's poem *Hymn to Proserpine*: "Laurel is green for a season, and love is sweet for a day; / But love grows bitter with treason, and laurel outlives not May." Laurel and love can also be, in English, suggestive of transience, the inevitability of disappointment, and the offering of ashgray lament ("Thou hast conquered, O pale Galilean; the world has grown grey from thy breath"), and a grammarian's indication and description of that strand in the language can affect its use, stimulating it, weaving it together with the more familiar and more positive strands.

Jews and vice and lack have gone as closely together in Christian speech as roses and love, laurel and victory, in English writing. When vices or defects are mentioned, Jews are likely to be spoken of, too; and, in the reverse direction, Christians tend strongly toward talk of wickedness and deceit and the like whenever Jews come up. But that is not the only thing to say about the Jews, the Synagogue, and the Church's grammar. It is also the case that when Israel is mentioned, Jesus is close at hand; that when Israel's god's promises to the people are characterized as irrevocable, involving a promise that has not been and cannot be taken back, as they are in Christian scripture, the Christian gaze is turned not only toward the Church but also toward the Synagogue; and that when popes and bishops and theologians say that the Synagogue is the Church's beloved elder brother, that the Church repents of its violence toward her, and that the two worship the same god and are addressed by the same god, the possibility comes to the fore, within the constraints of the Church's grammar, of linking the Jews and the Synagogue not with vice and deficiency but rather with virtue and proficiency. The grammatical remarks in this book may be a contribution to this disinterment—disinterment because the possibility of bringing talk of Jews and talk of holiness, goodness, and loveliness together is still quite deeply buried in the Christian archive. It needs digging up, digging out, dusting off, its grave clothes removed.

• • •

Jews have been represented by Christians not only verbally, and perhaps not most often verbally. There are many visual representations, too, in painting, sculpture, and drawing. One especially important issue in this area has to do with visual representations of Jesus. Sometimes, mostly when represented as an infant, Jesus is shown naked. Almost always, he is in such images also shown uncircumcised, which he would certainly not have been, and which the Church herself acknowledges he would not have been by celebrating his circumcision as a feast. Reluctance to depict Jesus naked and circumcised is an instance of a strong Christian tendency to erase, or shy away from, showing Jesus as an Israelite, born to an Israelite mother. That tendency is evident also when Jesus is represented, intentionally, as bearing physical characteristics that the representer does not imagine him to have had in his time and place——as a woman, perhaps, or as Scandinavian, or as Chinese, or as Maori. These images are typically supported and justified by a theology that emphasizes Jesus's humanity generically, rather than the particularity of his condition as an Israelite. If the god assumed human nature, the thought is, then Jesus can defensibly be represented as a human person with any appearance, located at any place and in any time. He is, after all, one of us, we humans, and his belonging to Israel can come to seem unimportant, not in need of being shown when he is represented. These ways of representing Jesus, perhaps most dramatically in images of the naked uncircumcised child who in other respects seems to be shown as the artist imagines first-century Israelites to have been, are evidence of fugal flight. It is difficult for the Church to tolerate the thought—much more, then, the image—of Jesus as a circumcised Israelite—a Jew, as we would now say. The physical evidence is therefore absent.

There is a good deal to be said for and against (mostly against, but not entirely so) representing Jesus as female, or European, or, most generally, as just like the one doing the representing. The only point to emphasize here is that refusal to represent, for example, the young Jesus as circumcised belongs to a Christian grammar of Israel that distances the Church, and therefore Jesus, from Israel. It is not that the Church would deny that Jesus was of Israel, nor that it is vital, from the Church's point of view, that this be so, nor that he was, of course, circumcised (the Church has a long and deep interest in Jesus's prepuce as one of the few possible relics of his flesh if his ascension is assumed, though that interest does not show much concern with Israel). It is rather that Jesus's Jewishness is not to be examined, not to be brought before the eyes, not to be attended to as evidence exactly of his Jewishness. If the grammar sketched here finds any acceptance, it will become easier to look at Jesus's circumcised penis and to see what it means for the Church, which is at least that the flesh Christians are cleaved to in their baptisms is circumcised, which is to say both Jewish and male.

The Christian grammar of Israel provided here (there can be others) is descriptive in the sense that it shows a lexicon and a syntax there to be seen. But it also has a normative edge. If the Church's tendency to display the Synagogue as everything she is not, to characterize her as a sink of depravity, belongs to her fugal flight from the Synagogue, then turning her gaze toward the Synagogue as the belovedly contrapuntal other, the dialect of the god's speech to the world that is the condition of the possibility of herself as a complementary dialect and that is now, and until the end, sufficiently distinct from herself that neither dialect can be rendered without remainder into the other—turning her attention to that grammar is what must happen if the fugue is to be resolved. It won't do to tell Christians to stop talking and writing about Jews as, by and large, they always have; the only thing that will do is to show a different way of talking and writing that is sufficiently attractive, sufficiently beguiling, that more Christians may want to engage in it. That is the normative edge: the fugue has been one of flight for long enough; it is time for it to become properly musical, so that Israel can, as Synagogue and Church, resound together. That resolution is a very long way off. Almost invisible, inaudible, impalpable. It is a proper object of hope.

• • •

There is also the question of representations of Jews and of the Synagogue in Christian liturgy. There they have been, for most of the Church's history since Israel's complication, depicted mostly negatively. They, or some among them, have been accused homiletically, and in liturgical art, and in Scripture, of various unpleasantnesses, including god-killing, legalism, blindness, stubbornness, ritual murder of Christian children, general malignity toward Christians, cunning, deceit, the carrying of infectious disease, and desecration of consecrated hosts; their baptism has been advocated and prayed for; their shunning and quarantine in ghettos and lazarettos has been called for; as, sometimes, particularly by preachers close to the gutter, has been their killing in retribution for imagined crimes and as a means of purifying the earth. These verbal pictures are neither pretty nor edifying, and they remain with us.

These unremittingly negative verbal presences of Jews in Christian liturgy are not the only kind. Jews are also sometimes, more often during the last two or three generations, spoken of positively, as still in covenanted relation with the god, with the consequence that the Synagogue can be called such things as the Church's older brother, or the Church's father in faith. It is sometimes said that Christians can learn from Jews, and that they may, and perhaps ought, participate with Jews in this or that activity, sometimes specifically liturgical, and sometimes more broadly halakhic. It is common enough now, in Catholic Churches in North America and Europe, to hear public prayer for the flourishing of the Synagogue and the Jews, and respectful observation that this or that synagogal festival is just now being celebrated and ought be held in prayer by Christians. During the last three or four decades, however, that sort of thing has been attenuated somewhat by a widely shared sense on the part of the European and North American intelligentsia that there is something amiss with the State of Israel's treatment of Palestinians and the question of Palestinian statehood, which can easily lead to the visceral sense that any expression of sympathy with Jews, or affirmation of what they do, is inseparable from hatred of Palestinians, or at least expressive of disordered political views.

There is, then, a range of ways in which Jews appear verbally in Christian liturgies. The tone is overwhelmingly negative, but not exclusively so: there is the occasional gleam of light. The balance will not change quickly or easily. The negative depictions of Jews mentioned are so widespread in the Christian archive, including the Church's Scripture, the living words of the god to the Church, spoken as such at every liturgical celebration, that it cannot be purified of them. It would be wrong-headed to try. Better to adjust the grammar, and in that way redirect the gaze. If the grammar of Israel advocated here begins to structure Christian talk and writing about the Synagogue and her Jews, many of the negative verbal depictions of Jews will fall away, or become marginalized as the dialect of a subset of Christians who have yet to learn how to speak properly about these matters—rather as there are still some speakers of English who talk about the planet we inhabit as if it were the center of the cosmos, the still point around which the galaxies turn. That sort of talk is by now difficult to enter into by most speakers, and those who use it as if it were not mark themselves as, by now, nonnative speakers on this topic. So also, with appropriate changes, for the still-prominent Christian idiolect that marks the Jew as a rat gnawing at the pilings supporting the Christian edifice, as here, in T. S. Eliot's poem, "Burbank with a Baedeker: Bleistein with a Cigar":

A lustreless protrusive eye
Stares from the protozoic slime
At a perspective of Canaletto.
The smoky candle end of time

Declines. On the Rialto once.
The rats are underneath the piles.
The Jew is underneath the lot
Money in furs. . . .

Or as a figure of tragedy like that carved on the western portal of the Cathedral of Notre Dame in Paris; or as someone desperately in need of baptism and explicit relation with Jesus. Should Christians come to see the Synagogue and the Church as coheirs to the god's promises and engaged upon the same task—being holy so that the world might be repaired—praying for the Jews' baptism, blaming them for Jesus's crucifixion, excising their liturgical and halakhic lives from the sphere of caresses given to the god, will come to seem less palatable, less possible as instance of Christian talk and writing, and less attractive as modes of speech. As the grammar takes root (it is early days), previously marginalized or unattractive or unavailable ways of talking about the Synagogue and her Jews will begin to show themselves, and to look lovely. The Church might, in her collects and prayers of the people, begin to show love of and respect for the Synagogue, and to express penitence for her sins against the Jews, and most especially for Jewish blood shed by Christian hands. Those are modes of verbal presence of the Jews in Christian liturgical life consonant with and nurtured by the grammar given here.

• • •

Another way in which Jews might be verbally present in Christian liturgies, at least for Catholic Christians, is by way of that part of the daily office now called the Office of Readings. Like every part of the office, this is structured around the reading (or chanting) of Psalms. (The Psalms are not, in the terms of this book, a Jewish verbal presence; they are, rather, part of Israel's scriptural archive held in common by Christians and Jews, Israel's two bodies; they are for the Church the very words of the god.) It includes, as well, a reading from elsewhere in the canon of Scripture, typically from the New Testament. And it includes a reading from the nonscriptural Christian archive, sometimes responsive to the scriptural reading, and sometimes not. The excerpts of this kind are from works by figures of some authoritative significance for the Church: saints, *doctores ecclesiae*, ecumenical councils, bishops, popes, speculative theologians, and so on. They come from works composed in a wide array of languages: Latin, Greek, Syriac,

French, Spanish, German, English, and so on. The week in which I am writing this paragraph is representative in the range of its selections: there is one excerpt from *Gaudium et Spes*, a work promulgated at the Second Vatican Council (1962–1965); one from Thomas Aquinas's exposition of John's Gospel (thirteenth century); one from John Chrysostom's homilies on the First Letter to the Corinthians (fourth century); two from Columbanus's instruction on Christ as the *fons vitae* (seventh century); and two from Augustine's *Confessiones* (fourth century). These works are not the god's words; they are not the god speaking directly to the reader or hearer of the office; they have varying degrees of authority as the Church understands these matters, and the principal point of their inclusion in this part of the office is instructional and inspirational: they provide instances of Christian writing about this or that topic of importance to the Christian life which might provoke thought or prayer or meditation on the part of those who read or hear them. The excerpts belong to the Christian part of Israel's archive, and they therefore also, in addition to the instructional and formational purposes they serve, provide a sense of the range and depth of that archive. They make the fact of it, its variety and complexity and historical depth, lively.

Israel's archive includes not only works by Christians, Jewish and not, but also works by unbaptized Jews. The Office of Readings could very well include excerpts from that part of the archive, and if it did, that would be a verbal presence of unbaptized Jews on the Christian liturgical stage. For example: during the season of Lent I often make it a practice to read, closely, a chapter or part of one from Maimonides's *Guide of the Perplexed* (in Shlomo Pines's English version). That is in part because Lent is, for me, often an occasion for thinking and praying about some of the topics on which Maimonides is especially sharp and instructive (naming the god, for instance), and I have wanted to be prodded into thinking and writing things about that topic which I would have been unlikely, without reading Maimonides, to have thought and written. But it is also in part because I take Maimonides to be a writer of weight for the Synagogue, and his works therefore to be instances of intellectually serious response to the god I acknowledge by someone versed in and formed by the Synagogue's long engagement with the intellectual gifts given it by that same god. My reading of Maimonides lies, therefore, at two difficult but fruitful intersections: between the analytical and the devotional (for me these are scarcely distinguishable), and between the Church and the Synagogue.

Excerpts from such works could easily become a regular part of the Office of Readings. Including works by unbaptized Jews in that office would, so far as I can see, require nothing more than administrative work on the part of the Roman dicastery responsible for these matters. There are no matters of doctrine or of canon law at stake; there is simply an extension of what Catholics may read or hear liturgically in this particular part of the daily office. The extension seems natural, perhaps even inevitable, if the grammar of Israel laid out in this writing is accepted, or even seriously entertained. Why not read, devotionally and analytically, what Jews, the other Israelites, have written and are writing about the Church's god? If the grammar here becomes standard, then the burden of proof shifts, from those who advocate the extension to those who oppose it, and it is hard to see how that burden could be met. According to the older grammars, by contrast, it is at least as hard to see why such a proposal would be made, much less accepted. If the Synagogue, with respect to philosophical, theological, or devotional writing, is considered primarily or only a place of lack and loss, then there is no reason to expect Christian formation or inspiration from reading or hearing the writing of unbaptized Jews on such topics. But those older grammars have no defensible place in the Church now, and so the proposal made here holds its place as at least prima facie plausible.

This suggestion about the verbal presence of unbaptized Jews in the lectionary can easily be extended to the homily. Words from the Jewish part of Israel's archive can be used by Christian preachers of all stripes to make points about the scriptural excerpts that have just been heard, or to indicate lines of halakhic or theological thinking. And it is not uncommon to hear this done in some of the Church's byways, if not yet on her highways. It is, or it used to be, common enough to hear Abraham Heschel or Martin Buber or Simone Weil (a complicated case: a self-denying Jew, and an unbaptized but aspirational Christian) mentioned or quoted, approvingly, in Catholic homilies or Anglican sermons, of which I have heard many during the past five decades. But it is also, and perhaps equally, common to hear gentile authorities—the Dalai Lama, for example, or some or another gentile poet or essayist or novelist—used in these ways, and that indicates an important difference between the proposal made here and the attitude evident in these more relaxed and expansive homiletical practices. It is that, according to the grammar given here, words and works belonging to the Jewish archive have a significance and an authority for the Church that those belonging to the gentile archive necessarily lack. What Jews say and write about Scripture or liturgy or halakhah or theology is, for Christians, familial, close and in-house, haimish, no matter its degree of profundity, its truth, or its concordance with the Church's doctrine and discipline. Jewish speech and writing are a theme in the fugue to which Christian speech belongs as a counter-theme. That is not so for gentile speech and writing, which is why I do not propose, and would oppose, the inclusion of excerpts from gentile writings in the lectionary of the Office of Readings. What Vasubandhu or Tsong-kha-pa or Dogen have written may be more profound, more subtle, more precise, and more conceptually and rhetorically elegant than anything in Israel's archive. It may be (I think it is) that Christians individually and the Church collectively have much to learn from close consideration of such gentile writing. But none of it belongs to Israel; none of it is a thread in the garment of holiness woven by the god for the world's redemption and repair. It is, instead, Egyptian gold: treasure necessary for the Church, but to be expropriated and reconfigured rather than set in a monstrance and admired. Its verbal presence in Christian preaching is unexceptionable, and may be both instructive and inspiring, but it is different in kind from the presence of Jewish words there, and the extent to which the grammar of Israel here proposed is internalized and used by the Church is the extent to which that difference will be marked—liturgically, particularly, but in other ways too. The rhetorical devices available for this are already available to preachers: the means they now use to distinguish Christian voices in their homilies from non-Christian ones could be the same as those they use to distinguish Israelite from non-Israelite voices. The boundary is not removed, but shifted.

• • •

Another possibility: unbaptized Jews whose lives or writings are of particular significance to the Church might be memorialized in the calendar of saints, with collects and prayers where appropriate. Were this to be done gradually, as local and universal church calendars are revised in the usual ways, such memorials and the reasons for them could become a topic in the training of priests and deacons and catechists so that they can understand and explain what such acts of remembering signify about the ecclesial grammar of Israel. Changes such as this, minor and gradual at first, might be effective in diffusing doctrinal developments among practicing but often largely uncatechized Christians. Many baptized Jews of exemplary significance for the Church already have their places in the calendar, for example, the apostles, Paul, and Teresa Benedicta of the Cross (Edith Stein). This proposal would extend the practice of memorializing Jews to unbaptized ones. Criteria for ecclesial decisions about which unbaptized Jews to memorialize should overlap largely with those the Church uses in deciding whom among the baptized to memorialize—exemplarity in holiness, or in capacity to instruct the Church are the obvious ones. Martyrs are always appropriate, and the number of unbaptized Jewish martyrs—those who have died because they were Jews, for Israel—is enormous; it would be especially appropriate for the Church to memorialize those killed by Christians simply for being Jews. Remembering those horrors with prayers of remorse, self-inculpation, and penitence, could be a vital contribution to the Church's clarity about the bloodily violent results of getting the grammar of Israel wrong.

An objection to this suggestion about memorialization is that baptism—being a Christian—is requisite for it. But that objection belongs to a grammar of Israel that takes the distance between Christians and unbaptized Jews to be of the same kind and extent as that between Christians and gentiles. In such a grammar, it is a solecism to advocate what I here suggest: it breaks a hard boundary. But if Jews and Christians since Israel's complication are both of Israel, complementarily so according to the figure of the fugue, then the suggestion made here is not only not a solecism, but appropriate, attractive, beautiful, lucidly convenient. The objection canvassed therefore reduces to a restatement of one grammar against another. It shows that one grammar commends the practice here advocated, while the other makes it impossible, almost invisible even as a possibility. That is an advantage for the grammar here advocated: according to it, and not according to its principal rival, the Church may with propriety and elegance liturgically memorialize, learn from, and penitentially confess her violence directed at those who worship the same god as herself and who remain intimate with that god.

The Synagogue might object to the Church memorializing unbaptized Jews in this way, and to her inclusion of Jewish writings in her nonscriptural lectionary. It might seem to the Synagogue that such practices expropriate the Jewishness of those being memorialized or read from by christianizing their words and works and lives. That, it seems, is largely why the Synagogue objects to the Church remembering Teresa Benedicta as a Christian martyr when in fact the Nazis killed her because she was a Jew. There is force to this objection, and, as ever, the Church should attend closely to what the Synagogue says about any memorialization of Jews on her part. Teresa Benedicta, however, was a baptized Jew, which adds a layer of complication to the questions about expropriation and christianization; the proposal here has to do with unbaptized Jews, which ought make it less tempting for the

Church to memorialize them, should she choose to do so, by erasing their Jewishness. It should also be remembered that according to the grammar given here, the condition of being a Jew is not expunged or overwritten by baptism; Edith Stein did not cease to be a Jew because she was baptized and came to be called Teresa Benedicta. Keeping that in mind makes expropriation by erasure, which, arguably, some ecclesial attitudes to and representations of her (and of others like her) still show, less attractive.

• • •

The Church and the Synagogue each belong to Israel, who is constituted since the fugal complication by the two of them together, each damaged, though differently, by flight and forgetfulness, each holy and beloved, though differently, each responsive to the god liturgically, halakhically, and theologically, though differently and in many respects noncompossibly. Each has learned since the violence of their separation to perpetuate herself differently, the Church only by recruitment, her face turned to the gentiles, and the Synagogue largely by procreation, her face turned to the god. Each serves the same purpose, which is holiness for the world's repair, and Jews and Christians therefore need one another to prosecute that purpose under the god's guidance, though Christians, because of the violence of their history with Jews, have more need of Jews than Jews have of Christians in this way as in every other. The Church lacks standing to intervene in the Synagogue's life in any way other than by penitential offerings. The Church has, however, principally for her own benefit, an interest in learning to represent the Synagogue, for her own benefit rather than the Synagogue's, as she is, which is as the god's beloved elect, and she may find ways to do this liturgically and homiletically. The extent to which she does this is the extent to which the fugal flight might modulate into a fugal harmony.

EXCURSUS
JESUS AS SAVIOR OF THE WORLD

JESUS, CHRISTIANS LIKE to say, is the savior of the world: no one comes to the Father except by way of him; and there is no name under heaven by which salvation may be had other than his. This and similar claims are central and proper to the Church's teaching and proclamation. If salvation is delectable and indefectible intimacy with the god of Israel, then certainly Christians must say that it involves Jesus, for Jesus is that god enfleshed, the second person of the Trinity that god is. Nothing written in this book calls language of this sort into question. It is one of the registers in which the Church talks about, and to, her god, and to abandon it would be to abandon Christian talk. When, at the end, the saved see and are seen by the god, this involves seeing and being seen by Jesus. And, according to the axiom that all the god's actions *ad extra* are undertaken by all three persons indivisibly, the world's repair undertaken by the god with Israel in hand involves Jesus in every particular. What Jesus does is what Israel does, and every well-ordered act of the Synagogue is, because of her election, resonant with and responsive to Jesus just because every well-ordered act of the Synagogue is resonant with and responsive to the god of Israel. Every Israelite who becomes delightedly and indefectibly intimate with Israel's god becomes therefore delightedly and indefectibly intimate with Jesus—and the Church is confident in her hope that all Israelites, Jews and Christians alike, will, at the end, be delightedly and indefectibly intimate with the god in this way. That is the grammar of the Church's faith. The Synagogue does not speak or write in this way, and it is essential to Israel in her complication that she should not, just as it is essential to Israel in her complication that the Church does not speak of and to the god as the

Synagogue does. The fugal flight is not yet a fugal harmony, and both voices are needed until it is. The Church must speak with clarity and precision in the theological register about who Jesus is and what Jesus does; but she has no need to persuade the Synagogue of Jesus here below, and every need not to. What she knows is Jesus, and he is a great good to know. But she is confident that she has more to learn about the god of Jesus Christ than knowing Jesus can teach her; she is confident as well that at the heart of what she has yet to learn about that god is what the Synagogue already knows. It is Jesus who, seen clear and heard close, teaches her that. The work of Jesus in reconciling the world to the Trinity the god is, which is also to himself, is being done, now, by bringing Synagogue and Church gradually into harmony so that the gentiles, without exception, may flow in to her. No Jew needs to know Jesus to come to the Father, for every Jew is already with the Father, and is there because of Jesus.

EXCURSUS
THE CHURCH AS SACRAMENT OF THE WORLD

SUPPOSE WE UNDERSTAND the Church, Jesus's postascension body here below, as the universal sacrament and instrument of Jesus's work in the world. On such an understanding, the Church is the body, the form of life, appointed by the god to make Jesus available to and present in the world; and because all repair (healing, holiness, health, *salus*, salutary salvation, redress of damage) is the work of Jesus, the scope of the Church's work is universal. If a sacrament is an outward and visible sign of an inward and invisible grace, then the Church, the confessing community of the baptized, is the sacrament of and for the world, where the sacrament's grace is reparative and the world is all that is the case. No exceptions. No no-go areas. No *hortus conclusus* where Jesus cannot go or in which he is walled up. This is the kind of thing Christians say at every level, from considered doctrinal claims of ecumenical councils to off-the-cuff remarks of half-prepared homilists. And it is what Christians should say when they talk about Jesus and the Church and the world and sacramentality in an elevated theological register. It is good Christian doctrine. But how is it compatible with the grammar of Israel offered here, according to which it is not only the case that the Synagogue's life with the god remains a blessing and a means appointed by the god for the world's repair, but also that there is no need for the Church to offer Jesus to the Synagogue—and reason for the Church not to do so? The answer is simple enough. It can be shown by considering how the words *Church* and *world* are to be taken in the sentence, *the Church is the sacrament of the world*—such consideration being what any half-trained scholastic would do. The

Church belongs to Israel, and since Israel's complication she has her complement in Israel, which is the Synagogue. During the time of Israel-as-complex (it will last until the end), the Synagogue's liturgical and halakhic life provides the Church's liturgical and halakhic life an essential element of its shape and meaning, as is also true in the reverse direction. It is not that Jesus cannot go where the Synagogue is. He is, inevitably, already there. It is that the mode of his presence there is incognito, and that the Church's presence in and to the Synagogue, the mode of her sacramental self-offering to the Synagogue, corresponds to that unknown, unnamed presence for the time being; it is one of self-abnegation in the service of one she neither names to nor presses upon the Synagogue. The Church is the sacrament of the world; but she is so within Israel as complement to the Synagogue, whose work in repairing the world, appointed and guided as it is by the god of Israel who is the god of Jesus, she can only complement by serving it with the recognition that the reparative work of the sacrament can be done and is being done and must be done without the name. The Church's sacramental presence among the gentiles is, by contrast, with the name: Jesus asks to be named there, just as he asks not to be named in the Synagogue. The world is, now, tripartite, and the Church's sacramental presence is, when she is doing what she should, distinct in each part. In the Synagogue she is presently absent in name and face because the Synagogue is her complement in Israel; among the gentiles she is presently present in name and face because the gentiles are not of Israel and they can come to be by seeing Jesus; in and to herself she is Jesus's beloved who calls his name and is named by him.

EXCURSUS
THE INTERPRETATION OF SCRIPTURE

THE CHURCH READS the canon of Scripture from beginning to end as a witness to Jesus. Sometimes the witness is explicit and sometimes implicit; sometimes in prophetic voice and sometimes as fulfillment; sometimes as figure and sometimes as figured. Jesus appears in Scripture in many ways, but is always there. Not to see him there, as the Synagogue does not when she reads from her Torah scrolls and interprets what she hears, is not to see a figure really, if implicitly, present. Any reading of what the Church calls the Old Testament and the Synagogue the Tanakh that is blind to Jesus is blind to an important presence in the text. So the Church says, and so she ought say. Her long history of scriptural interpretation is in significant part predicated upon assumptions about Jesus's presence in the entirety of the text, and the arrangement of scriptural texts in her lectionaries shows how formative of her liturgical life with the god those assumptions have been and remain. She cannot abandon them without abandoning herself. For her not to read *ecce, virgo concipiet et pariet filium et vocabit nomen eius Emmanuel*, among many other Old Testament texts, as if it spoke of Jesus (not only of Jesus, but at least of Jesus), would be a solecism. What follows from this for the Church's understanding of the Synagogue's reading and interpretation of the Tanakh? Certainly that what the Synagogue sees and identifies there is not all that is to be seen and identified there; and certainly that to fail to see Jesus there is to fail to see a figure of importance (an understatement). Saying those things is entirely compatible with the Christian grammar of Israel offered here. But that grammar, coupled with an assumption about the scriptural text which the Church holds dear (and which perhaps the Synagogue does too) provides something more to say, something which removes the possibility of taking the Church's recognition of Jesus in Scripture and the Synagogue's nonrecognition of him there as a simple indication of the Church's sightedness and the Synagogue's blindness so far as Scripture is concerned. The assumption is that Scripture is *locutio divina*, the speech of the god to Israel. This entails that it is inexhaustible. No reading of it, as a whole or in part, can exhaust it, and every reading of it, as a whole or in part, is therefore blind to some among its meanings. That is as true of the Church's readings as of the Synagogue's. The grammar of Israel shown here adds to this assumption the thought that the Synagogue's sixteen-hundred-year-long (or so) engagement with the Tanakh, independent (mostly) of the Church, is intended by the god and delighted in by the god, and it frames that claim with the broader one that the work of the Synagogue and that of the Church together constitute the work of Israel since the complication. These claims suggest that, first, there is and must be much in the text of Scripture to which the Church is blind (because of Scripture's inexhaustibility); and, second, that some of what she fails to see in Scripture is evident to the Synagogue (because of complementarity). It is not that the Church is sighted and the Synagogue blind when each looks at Scripture. It is that each is blinkered, and that the harmonic resolution of Israel's internal fugal flight will involve each beginning to see something of what the other sees. The Church, because of the demand for penitence and penance with respect to the Synagogue, a demand heavy upon her, must now assume that the Synagogue is less blind than she about the riches of the canon of Scripture. She should therefore be eager to learn from the Synagogue what is in the Tanakh, as pupil to teacher, grateful to be taught.

EXCURSUS
ANTISEMITES AND PHILOSEMITES

ANTISEMITES AND PHILOSEMITES are alike in responding to Jews as if it matters that they are Jews. When antisemites and philosemites take themselves to be faced by a Jew or Jews, their actions are responsive to that feature of the situation. Jews, for them, are a distinctive subset of human creatures, and to be faced with one or more of them is likely, other things being equal, to prompt distinctive responses. Antisemites, when faced with Jews, respond hatefully, contemptuously, violently, lethally, condescendingly, and so on. Philosemites respond lovingly, imitatively, submissively, respectfully, admiringly, and so on. The adverbs (many more are possible) are intended to suggest not attitudes or judgments, which may or may not be present, but kinds of behavior; the behaviors in question may involve direct fleshly or verbal contact with Jews (the blow or the caress; the insult or the compliment), or they may involve more distanced legal or institutional arrangements (expulsion from or welcome into a body politic; restriction from or opening of access to institutions). As these words are used here, antisemitic and philosemitic activity is present ideal-typically when it responds directly to the physical presence of human creatures taken to be Jews. When Jews are talked or written about in their absence, or when, in contexts where there are no Jews, political or legal or social arrangements are made for them, something different occurs—not better or worse; simply different. There is no bright line here; but the paradigmatic cases of antisemitic and philosemitic behavior occur in the presence, or close to the presence, of those taken to be Jews. Not all human creatures are either antisemites or philosemites. Many, it seems, find Jews insufficiently distinctive to prompt either kind of response.

Jews, for such people, are at most a curiosity, more often an irrelevance, and in any case incapable of prompting love or hatred. Antisemites and philosemites are to be found among all human creatures—Christians, Jews, and gentiles. Non-Jewish Christians are the case of interest here. Most of these have been, as most still are, antisemites, in the sense that the perceived presence of Jews prompts in them actions of the negative kinds mentioned; all however should be philosemites, as some have been and some are. It belongs to fundamental ecclesial grammar to say this. Jews and Christians together constitute Israel; they worship the same god; they are of the same lineage; they have the same purpose; Jews are the god's particular intimates, held closer and more lovingly than Christians; the Church has seriously and systematically damaged the Synagogue; for non-Jewish Christians Jews are their closest intimates outside the Church, toward whom penitential and sacrificially loving behaviors are, for the long time being, the most appropriate. Christian antisemites are, in virtue of being so, doing damage to Israel, to the Synagogue, to the Church, and to themselves. But it doesn't follow from this that all non-Jewish Christian philosemitisms are to be celebrated or advocated by Christians. They can be disordered, as is often the case for imitative philosemitisms. Christians may be led by what they take to be love or respect for Jews, to copy them: to do what they do, as lovers often copy their beloveds in this or that way. That can lead to Christian imitations of Jewish liturgies, Christians speaking to the god as if they were Jews, Christians observing parts of the Synagogue's halakhah, and so on. At best, these imitative behaviors are in bad taste, like adopting your neighbors' habits of dress, speech, gait, and cuisine so that you become indistinguishable from them. At worst, they become antisemitic even when they seem to those who perform them not to be—celebrations of Succoth, for example, by non-Jewish Christians require such Christians to speak and act as if they were Jews, and show a perhaps culpable ignorance of the Church's history with the Synagogue; the mezuzah on the wall of a non-Jewish Christian house is like a cigar-store Indian, as the sukkah in a non-Jewish Christian back yard is like a health-spa sweatlodge. If it is a solecism for a Christian to act as an antisemite of any kind, and as a philosemite of the mimetic kind, which types of philosemitic activity are grammatical? If Christians should, in order to act in accord with Israel's grammar, act philosemitically, what might this look like? Formally speaking, the answer is easy enough: Christian philosemites are those in whom the perceived presence of Jews prompts puzzled, admiring, and penitential actions, closely braided together; and in whom the perceived presence of Jews prompts action that shows greater concern with their flourishing than with that of any others, Christian or gentile. Giving substance to this form is harder, and requires detailed analysis and depiction of particular circumstances. It is among the more important tasks of the Church now, and for the foreseeable future, to provide teaching and catechesis that instructs non-Jewish Christians in what well-ordered Christian philosemitism looks like in particular circumstances. Among the most important resources for the Church in doing these things will be close attention to what the Synagogue has to say about what, now, Christian philosemitism should look like. It may be that from the Synagogue's point of view, or from the point of view of some Jews, it won't look like much. Sometimes, the best thing lovers can do for their beloveds, or friends for their friends, is to leave them alone; it may be that ecclesial philosemitism now asks of the Church little more than to do that for the Synagogue. That would certainly be a penitential act of love on the Church's part. It would please Jesus.

WORKS CONSULTED

THIS BOOK TRESPASSES the boundaries of many scholarly fields and subfields (biblical interpretation, the history of the Synagogue, the history of the Church, the history of the Jews, the philosophy of taxonomy, Christian theology and canon law, Jewish theology and philosophy, Zionism, literary theory, and more), to each of which belongs a large literature of which I have read only a small portion. The list below, therefore, is nothing like a systematic guide to any of those literatures. It contains only those works mentioned in the text of this book, as well as those works I found especially informative or stimulating (the latter both positively and negatively) in preparing to write it.

I owe a special debt to the work of Daniel Boyarin, as will be evident to those who know it; to that of David Burrell, who long ago guided in person my early thinking about some of these matters; to that of Gavin D'Costa, whose sterling work on recent developments in Catholic doctrine on matters to do with Israel is unrivaled; and to that of David Novak, both on the page and in person. I'm grateful, too, to Lauren Winner, Philip Porter, and Brendan Case, each of whom was kind enough to read all or part of the manuscript at various stages, and to give me helpful comments.

The spirit of Wittgenstein, that obsessive baptized Jew, hovers over and under and around everything written here: my debt to him is beyond measure. The works in this list from which I got the most intellectual and aesthetic pleasure are Steinberg's *Sexuality* and Wieseltier's *Kaddish*. Those books are both relatively marginal to the enterprise under way here, and are profoundly dissimilar in style and purpose from one another, but each is a delight because it has verve, seriousness, and flavor, and because it is genuinely and constructively engaged with its topic—something surprisingly rare in scholarly work. The book on this list that has entered me most deeply and ineradicably, in ways I can no longer recall or fully disinter (I first read it in 1984), is Steiner's *Portage*. I hope that any reader of this book will at least seek out Steinberg's and Steiner's and Wieseltier's works.

Popes appear in this list under their given rather than their papal names; others with honorific titles (rabbis, bishops, saints, and others) appear without them. I prefer, here, to honor these people as writers rather than as holders of other offices. The details given for each item are of the particular version I read; when the first publication or composition date is widely different from the date of the item I read, I indicate that.

Anderson, Gary A., and Joel S. Kaminsky, eds. *The Call of Abraham: Essays on the Election of Israel in Honor of Jon D. Levenson*. Notre Dame, IN: University of Notre Dame Press, 2013.

Anselm of Canterbury. *S. Anselmi Cantuariensis Archiepiscopi Opera Omnia*. Vol. 5. Edited by F. S. Schmitt. Edinburgh: Thomas Nelson, 1949.

Arendt, Hannah. *The Jew as Pariah: Jewish Identity and Politics in the Modern Age*. Edited by Ron H. Feldman. New York: Grove Press, 1978. Essays composed at various dates between 1943 and 1966.

Baker, Cynthia A. *Jew*. New Brunswick, NJ: Rutgers University Press, 2017.

Baron, Lori, Jill Hicks-Keeton, and Matthew Thiessen, eds. *The Ways That Often Parted: Essays in Honor of Joel Marcus*. Atlanta: Society of Biblical Literature Press, 2018.

Batnitzky, Leora. "Rethinking Christian and Jewish Exceptionalisms." *Modern Theology* 38, no. 1 (2022): 63–80.

Becker, Adam H., and Annette Yoshiko Reed, eds. *The Ways That Never Parted: Jews and Christians in Late Antiquity and the Early Middle Ages*. Minneapolis: Fortress Press, 2007.

Benamozegh, Elia. *Israel and Humanity*. Translated by Maxwell Luria. Mahwah: Paulist Press, 1995. First published in French in 1914.

Bergoglio, Jorgé Francesco. "Visit to the Synagogue of Rome." Address of January 17, 2016. www.vatican.va.

Boyarin, Daniel. "'This We Know to Be the Carnal Israel': Circumcision and the Erotic Life of God and Israel." *Critical Inquiry* 18 no. 3 (1992): 474–505.

Boyarin, Daniel. *Border Lines: The Partition of Judeo-Christianity*. Philadelphia: University of Pennsylvania Press, 2004.

———. *Judaism: The Genealogy of a Modern Notion*. New Brunswick, NJ: Rutgers University Press, 2019.

———. "Rethinking Jewish Christianity: An Argument for Dismantling a Dubious Category (to Which Is Appended a Correction of My *Border Lines*)." *Jewish Quarterly Review* 99, no. 1 (2009): 7–36.

———. "Semantic Differences; or, 'Judaism'/'Christianity.'" In Becker and Reed, *Ways That Never Parted*, 65–85.

———. *Socrates and the Fat Rabbis*. Chicago: University of Chicago Press, 2009.

———. "Why Ignatius Invented Judaism." In Baron et al., *Ways That Often Parted*, 309–24.

Boyarin, Daniel, and Jonathan Boyarin. "Diaspora: Generation and the Ground of Jewish Identity." *Critical Inquiry* 19, no. 4 (1993): 693–725.

Breiterman, Zachary. "Zionism." In Kavka et al., *Cambridge History*, 606–34.

Bullivant, Stephen. "Sine Culpa? Vatican II and Inculpable Ignorance." *Theological Studies* 72 (2011): 70–86.

Burrell, David B. *Knowing the Unknowable God: Ibn-Sina, Maimonides, Aquinas*. Notre Dame, IN: University of Notre Dame Press, 1992.

———. *Towards a Jewish-Christian-Muslim Theology*. Chichester: Wiley-Blackwell, 2011.

Codex Iuris Canonici / Code of Canon Law. 1983. Latin and English text, with revisions subsequent to 1983, at https://tinyurl.com/446ky9f9.

Cohen, Jeremy. *Living Letters of the Law: Ideas of the Jew in Medieval Christianity*. Berkeley: University of California Press, 1999.

Cohen, Shaye J. D. *The Beginnings of Jewishness: Boundaries, Varieties, Uncertainties*. Berkeley: University of California Press, 2001.

Cole, Teju. *Black Paper*. Chicago: University of Chicago Press, 2021.

———. *Fernweh*. London: Mack Books, 2020.

Commission for Religious Relations with the Jews. "'The Gifts and Calling of God Are Irrevocable' (Rom. 11:29)—a Reflection on Theological Questions Pertaining to Catholic-Jewish Relations on the Occasion of the 50th Anniversary of 'Nostra Aetate' (No. 4)." Released December 10, 2015, over the names of Kurt Koch, Brian Farrell, and Norbert Hoffman. At www.christianunity.va.

———. "Guidelines and Suggestions for Interpreting the Conciliar Declaration Nostra Aetate (n. 4)." Released December 1, 1974 over the names of Joseph Willebrands and Pierre-Marie de Contenson. At www.christianunity.va.

———. "Notes on the Correct Way to Present the Jews and Judaism in Preaching and Catechesis in the Roman Catholic Church." Released June 24, 1985, over the names of Joseph Willebrands, Pierre Duprey, and Jorge Mejia. At www.christianunity.va.

———. "We Remember: A Reflection on the Shoah." Released March 16 1998, over the names of Edward Idris Cassidy, Pierre Duprey, and Remi Hoeckman. At www.christianunity.va.

Connelly, John. *From Enemy to Brother: The Revolution in Catholic Teaching on the Jews, 1933–1965*. Cambridge, MA: Harvard University Press, 2012.

Couzin, Robert. "Uncircumcision in Early Christian Art." *Journal of Early Christian Studies* 26, no. 4 (2018): 601–29.

Cunningham, Philip A. *A Story of Shalom: The Calling of Christians and Jews by a Covenanting God.* Mahwah, NJ: Paulist Press, 2001.

Dahan, Gilbert. *Les intellectuels chrétiens et les juifs au moyen âge*. Paris: Cerf, 2007. First published 1990.

———. *La polémique chrétienne contre le judaïsme au moyen âge*. Paris: Seuil, 1991.

D'Costa, Gavin. *Catholic Doctrines on the Jewish People after Vatican II*. New York: Oxford University Press, 2019.

———. "The Mystery of Israel: Jews, Hebrews, Hebrew Catholics, Messianic Judaism, the Catholic Church, and the Mosaic Ceremonial Law." *Nova et Vetera* 16, no. 3 (2017): 939–77.

———. *Vatican II: Catholic Doctrines on Jews and Muslims*. Oxford: Oxford University Press, 2014.

D'Costa, Gavin and Faydra L. Shapiro, eds. *Contemporary Catholic Approaches to the People, Land, and State of Israel*. Washington, DC: Catholic University of America Press, 2022.

Di Segni, Riccardo. "Steps Taken and Questions Remaining in Jewish-Christian Relations Today." Partial transcript of a talk given at the Pontifical Gregorian University on October 19, 2004. At https://tinyurl.com/2p8zr4u5.

Eliot, George. *Daniel Deronda*. London: Penguin Classics, 1996. First published 1876.

Eliot, T. S. *The Poems of T. S. Eliot*. Edited by Christopher Ricks and Jim McCue. 2 vols. Baltimore: Johns Hopkins University Press, 2015.

Farrow, Douglas. "For the Jew First: Reaffirming the Pax Paulinica." In *Theological Negotiations: Proposals in Soteriology and Anthropology*, edited by Douglas Farrow, 209–50. Grand Rapids: Baker Academic, 2018.

Feingold, Lawrence. *The Mystery of Israel*. 3 volumes. St. Louis: Miriam Press, 2010.

Finkielkraut, Alain. *Le juif imaginaire*. Paris: Seuil, 1983. First published 1980.

Frederiksen, Paula. *Augustine and the Jews: A Christian Defense of Jews and Judaism*. New Haven, CT: Yale University Press, 2010. First published 2008.

Frymer-Kensky, Tikva, David Novak, Peter W. Ochs, and Michael A. Signer. "Dabru Emet: A Jewish Statement on Christians and Christianity." A full-page advertisement in *The New York Times*, September 10, 2000.

Frymer-Kensky, Tikva, David Novak, Peter W. Ochs, David Fox-Sandmel, and Michael A Signer, eds. *Christianity in Jewish Terms*. Boulder, CO: Westview Press, 2000.

Gregerman, Adam. *Building on the Ruins of the Temple: Apologetics and Polemics in Early Christianity and Rabbinic Judaism*. Tübingen: Mohr Siebeck, 2016.

Gregerman, Adam. "The Desirability of Jewish Conversion to Catholicism." *Horizons* 45 (2018): 249–86.

Harkins, Franklin T, ed. *Transforming Relations: Essays on Jews and Christians throughout History in Honor of Michael A. Signer.* Notre Dame, IN: University of Notre Dame Press, 2010.

Hayes, Christine E. *Gentile Impurities and Jewish Identities: Intermarriage and Conversion from the Bible to the Talmud.* New York: Oxford University Press, 2002.

Herbert, George. *The English Poems of George Herbert.* Edited by Helen Wilcox. Cambridge: Cambridge University Press, 2007.

Hesse, Herman. *Das Glasperlenspiel.* Zürich: Fretz and Wasmuth, 1943.

Horn, Dara. *People Love Dead Jews: Reports from a Haunted Present.* New York: Norton, 2021.

Kaminsky, Joel S. "Can Election Be Forfeited?" In Anderson and Kaminsky, *Call of Abraham*, 44–66.

Kasper, Walter. "The Commission for Religious Relations with the Jews: A Crucial Endeavour of the Catholic Church." Address of November 6, 2002 at Boston College. www.vatican.va.

———. "The Jewish-Christian Dialogue: Foundations, Progress, Difficulties, and Perspectives." Address of November 21, 2001 at the Israel Museum in Jerusalem. www.vatican.va.

Kavka, Martin, Zachary Breiterman, and David Novak, eds. *The Cambridge History of Jewish Philosophy.* Volume 2: *The Modern Era.* Cambridge: Cambridge University Press, 2012.

Kepnes, Stephen. "Liturgy." In Kavka et al., *Cambridge History*, 519–37.

Kessler, Herbert L. "Shaded With Dust: Jewish Eyes on Christian Art." In Kessler and Nirenberg, *Judaism and Christian Art*, 74–114.

Kessler, Herbert L. Kessler and David Nirenberg, eds. *Judaism and Christian Art: Aesthetic Anxieties from the Catacombs to Colonialism.* Philadelphia: University of Pennsylvania Press, 2011.

Kinzer, Mark S. *Searching Her Own Mystery: Nostra Aetate, the Jewish People, and the Identity of the Church.* Eugene, OR: Cascade Books, 2015.

Korn, Eugene B. and John T. Pawlikowski, eds. *Two Faiths, One Covenant? Jewish and Christian Identity in the Presence of the Other.* Lanham, MD: Rowman and Littlefield, 2005.

Kupfer, Marcia. "Abraham Circumcises Himself: A Scene at the Endgame of Jewish Utility to Christian Art." In Kessler and Nirenberg, *Judaism and Christian Art*, 143–82.

Levenson, Jon D. "Miscategorizing Chosenness." In *Partners with God: Theological and Critical Readings of the Bible in Honor of Marvin*

A. Sweeney, edited by Shelley L. Birdsong and Serge Frolov, 327–43. Claremont, CA: Claremont Press, 2017.

———. "The Universal Horizon of Biblical Particularism." In *The Bible and Ethnicity*, edited by Mark G. Brett, 143–69. Leiden: Brill, 1996.

Levering, Matthew. *Christ's Fulfillment of Torah and Temple: Salvation According to Thomas Aquinas*. Notre Dame, IN: University of Notre Dame Press, 2002.

———. *Engaging the Doctrine of Israel: A Christian Israelology in Dialogue with Ongoing Judaism*. Eugene, OR: Cascade Books, 2021.

Lux, Richard C. *The Jewish People, the Holy Land, and the State of Israel: A Catholic View*. Mahwah, NJ: Paulist Press, 2010.

Maimonides, Moses. *The Guide of the Perplexed*. Translated by Shlomo Pines. Chicago: University of Chicago Press, 1963.

Manuel, Frank Edward. *The Broken Staff: Judaism through Christian Eyes*. Cambridge, MA: Harvard University Press, 1992.

Maritain, Jacques. *Le mystère d'Israël et autres essais*. Paris: Declée de Brouwer, 1965.

Marshall, Bruce D. "Quasi in Figura: A Brief Reflection on Jewish Election, after Thomas Aquinas." *Nova et Vetera* 7 (2009): 477–84.

———. "Christ and Israel: An Unsolved Problem in Catholic Theology." In Anderson and Kaminsky, *Call of Abraham*, 330–50.

———. "Religion and Election: Aquinas on Natural Law, Judaism, and Salvation in Christ." *Nova et Vetera* 14, no. 1 (2016): 61–125.

Marx, Karl. "Zur Judenfrage." *Deutsch-Französische Jahrbücher* 1 (1844): 347–77.

Mason, Steve. "Jews, Judaeans, Judaizing, Judaism: Problems of Categorization in Ancient History." *Journal for the Study of Judaism* 38, nos. 4–5 (2007): 452–512.

Matter, E. Ann. "Wandering to the End: The Medieval Christian Context of the Wandering Jew." In Harkins, *Transforming Relations*, 224–40.

Michaels, Walter Benn. *The Shape of the Signifier: 1967 to the End of History*. Princeton, NJ: Princeton University Press, 2004.

Miller, David M. "Ethnicity, Religion, and the Meaning of *Ioudaios* in Ancient 'Judaism.'" *Currents in Biblical Research* 12, no. 2 (2014): 216–65.

———. "Ethnicity Comes of Age: An Overview of Twentieth-Century Terms for *Ioudaios*." *Currents in Biblical Research* 10, no. 2 (2012): 293–311.

———. "The Meaning of *Ioudaios* and Its Relationship to Other Group Labels in Ancient 'Judaism.'" *Currents in Biblical Research* 9, no. 1 (2010): 98–126.

Moyaert, Marianne. "The Gifts and Calling of God are Irrevocable." *Irish Theological Quarterly* 83 (2018): 24–43.

Nirenberg, David. *Aesthetic Theology and Its Enemies: Judaism in Christian Painting, Poetry, and Politics*. Waltham, MA: Brandeis University Press, 2015.

———. *Anti-Judaism: The Western Tradition*. New York: Norton, 2013.

Nova Vulgata Bibliorum Sacrorum. Editio typica altera. Vatican City: Libreria Editrice Vaticana, 2005. Edition first published 1986.

Novak, David. *Covenantal Rights: A Study in Jewish Political Theory*. Princeton, NJ: Princeton University Press, 2000.

———. "Creation." In Kavka et al., *Cambridge History*, 371–98.

———. *The Election of Israel: The Idea of the Chosen People*. Cambridge: Cambridge University Press, 1995.

———. "The End of the Law." In Harkins, *Transforming Relations*, 34–49.

———. *Halakhah in a Theological Dimension*. Chico, CA: Scholars Press, 1985.

———. *Zionism and Judaism: A New Theory*. Cambridge: Cambridge University Press, 2015.

Pawlikowski, John T. "A Catholic Response to Gavin D'Costa." *Theological Studies* 73 (2012): 629–40.

Pawlikowski, John T., and Hayim Goren Perelmuter, eds. *Reinterpreting Revelation and Tradition: Jews and Christians in Conversation*. Lanham, MD: Rowman and Littlefield, 2000.

Peterson, Erik. "The Church from Jews and Gentiles." In *Theological Tractates*, edited and translated by Michael J. Hollerich, 40–67. Stanford, CA: Stanford University Press, 2011; composed ca. 1932.

Pomplun, Trent. "Quasi in Figura: A Cosmological Reading of the Thomistic Phrase." *Nova et Vetera* 7 (2009): 505–22.

Ratzinger, Joseph. "Address at the Great Synagogue of Rome." Address given January 27, 2010. At https://tinyurl.com/yc7c848u.

———. "Address to Dr. Riccardo Di Segni, Chief Rabbi of Rome." Address given January 16, 2006. At https://tinyurl.com/yc7c848u.

———. "Grace and Vocation Without Remorse: Comments on the Treatise 'De Iudaeis.'" Translated by Nicholas J. Healey Jr. *Communio* 45 (2018): 163–84.

Ravitsky, Aviezer. *Messianism, Zionism, and Jewish Religious Radicalism.* Translated by Michael Swirsky and Jonathan Chipman. Chicago: University of Chicago Press, 2006. First published, in Hebrew, in 1993.

Raz-Krakotzkin, Amnon. *The Censor, the Editor, and the Text: The Catholic Church and the Shaping of the Jewish Canon in the Sixteenth Century*. Philadelphia: University of Pennsylvania Press, 2007.

Rose, Jacqueline. *The Question of Zion.* Princeton, NJ: Princeton University Press, 2007.

Rowe, Nina. *The Jew, the Cathedral and the Medieval City: Synagoga and Ecclesia in the Thirteenth Century*. Cambridge: Cambridge University Press, 2011.

Rozen-Zvi, Ishay, and Adi Ophir. "Goy: Toward an Etymology." *Dine Israel* 28 (2011): 69–122.

Rosenzweig, Franz. *The Star of Redemption*. Translated from the second edition of 1930 by William W. Hallo. Notre Dame, IN: University of Notre Dame Press, 1985.

Sagi, Avi. "Halakhah." In Kavka et al., *Cambridge History*, 501–18.

Sagi, Avi, and Zvi Zohar. *Transforming Identity: The Ritual Transition from Gentile to Jew—Structure and Meaning*. New York: Continuum, 2007.

Sandmel, David Fox. "Philosemitism and 'Judaizing' in the Contemporary Church." In Harkins, *Transforming Relations*, 405–20.

Sartre, Jean-Paul. *Refléxions sur la question juive*. Paris: Gallimard, 1985. First published 1946.

Schenk, Calvin E, eds. *Who Do You Say That I Am? Christians Encounter Other Religions.* Notre Dame, IN: University of Notre Dame Press, 2004.

Scholem, Gershom. *Major Trends in Jewish Mysticism*. New York: Schocken, 1946.

Seidman, Naomi. *Faithful Renderings: Jewish-Christian Difference and the Politics of Translation*. Chicago: University of Chicago Press, 2006.

Shanks, Hershel. *Christianity and Rabbinic Judaism: A Parallel History.* 2nd ed. Washington, DC: Biblical Archaeology Society, 2011.

Signer, Michael A. "Blindness or Insight? The Jewish Denial of Jesus Christ." In Schenk, *Who Do You Say?*, 187–206.

———. *Memory and History in Christianity and Judaism*. Notre Dame, IN: University of Notre Dame Press, 2001.

———. "One Covenant or Two: Can We Sing a New Song?" In Pawlikowski and Perelmuter, *Reinterpreting Revelation*, 3–23.

Soulen, Kendall. *The God of Israel and Christian Theology*. Minneapolis: Fortress Press, 1996.

———. *Irrevocable: The Name of God and the Unity of the Christian Bible*. Minneapolis: Fortress Press, 2022.

Steinberg, Leo. *The Sexuality of Christ in Renaissance Art and in Modern Oblivion*. 2nd ed. Chicago: University of Chicago Press, 1997.

Steiner, George. *The Portage to San Cristóbal of A. H.* Chicago: University of Chicago Press, 1999. First published 1979.

Swinburne, Algernon Charles. *Poems and Ballads*. London: Savill and Edwards, 1866.

Ticciati, Susannah. "The Future of Biblical Israel: How Should Christians Read Romans 9–11 Today?" *Biblical Interpretation* 25, nos. 4–5 (2017): 497–518.

Tokarczuk, Olga. *The Books of Jacob*. Translated from Polish by Jennifer Croft. New York: Riverhead Books, 2022. First published 2014.

Trigano, Shmuel. "Jews alongside Non-Jews." In Kavka et al., *Cambridge History*, 538–78.

Wasserman, Mira Beth. *Jews, Gentiles, and Other Animals: The Talmud after the Humanities*. Philadelphia: University of Pennsylvania Press, 2017.

Weil, Simone. "Lettre à un religieux." In *Oeuvres*, edited by Florence de Lussy, 985–1016. Paris: Gallimard, 1999. Composed 1942.

Wieseltier, Leon. "The Exclamation Point." *Liberties* 2, no. 1 (2021): 357–86.

———. *Kaddish*. New York: Knopf, 1998.

Winner, Lauren F. *Wearing God: Clothing, Laughter, Fire, and Other Overlooked Ways of Meeting God*. New York: HarperOne, 2015.

Wittgenstein, Ludwig. *Culture and Value*. Translated by Peter Winch. Chicago: University of Chicago Press, 1980. Composed between 1914 and 1951.

———. *Philosophische Untersuchungen*. Translated by G. E. M. Anscombe, P. M. S. Hacker, and Joachim Schulte. 4th ed. Chichester: Wiley-Blackwell, 2009. First published 1953.

———. *Tractatus Logico-Philosophicus*. London: Routledge and Kegan Paul, 1922.

Wojtyla, Karol. "Address at the Great Synagogue of Rome." Address given April 14, 1986. At https://tinyurl.com/66fw6wbe.

Wyschogrod, Michael. *The Body of Faith: God in the People Israel*. Northvale, NJ: Jason Aronson, 1996. First published 1983.

Yuval, Israel Jacob. *Two Nations in Your Womb: Perceptions of Jews and Christians in Late Antiquity and the Middle Ages*. Translated by Barbara Harshav and Jonathan Chipman. Berkeley: University of California Press, 2008.

INDEX OF SUBJECTS AND NAMES